THEORY AND INTERPRETATION OF NARRATIVE
James Phelan, Peter J. Rabinowitz, and Robyn Warhol, Series Editors

Thomas Hardy's Brains

PSYCHOLOGY, NEUROLOGY, AND HARDY'S IMAGINATION

Suzanne Keen

THE OHIO STATE UNIVERSITY PRESS | COLUMBUS

Library of Congress Cataloging-in-Publication Number
2013032860

ISBN-13: 978-0-8142-1249-3 (cloth : alk. paper)
ISBN-10: 0-8142-1249-2 (cloth : alk. paper)
ISBN-13: 978-0-8142-9352-2 (cd-rom)
ISBN-10: 0-8142-9352-2 (cd-rom)

Cover design by Laurence J. Nozik
Type set in Adobe Sabon
Typesetting by Juliet Williams
Printed by Thomson-Shore, Inc.

9 8 7 6 5 4 3 2 1

to The Thomas Hardy Association

CONTENTS

ACKNOWLEDGMENTS

My Hardy debts run deep. I began reading him as a teenager, when my mother, Sally Whitcomb Keen, put *The Return of the Native* in my hands. I had already visited Hardy country, though to a ten year old in 1972 the barrows and downs spoke of Tolkien and Rosemary Sutcliff, and I couldn't yet know how much Hardy those writers had absorbed. Hardy country was also Whitcomb country, where the ancestral barn and deconsecrated parish church still stand. My Whitcombs (the Robert line) left Dorset in the seventeenth century, long before William Barnes and Thomas Hardy made their neighborhood a part of Wessex. Many years later, James and Helen Gibson dropped me off at the village of Whitcomb during the biennial Hardy Conference. I was five months' pregnant, and they didn't think I should walk. Though I had not yet published a word about Hardy, the scholars and readers at the Hardy Conference welcomed me into their community. The Thomas Hardy Association opened in cyberspace in 1996, and has proven an important forum and resource for Hardyans worldwide.

I am grateful for the suggestions and encouragement of Ian Duncan, Susan Stanford Friedman, Richard Fulton, Patrick Leary, Phillip Mallet, Rosemarie Morgan, Alan Palmer, Claude Rawson, Kristin Ross, the late Bob Schweick, Linda Shires, Meir Sternberg, Lisa Zunshine, and several anonymous press readers. Editorial assistant Chelsi Hewitt gave the manuscript a lick, spit, and polish. A Lenfest Summer Research Grant from

Washington and Lee University enabled me to visit Widener Library at Harvard University to consult its superb collection of nineteenth-century periodicals. A Hewlett-Mellon Grant from Washington and Lee University supported a year's sabbatical for writing, for which I owe thanks to Provost June Aprille and Dean of the College Hank Dobin, members of the President's Advisory Committee, and the most munificent of donors, Gerry and Marguerite Lenfest.

Earlier versions of chapter 5, and small parts of other chapters appeared previously in BRANCH: Britain, Representation and Nineteenth-Century History, ed. Dino Franco Felluga, "'Altruism' Makes a Space for Empathy, 1852" (July 2012); in *Poetics Today,* ed. Meir Sternberg, "Empathetic Hardy: Bounded, Ambassadorial, and Broadcast Strategies of Narrative Empathy" 32.2 (Summer 2011), 349–89; in *Style,* ed. John V. Knapp, "Response to Alan Palmer," 45.2 (Summer 2011), 357–59; and in *The Ashgate Research Companion to Thomas Hardy,* ed. Rosemarie Morgan, "Psychological Approaches to Thomas Hardy," (Ashgate, 2010), 285–300. I am grateful to the editors for their permission to reproduce portions or revised versions of those essays here.

ABBREVIATIONS
FOR HARDY'S WORKS

Desperate Remedies (1871)	DR
Under the Greenwood Tree (1872)	UGT
A Pair of Blue Eyes (1873)	PBE
Far from the Madding Crowd (1874)	FFMC
The Hand of Ethelberta (1876)	HE
The Return of the Native (1878)	RN
The Trumpet Major (1880)	TM
A Laodicean (1881)	L
Two on a Tower (1882)	TT
The Mayor of Casterbridge (1886)	MC
The Woodlanders (1887)	W
Wessex Tales (1888)	WT
A Group of Noble Dames (1891)	GND
Tess of the d'Urbervilles (1891)	Tess
Life's Little Ironies (1894)	LLI
Jude the Obscure (1895)	Jude
The Well-Beloved (1897)	W-B
Wessex Poems (1898)	WP

Poems of the Past and Present (1901[2])	*PPP*
The Dynasts (1904, 1906, 1908)	*Dynasts*
Time's Laughingstocks (1909)	*TL*
A Changed Man (1913)	*CM*
Satires of Circumstance (1914)	*SC*
Moments of Vision (1917)	*MV*
Late Lyrics (1922)	*LL*
Human Shows (1925)	*HS*
Winter Words (1928)	*WW*

The Collected Letters of Thomas Hardy (ed. Millgate and Purdy)	*Letters*
The Early Life of Thomas Hardy, 1840–1891 (F. E. Hardy)	*Early Life*
The Later Years of Thomas Hardy, 1892–1928 (F. E. Hardy)	*Later Years*
The Life and Work of Thomas Hardy (ed. Millgate)	*Life and Work*
The Literary Notebooks of Thomas Hardy (ed. Björk)	*Literary Notebooks*
The Personal Notebooks of Thomas Hardy (ed. Taylor)	*Personal Notebooks*
Thomas Hardy's "Facts" Notebook (ed. Greenslade)	*"Facts" Notebook*
Thomas Hardy's "Poetical Matter" Notebook (ed. Dalziel and Millgate)	*"Poetical" Notebook*

A NOTE ABOUT EDITIONS

In parenthetical page number citations, I refer whenever possible to the Oxford World Classics paperbacks of Hardy's fiction, a set of critical editions published under the general editorship of Simon Gatrell, reissued in 2009 with identical pagination. When not available, as in *The Hand of Ethelberta*, I fall back on New Wessex Editions. In several cases comparison with the Penguin editions, which print the first edition or manuscript version of Hardy's works, requires citation of an alternative text. Notes indicate this deviation from my usual practice. For the poetry, I rely on Samuel Hynes, ed., *The Complete Poetical Works of Thomas Hardy*, v. 1–5 (Oxford: Clarendon Press, 1982–95), indicated by volume number and original edition title abbreviation, e.g., for a poem originally published in *Wessex Poems*, (WP, v. 1, 81–2). Part and line numbers in citations from *The Dynasts* refer to volumes 4 and 5 of Hynes's edition. For Hardy's life as he recorded it, I rely on the standard edition, *The Life and Work of Thomas Hardy*, edited by Michael Millgate, based on "materials previously drawn upon for *The Early Life of Thomas Hardy, 1840–1891*, and *The Later Years of Thomas Hardy, 1892–1928*, published over the name of Florence Emily Hardy." Throughout I have relied upon two electronic concordances, Martin Ray's CD-ROM *A Variorum Concordance to the "Complete Poems"* (1999) and Mitsuharu Matsuoka's web-based *The Victorian Literary Studies Archive Hyper-Concordance*.

"He considered that he knew fairly well . . . the life of an isolated student cast upon the billows of London with no protection but his brains."

   —Hardy recalling his younger self, c. 1867 (*Life and Work* 58)

"Dr. Grosart finds abundant evidence that the facts and mysteries of nature and human nature have come urgently before Mr. Hardy's penetrative brain."

   —quoted by Hardy, February 1888 (*Life and Work* 213–14)

"His back, his legs, his hands, his face, were longing to be out of the world. His brain was not longing to be, because, like the brain of most people, it was the last part of his body to realise a situation."

   —Thomas Hardy, March 1890 (*Life and Work* 224)

Psychological Hardy

"He was lying on his back in the sun, thinking how useless he was, and covered his face with his straw hat. The sun's rays streamed through the interstices of the straw, the lining having disappeared. Reflecting on his experiences of the world so far as he had got he came to the conclusion that he did not wish to grow up": psychological Hardy began as dissociated Hardy (*Life and Work* 20). Later he would give this experience of daydream and alienation to his character Jude Fawley (*Jude* 12). Entranced by the intensification of the color when evening sun hit the Venetian red walls at Bockhampton (*Life and Work* 20), dancing to conceal his weeping at the sound of certain airs (19), aesthetic Hardy responded to sensations feelingly. Developmentally delayed Hardy, though a precocious reader (19), remarked in old age that "a clue to much of his character and action throughout his life is afforded by his lateness of development in virility . . . a child till he was sixteen, a youth till he was five-and-twenty, and a young man until he was nearly fifty" (37). Young adult Hardy, while busy becoming the writer Thomas Hardy, was also a traumatized Hardy, who lost his close friend and mentor Horace Moule to suicide in 1873 (Millgate, *Biography Revisited* 141–44), and a repressed Hardy, who granted liberties to his fictional characters that he never allowed himself.

Lacking the Freudian terminology did not prevent Hardy from recognizing his repressive habits. He wrote of himself, "I have a faculty ɔssibly not uncommon) for burying an emotion in my heart or brain Ɪⱼr forty years, and exhuming it at the end of that time as fresh as when interred" (*Life and Work* 408). The love in the elegiac "Emma" poems may have been exhumed in just this fashion even as he consigned his dead wife to the clay (*SC* v. 2, 47–70). Puzzling over his own disposition, the poet Hardy lets his reader see a telepathic Hardy, drafting a poem about his cousin, unaware she is dying (*WP* v. 1, 81–82), and a grieving Hardy, hearing voices: "Woman much missed, how you call to me, call to me" (*SC* v. 2, 56, l. 1). Less flattering images of the author emerge from later biographies, where we can catch glimpses of neurotic Hardy, delusional Hardy, passive-aggressive Hardy, status-conscious Hardy. His own words sometimes convict him of harsh judgments about humanity: "You may regard a throng of people as containing a certain small minority who have sensitive souls," he wrote in 1887, "these, and the aspects of these being what is worth observing. So you divide them into the mentally unquickened, mechanical, soulless; and the living, throbbing, suffering, vital. In other words into souls and machines, ether and clay" (*Life and Work* 192). Hardy was proud to go undetected as an observer and judge of men: "none of the society-men who met him suspected from his simple manner the potentialities of observation that were in him" (408). He wore his "unconscious air" like a cloak of invisibility, and he saw through men like glass (408).

In 1883, the Victorian sexologist Havelock Ellis wrote an extensive essay on Thomas Hardy's work up to that date, defining the novelist as "a psychologist who is also an artist." Placing Hardy in a genealogy of writers from Jane Austen to Charlotte Brontë to George Eliot, Ellis argues that the "most serious work in English fiction" gives "a foremost place to the elements of art and psychology" (Ellis 164). Ellis's *Westminster Review* essay initiates the persistent practice of responding to Hardy with terms drawn from a variety of psychological schools. Often readers persuaded of Hardy's modernity have seen him presciently foreseeing psychological concepts of later times, even developments fifty years hence. For instance, Rosemary Sumner shows how Hardy anticipates aspects of Freud, Jung, behaviorist operant conditioning, and (in the literary field) the psychological interests of Lawrence and Proust.[1] Readings attentive to Hardy's saturation in folk beliefs document his interest in psychic phe-

---

1. See Rosemary Sumner, *Thomas Hardy, Psychological Novelist* (1981). See also Peter Allan Dale, who discusses Freudian sublimation in *Jude* (1895), regression, narcissism, and the repetition compulsion in *The Well-Beloved* (1897) in *In Pursuit of a Scientific Culture: Science, Art, and Society in the Victorian Age* (1989), 262, 264–67, 271.

nomena, including dreams, hallucinations, premonitions, psychosomatic illnesses, and telepathy (Pinion 158–61). Speculative psychological readings of Hardy's work have often put the author on the couch, for Freudian or Jungian analysis. Hardy's careful scripting of his life records in the two-volume biography that first appeared as the work of his widow, Florence Emily Hardy,[2] has not prevented his biographers from reading the lacunae, or buried clues, to reveal the secrets of this most self-conscious man. Nor are the extant materials exhausted: the most recent biographies, Ralph Pite's *Thomas Hardy: The Guarded Life* (2007) and Claire Tomalin's *Thomas Hardy: The Time-Torn Man* (2006) offer alternative psychological portraits of the author, Tomalin's especially attentive to his relations with significant women, Pite's alert to the writer's flaws and contradictions. Evoking Freudian terminology, W. H. Auden described his relationship with Thomas Hardy as an instance of "transference," reporting that he was once in love with Hardy as a poetical father (Auden 135, 142), and the diagnostic impulse underlies some fine analyses of his writerly craft, as when Tom Paulin or Lawrence Jay Dessner explain the idiosyncrasies of Hardy's perceptions.

To link Thomas Hardy with psychology and the psychological, then, is a traditional practice that has persisted for over a century. Hardy's characters have frequently been examined in psychological terms derived from Freudian diagnostic schemas, so, for instance, Albert Guérard describes Hardy's protagonists as "neurotic voyagers" or "impotent spectators" in a 1949 psychoanalytic study.[3] More recent studies employing psychoanalytic approaches have continued to discuss aspects of Hardy's representations of human relations, as in Christopher Lane's fine book, *The Burdens of Intimacy: Psychoanalysis and Victorian Masculinity* (1999). Jungian, Horneyan and Lacanian readings have also made their way into print.[4] Tim Armstrong's Derridean discussion of

---

2. F. E. Hardy, *The Early Life of Thomas Hardy, 1840–1891* (1928), and *The Later Years of Thomas Hardy, 1892–1928* (1930).

3. Albert Guérard, *Thomas Hardy: The Novels and Stories* (1949). For more recent psychological schematizations of Hardy's fictional characters, see Geoffrey Thurley, *The Psychology of Hardy's Novels: The Nervous and the Statuesque* (1975), a typological analysis of character and relational dynamics in Hardy's longer fiction according to psycho-physiological traits. Frank R. Giordano, Jr., offers a typology of Hardy's melancholics and suicides in *"I'd Have My Life Unbe"*: *Thomas Hardy's Self-destructive Characters* (1984).

4. For Jungian and Lacanian approaches, see Owen Schur's Lacanian reading of *The Woodlanders* and *The Well-Beloved* in *The Regulation of Consciousness in the English Novel: Desire and Power* (2002) and Byunghwa Joh's Jungian diagnosis, *Thomas Hardy's Poetry: A Jungian Perspective* (2002). Bernard J. Paris offers a Horneyan reading of *The Mayor of Casterbridge* in *Imagined Human Beings: A Psychological Approach to Character and Conflict in Literature* (1997).

the "trauma of *becoming-historical*" has rewarding readings of "The Convergence of the Twain" and the Emma poems (Armstrong 2), and William A. Cohen applies Deleuze and Guattari's "faciality" to Hardy's materialist representations of bodies, faces, and places in *The Return of the Native* (1878) (Cohen 437–52). Tess, Sue Bridehead, Bathsheba Everdene and Eustacia Vye have all attracted psychoanalytic commentary, only some of it acknowledging the fictionality of these female characters.[5] Treatments of Hardy's representations of gender and sexuality often rely on psychological and psychoanalytic concepts to ground interpretations.[6] An especially rich area of commentary treats Hardy's representations of the senses and sensation, as for instance in John Hughes's work on eyes and glances.[7] One of the finest books ever written about Hardy's work, J. Hillis Miller's *Thomas Hardy: Distance and Desire* (1970), treats Hardy the writer psychologically, interpreting his distancing use of narrators, his characters' mind-reading abilities, his characteristic patterns of approach and withdrawal, and his unconscious emotional transfiguration of the physical world, "storing up feelings in houses, in furniture, in musical instruments, in a certain glade by a stream, or in a given spot by the seacliffs" (Miller *Distance and Desire* 244).

The psychological theories and psychoanalytic techniques that have been visited upon Hardy, his family members, his wives, and his fictional characters have nearly all belonged to the later twentieth century. This book resituates the Hardy that Havelock Ellis noticed in his own time, in the context of the later nineteenth and early twentieth centuries. Thomas Hardy's representations of brains were conceived in light of Victorian brain science, his imagery of nerves depicted in keeping with Victorian

---

5. Hardy's Tess is especially vulnerable to being read as "woman," rather than a word mass, in E. M. Forster's term. Possibly Hardy starts the hare with his subtitle, "A Pure Woman." See, for example, Peter J. Casagrande, *Tess of the d'Urbervilles: Unorthodox Beauty* (1982), and Arthur Efron, *Experiencing Tess of the d'Urbervilles: A Deweyan Account* (2005).

6. See, for example, Penny Boumelha, *Thomas Hardy and Women: Sexual Ideology and Narrative Form* (1982); the essays by Brady, Higonnet, Langland, and Sadoff in Margaret Higonnet, ed., *The Sense of Sex: Feminist Perspectives on Hardy* (1993); Rosemarie Morgan, *Women and Sexuality in the Novels of Thomas Hardy* (1988); and Kaja Silverman, "History, Figuration and Female Subjectivity in *Tess of the d'Urbervilles*" (1984).

7. See John Hughes, "Visual Inspiration in Hardy's Fiction," in *Palgrave Advances in Thomas Hardy Studies,* edited by Phillip Mallett (2004); on the psychology of perception in Hardy, see J. B. Bullen, *The Expressive Eye: Fiction and Perception in the Work of Thomas Hardy* (1986). On the sense of hearing, see Mark Asquith's superb *Thomas Hardy, Metaphysics and Music* (2005).

medical neurology. As I demonstrate in chapter 1, "Psychological Influences on Hardy," the writer was a serious student of the psychology of human behavior, which he sought out in diverse sources beginning with reading he did in his early 20s. I rely throughout this book on sources such as Hardy's *Literary Notebooks,* collections of reading notes taken from the 1860s onward, to document Hardy's intellectual curiosity and studious habits. From these notes and from his published works a different picture of psychological Hardy emerges, one more in control of the imagistic schemas of brain and mind, emotions and motive, than has always been credited. Hardy knew the work of Henry Maudsley,[8] T. H. Ribot, and Henry Head; strongly influenced by Herbert Spencer, he also carefully read G. H. Lewes, his guide to Spinoza and Comte; he encountered both Alexander Bain and William James.

Influence studies document Hardy's magpie gatherings of ideas, with some strands standing out: his agnosticism, his Darwinism, and his early interest in the systems of Charles Fourier and Comte's Positivism. Hardy denied he was a pessimist, preferring the label "evolutionary meliorist" ("Preface," *LL* v. 2, 319); he also insisted that he was not a Positivist (*Letters* v. 3, 53) though he certainly knew Comte's work. He was of no one school. The separate impact of John Stuart Mill, Charles Darwin, Herbert Spencer, Charles Fourier, as well as Auguste Comte have frequently been noted by Hardy critics.[9] A few scholars and critics of Hardy's poetry describe his monist and materialist influences, including Eduard von Hartmann.[10] What has not been clear in these earlier studies is how Hardy's extraction of elements of an affective human psychology from diverse sources coheres, and develops, as the discipline itself becomes established during Hardy's working life. Although Hardy refers directly to major psychological areas of research in his work, most studies of Hardy's influences emphasize his reading in philosophy and

---

8. Sally Shuttleworth has recently drawn attention to the importance of Maudsley to Hardy, in *The Mind of the Child: Child Development in Literature, Science, and Medicine, 1840–1900* (2010) 335–52.

9. See Lennart A. Björk, editor of Hardy's *Literary Notebooks,* the authority in this area. For instance, in his introduction to the *Notebooks,* Björk argues that Hardy's view of human nature is indebted to Fourier's psychology, with its emphasis on emotionality (v. 1, xxvi; see also the first entries of the *Notebooks,* in which Hardy diagrams Fourier (v. 1, 3–4).

10. Though Wickens's point is to demonstrate the plurality of voices and divergent views within the poem, he offers a thorough study of Hardy's monist influences. See G. Glen Wickens, *Thomas Hardy, Monism, and the Carnival Tradition: The One and the Many in* The Dynasts (2002). See also J. O. Bailey, *Thomas Hardy and the Cosmic Mind* (1956), Susan Dean, *Hardy's Poetic Vision* (1977), and Walter Wright, *The Shaping of* The Dynasts (1967).

science over his familiarity with psychology.[11] Up until now, Hardy has been understood neither as a student of psychology nor as a reader of neurology, Victorian brain science.

This neglect of Hardy's brains and nerves has persisted even though J. Hillis Miller, Susan Dean, and Samuel Hynes long ago pointed out the neurological imagery in *The Dynasts* (1904–8).[12] Indeed, Hardy's thinking about the psychology of motives and the place of humans in the universe reaches its imagistic and dramatic fulfillment in *The Dynasts*. Medical neurologists were thoroughgoing materialists by Hardy's time, but his epic drama is one of the first modern texts to represent the monist idea of the universe in explicitly neurological imagery of hyperastronomical scale.[13] The groundwork for this representation occurred much earlier in Hardy's career, for he conceived the poem and conducted research that would shape it, and the novels of the 1880s, decades earlier. At the beginning of his writing career, Hardy's representations of psychology drew not on the cutting edge science of neurons and their ejections, but on ideas about brain and behavior that prevailed in earlier decades of the nineteenth century, including Cartesian hydraulic theories of mind and phrenology, an early—now discredited—theory of brain localization focused on examining protrusions of the skull.[14] That he was not satisfied with these theories shows in his satirical representations. In 1863 Hardy himself had his skull examined by the phrenologist Cornelius Donovan, who predicted that "his would lead him to no good" (*Life and Work* 43). Like fortune-tellers, phrenologists were savvy readers of faces, clothing, postures, and accents. In 1863 Thomas Hardy was an unknown, evidently provincial young man, presenting for class reasons few external cues of affluence or prospects that Donovan could pick up and attribute to skull protrusions. In any case the phrenologist missed an

11. Björk's work is a significant exception. See his essay, "Hardy's Reading," in *Thomas Hardy: The Writer and His Background*, ed. Norman Page (1980) 102–27, and his monograph, *Psychological Vision and Social Criticism in the Novels of Thomas Hardy* (1987).

12. See Miller, *Distance and Desire* 267; Susan Dean, *Hardy's Poetic Vision in The Dynasts: The Diorama of a Dream* (1977) 257–58; and Samuel Hynes, *The Pattern of Hardy's Poetry* (1961) 161.

13. On the Romantic precursors to twentieth-century "mathematically sublime" conceptions of the brain, see Alan Richardson, *The Neural Sublime: Cognitive Theories and Romantic Texts* (2010) 36–37.

14. The 1840s were the heyday of British phrenology. Through it was mostly abandoned in Britain by the 1850s, the early advocates having died or moved on, there was a phrenologist practicing in Bristol from 1861 to 1901. See John Van Wyhe's website, "The History of Phrenology: A Chronology," *The Victorian Web*, ed. George Landow.

opportunity to recognize Hardy's genius, and that may have motivated Hardy to take a satirical perspective on phrenology.

In Hardy's second published book, *Under the Greenwood Tree* (1872), the aspirant novelist mocks the popular science of phrenology in a scene of character analysis carried out by analyzing the bumps and deformities of a cobbler's wooden last, a model of a foot used to produce custom fit shoes. Where other Victorian novelists (such as Charlotte Brontë and George Eliot) solemnly called upon their readers' enthusiasm for phrenology by reporting their characters' high brows and prominent organs of veneration,[15] Hardy brings them down to earth with a homely scene of personality-revealing foot models. The cobbler holds up the wooden last and comments on the character whose foot it reveals:

> "Yes, a very queer natured last it is now, 'a b'lieve," he continued, turning it over caressingly. "Now you notice that there"—(pointing to a lump of leather bradded to the toe), "that's a very bad bunion that he've had ever since 'a was a boy. Now this remarkable large piece" (pointing to a patch nailed to the side), shows a' accident he received by the tread of a horse, that squashed his foot a'most to a pomace. The horseshoe came full-butt on this point you see. (*UGT* 24)

The history of a body and the character owning that history show in the bumps and abrasions on the last. The bumps point outward, to experience, not inward to character. Phrenologists believed that they could read the impress of the brain from protrusions of the skull, gaining insight to character expressed by shapes of prominent brain areas. In Hardy's analogy, the leather shoe corresponds to the body, and these exterior shells are represented by an image of their interior shapes—parts marked both by heredity and experiences. Yet the shoemaker who decodes the record of two lives from the wooden last knows both men as individuals and presents a history shaped more profoundly by circumstances than by innate character. In 1877 Hardy wrote in his notebook "An object or mark raised or made by man on a scene is worth ten times any such formed by unconscious Nature. Hence clouds, mists, and mountains are unimportant beside the wear on a threshold, or the print of a hand" (*Life and Work* 120). Though Hardy came to believe in an indifferent universe

---

15. See Sally Shuttleworth, "Psychological Definition and Social Power: Phrenology in the Novels of Charlotte Brontë" (1989); Nicholas Dames, "The Clinical Novel: Phrenology and *Villette*" (1996); T. R. Wright, "From Bumps to Morals: The Phrenological Background to George Eliot's Moral Framework" (1982).

in which the actions of humans shrink to meaninglessness against the backdrop of the cosmos, he was nonetheless a most humane artist, fascinated by the particular tokens of human habitation, motivation, desire, passion, or prejudice. Always an attentive reader of the marks human beings made as they passed through their habitations, Hardy could call up memories from what they left behind. Though he gave some credence to physiognomy, inviting readers to judge characters by their faces, hair, and clothing, Hardy did not endorse the access to interior character and personality through external signs, as promised by phrenology. Instead he brought a Darwinian sense of the processes of coadaptation to his description of the interactions of character and environment, while character itself he saw as shaped by both heredity and human instincts.

While physical traits and personal histories are widely knowable to the community in *Under the Greenwood Tree,* the insides of others' minds remain generally mysterious. William A. Cohen's assertion that few could have been tempted "to read Thomas Hardy as a psychological realist" registers, not for the first time, Hardy's reticence about characters' thoughts (Cohen 437). A century earlier, Havelock Ellis noted, "Generally, [Hardy] is only willing to recognize the psychical element in its physical correlative"; Ellis comments aptly that "This dislike to use the subjective method or to deal directly with mental phenomena is a feature in Mr. Hardy's psychology which has left a strong mark on his art" (Ellis 175). In the loquacious culture of *Under the Greenwood Tree,* silence gains value as inscrutability. A character comments of another: "that man's dumbness is wonderful to listen to," and the feeble-minded Leaf is unusual in that his thoughts show on his exterior: "'A do look at me as if 'a could see my thoughts running round like the works of a clock'" (*UGT* 91). Less impaired characters read each other's intentions by interpreting their bodies, but the conclusion of *Under the Greenwood Tree* emphasizes how characters continue to keep secrets from one another. *Under the Greenwood Tree* shows early Hardy making reference to the brain as a container of knowledge and as a delicate organ vulnerable to shocks, but maintaining unusual reticence (for a Victorian novelist) about the contents of characters' minds. In this combination, Hardy's fiction presciently models a theory of embodied cognition emphasizing affect, read by other characters through external signs in the pervasive activity of intermental thought. These convictions about human psychology show in Hardy's narrative techniques from his earliest novels.

The difference made by Hardy's neurological turn can be seen in contrasting passages from his first published novel *Desperate Remedies* and his last major work, the Napoleonic poem, *The Dynasts*. When Cytherea suffers from a shock, Hardy employs a gendered physiology typical of the genre of sensation fiction: "She thought and thought of that single fact which had been told her—that the first Mrs. Manston was still living—till her brain seemed ready to burst its confinement with excess of throbbing" (*DR* 255).[16] This relatively crude image of brain-as-contents-of-a-skull contrasts with Hardy's clinical imagery of brain and nerves in *The Dynasts*. Pulling back from the battlefield, the stage directions assert "the scene becomes anatomized and the living masses of humanity transparent"; with "preternatural clearness," the readers of *The Dynasts* can see what the human agents never perceive: the "controlling Immanent Will appears therein, as a brain-like network of currents and ejections, twitching, interpenetrating, entangling, and thrusting hither and thither the human forms" (*Dynasts* v. 4, 160). He projects the image of a living brain through the agency of the Spirit of the Years, who in scientific showman's manner, visually demonstrates the Immanent Will's electric animation of human agents. This shows the combatants on both sides in subjection to the Will, superimposed on the scene as "the interior of a beating brain lit by phosphorescence" (*Dynasts* v. 5, 61).

Though Hardy's last great work comes out between 1904 and 1908, its underpinning philosophy and imagery of a brain-like Will controlling human agency through its ejects preoccupied Hardy over two decades earlier. In the 1880s his notes frequently describe human beings as somnambulists, sleepwalkers hallucinating their idea of the world, acting automatically without realizing what their actions mean (*Life and Work* 190, 192). Though these Huxleyan views of automatism[17] (combined with Hardy's narrative reticence about his characters' mind-stuff) discourage a naturalistic psychological reading of his fictional characters, they ground a study of the philosophical and scientific sources of *The Dynasts* as relevant to Hardy's fiction from the 1880s onwards. What else had changed? From the 1870s to the turn of the twentieth century, the tools and techniques for studying the structures and function of the nervous system developed rapidly, and in the same period, Hardy moved steadily towards realizing a more physiologically accurate rendering of brains and nerves. The philosophical and scientific sources of *The Dynasts* thus become pertinent to the major fiction from *The Mayor of Casterbridge* (1886)

---

16. See Rachel Malane, *Sex in Mind: The Gendered Brain in Nineteenth-Century Literature and Mental Sciences* (2005).

17. T. H. Huxley, "On the Hypothesis That Animals Are Automata, and Its History" (1874).

through *Jude the Obscure* (1895) and several of Hardy's important essays on the art of fiction.

The turning point from a brain-capacity model to a neurological conception can be detected in the mid 1880s, when Hardy began serious research for his Napoleonic poem. The change shows up nearly immediately in his fiction. In *The Woodlanders* (1887), Hardy has a character gaze at a slice of brain under a microscope, materializing brains as neural tissue. Dr. Fitzpiers scandalously attempts to secure rights to an interesting subject's brain so he can dissect it after her decease.[18] He expresses interest in the specimen because it is large, for a woman's brain (*W* 46). What might Dr. Fitzpiers seek to see in Grammer's brain under his miscroscope? We may infer from his interest in brain capacity that Fitzpiers would have weighed the brain; he might also have traced the convolutions of the cerebral cortex. He could have observed dendrites and myelinated and unmyelinated axons of nerve cells, white and gray matter of the cerebral cortex, and the appearance of degenerating nerve fibers, though probably not the tissue loss of senility, for Grammer is as sharp as can be. Fitzpiers reads her hesitancy to submit to his will as a sign of "nervous disease" (119). Depending on his skill and his lab equipment, Fitzpiers might know how to use stains: in 1873, Camillo Golgi had published his method for staining techniques that enabled the study of neuroglia. In 1885, Theodor Meynert published *Psychiatry: A Clinical Treatise on the Diseases of the Forebrain;* perhaps Fitzpiers studied that diagnostic work, though Hardy does not specify. Indeed, when Fitzpiers speaks of his research, he flirtatiously chides Grace for starting back from the miscroscope where a slice of John South's brain lies sectioned: "'Here I am'" complains the scientist "'endeavoring to carry on simultaneously the study of physiology and transcendental philosophy, the material world and the ideal, so as to discover if possible a point of contact between them; and your finer sense is quite offended!'" (119).

Searching for the location of that point of contact—Descartes proposed the pineal gland because of what he perceived about its shape and location—had been a project of theorizing dualists, but as Fitzpiers makes clear, the idealists' search involves scrutiny of material evidence. Grace recoils from the anatomized brain section while her "finer sense" fails to warn her against Fitzpiers's designs (*W* 199). That an opportunistic man-on-the-make such as Fitzpiers should profess interests in the transcen-

---

18. See the discussion of the rapid advances in nineteenth-century neurology in Gordon Shepherd, *Foundations of the Neuron Doctrine* (1991).

dental and the ideal in the midst of a seductive routine suggests Hardy's skepticism about philosophical interpretations of psychological discoveries and the men who make them. A user of girls and old folks, Fitzpiers the psychological investigator possesses up-to-date knowledge of research methods but shows no sign of the conscience whose location in brain cells he would like to identify. Unlike the hypocritical Fitzpiers, Hardy endorses an anti-supernaturalist, materialist view from medical psychology that carries with it no implicit idealism. He transposes neurological theory onto his figurations of a monist universe, with no motive metaphysics, but only an impercipient cosmic unity that neither notices nor cares for the human creatures impelled by its impulses. This frame of reference only heightens the poignancy of Hardy's embodied, affective psychology, which owes less to anatomy and more to behavioral observation for its diagnoses of the human condition.

A focus on the psychological Hardy participates in two related critical projects. First, it extends the investigation of science and literature's interpenetration during the Victorian period, before the disciplinary breach that C. P. Snow announced in 1959 with the phrase "the two cultures."[19] Educated men and women of Hardy's time brought the resources of both scientific and humanistic ways of thinking to bear on their philosophical, theological, and political questions. Though the importance of Darwin to Hardy and his contemporaries has long been recognized,[20] recent work in Victorian studies has begun to demonstrate how profoundly realms of scientific psychology and literature interpenetrated.[21] Vanessa L. Ryan's *Thinking without Thinking in the Victorian Novel* (2012) takes the important step of restoring the "prehistory of neural science" to cognitivist discussions of Victorian novelists (Ryan 2). Notable recent literary work on Victorian psychology has focused on the

19. C. P. Snow, *The Two Cultures and the Scientific Revolution* (1961). For the restoration of the one culture of the Victorians, see Gillian Beer's *Open Fields: Science in Cultural Encounter* (1996).

20. Hardy honored Darwin by attending his funeral in Westminster Abbey (*Life and Work* 158). Canonically, see Gillian Beer, *Darwin's Plots: Evolutionary Narrative in Darwin, George Eliot, and Nineteenth-Century Fiction* (2000), and George Levine, *Darwin and the Novelists: Patterns of Science in Victorian Fiction* (1988).

21. Rick Rylance recovered for literary study the interaction of science and literature through his portrait of G. H. Lewes in *Victorian Psychology and British Culture, 1850–1880* (2000). See also George Levine, *Dying to Know: Scientific Epistemology and Narrative in Victorian England* (2002); Nicholas Dames, *The Physiology of the Novel: Reading, Neural Science, and the Form of Victorian Fiction* (2007); and Anne Stiles, "Victorian Psychology and the Novel."

emotions,[22] on amnesia and displaced memories,[23] mesmerism,[24] on sensation fiction,[25] and, preeminently among the psychological realists, on George Eliot.[26] The wide applicability of Alan Richardson's path-breaking work on Romantic poetry and early-nineteenth-century science of the mind, which has proven pertinent to all the major canonical poets,[27] encourages a cognitive literary historicism, or cultural cognitivism of Victorian literature. As Nicholas Dames concludes in a review of Anne Stiles's edited collection, *Neurology and Literature: 1860–1920*, "to become more robust . . . the study of neurology and literature will have to turn outside its immediately relevant canon to make risky engagements with the canons of others."[28] This book takes a step in the direction indicated by Dames, showing Hardy to be deeply engaged with the medical neurology and psychology of his time, reading their texts and conversing in person with physicians and scientists. For although Hardy's reading is well documented and his influences much studied, he has not been understood as participating in the literary articulation of contemporary brain science.

Hardy was proud of his early reading and recognition of Darwin (*Life and Work* 158), and although he never claimed to be a scientist himself, he shared the materialist worldview that many regarded as the inevitable response to Darwin. Thus one project undertaken here can be characterized as historical and contextual, operating quite traditionally by scrutinizing Hardy's sources and influences and by tracing the representational path of his imagery and characterization related to brains and nerves. It recovers the Victorian science of brain and mind with which Thomas Hardy engaged throughout his career. It participates in developing a cultural history of the emotions and their disorders, by examining the representation of emotional behavior and psychological ailments in the

---

22. See Jill L. Matus's overview of this area, "Victorian Framings of the Mind: Recent Work on Mid-Nineteenth Century Theories of the Unconscious, Memory, and Emotion" (2007); see also Rachel Ablow, "Victorian Feelings and the Victorian Novel" (2007).

23. See Gillian Beer, "Origins and Oblivion in Victorian Narrative" (1986); Nicholas Dames, *Amnesiac Selves: Nostalgia, Forgetting, and British Fiction, 1810–1870* (2001); and Athena Vrettos, "Displaced Memories in Victorian Fiction and Psychology" (2007).

24. See Alison Winter, *Mesmerized: Powers of Mind in Victorian Britain* (1998).

25. See Anne Stiles, ed., *Neurology and Literature, 1860–1920* (2007).

26. See Michael Davis, *George Eliot and Nineteenth-Century Psychology: Exploring the Unmapped Country* (2006).

27. Alan Richardson, *British Romanticism and the Science of the Mind* (2001) and *The Neural Sublime: Cognitive Theories and Romantic Texts* (2010).

28. Nicholas Dames, review of Anne Stiles, ed., *Neurology and Literature, 1860–1920* (2009) 554.

work of an informed observer. It opens up questions about what Hardy might have absorbed from his wider intellectual circle, particularly from club contacts (many physicians and scientists belonged to Hardy's club, the Athenaeum). It supports the picture of a writer at least as scientific as philosophical, established by the influential work of Gillian Beer and George Levine.

The second project to which a focus on psychological Hardy contributes can be termed "cognitive," since cognitive literary studies should be understood as embracing affect as well as cognitive schemas.[29] Three factors make my interdisciplinary approach to Hardy relevant to cognitivists. First, I engage with other scholars who share my conviction that historical and cultural contexts inflect expressions that may originate from our embodied consciousness. Thus I join a conversation going on in the new field of cognitive historicism, in which Alan Palmer, Alan Richardson, Vanessa Ryan, Blakey Vermeule, and Lisa Zunshine supplement contextual and historicist readings of literary texts with insights drawn from cognitive psychology and evolutionary psychology.[30] Second, by writing a case study of a well-known individual author, I assess the worthiness of the new tools and techniques of literary cognitivism. As Dale Kramer wisely observes, Hardy's "works tend to test the validity of matured theories more than they offer early opportunities for theoretical display" (Kramer xvi). I believe the time has come to evaluate some of the claims of literary cognitivism with regards to the works of a writer who was well aware of the psychology of his day. Lisa Zunshine acknowledges that cognitive literary studies works best for literary scholars when it provides tools and theoretical frames that illuminate the works and writers that we study. She advocates a contextual cognitivism, attentive to both cultural contexts and historical particulars that shape and govern the expression of schemas and other products of our embodied minds.[31] That Thomas Hardy himself articulated an emotional, embodied Theory of Mind that has much in common with the model now in vogue makes the third reason, in the form of a question: to what degree does Hardy's prescient modernity inhere in his materialist, neurological turn? In this book

---

29. See Suzanne Keen "Introduction: Narrative and the Emotions" (2011).

30. See Alan Richardson and Ellen Spolsky, eds., *The Work of Fiction: Cognition, Culture, and Complexity* (2004); Vanessa Ryan, *Thinking without Thinking in the Victorian Novel (2012)*; Blakey Vermeule, *Why Do We Care about Fictional Characters?* (2010); Lisa Zunshine, ed., *Introduction to Cognitive Cultural Studies* (2010); and Alan Palmer, *Social Minds in the Novel* (2010).

31. See Zunshine, "What Is Cognitive Cultural Studies?" (2010).

I explore Hardy's knowledge of the psychology and neurology of his own time, observing the changing imagery of brain and nerves he employed in over a half century of writing.

Old school concordance users and tracers of motifs will not be surprised to learn that Hardy's words reward attention.[32] Hardy's verbal craftsmanship, at its most exquisite and awkward in his short lyrics, is always a prominent feature of his fictional worldmaking and his characterization of imaginary beings. No nineteenth-century novelist has a more expansive and evocative vocabulary, with its working antiques, its inspired coinages, its pungent local terms, and its contemporary technical language. Hardy spends generously from his word-hoard, and it remains intact for the critic to plunder. Close work with words also rewards those interested in psychology and cognitive schemas. Ralph Elliott notices that Hardy's coined compound words, a characteristic feature of his style, "describe emotional states of mind" and "psychological upheavals" (Elliott 178). Elliott observes that "Certain elements tend to recur in this group of epithets: heart, life, mind, thought, nature, nerve, passion, soul, spirit" (178).

As this diction demonstrates, Hardy's interest in the human condition of living with emotion-driven brains shows forth vividly in the novels. Concordance data shows that Hardy's first published novel, the sensation fiction *Desperate Remedies* (1871) employs the words "brain" or "brains" two dozen times, often in hydraulic imagery of pressurized brain fluids. *The Woodlanders* comes in second with thirteen mentions. All but two books Hardy published mention brains,[33] and towards the end of his career, Hardy's use of the word "brain" peaks in *The Dynasts*, with twenty-six occurrences. Examining the correlative imagery associated with the word "brain" reveals a range of interests. Hardy often uses the word to mean intelligence or the vehicle of character, but also he refers to the organ that fills the skull. This shows not only in his metonyms for brain capacity, but also in references to diseases. Brains suffer perturbation, shriveling up, liquefaction, and suicidal blowing out. Eventually these physical brains in Hardy's imagery yield to a cellular image of networks of pulsing nerves, in a tightening focus on the microscopic that accompanies Hardy's artistic ambitions to represent the whole cosmos.

---

32. Especially useful are Martin Ray's *A Variorum Concordance to the "Complete Poems"* (1999) and Mitsuharu Matsuoka's web-based *The Victorian Literary Studies Archive Hyper-Concordance*.

33. The exceptions are *The Trumpet Major* (1880) and *The Well-Beloved* (1897).

When does Hardy start thinking about the miniature world under the microscope as a metaphor for universe and mind? The concordance is once again informative. While most of the instances of word "microscope" occur just where we would expect them, in *The Woodlanders* (a microscope is Dr. Fitzpiers's primary scientific instrument), as early as *The Return of the Native* Hardy employs the microscopic to characterize the actions of a mind. Eavesdropping on the furze stackers, and learning from the heathmen's conversation that Clym Yeobright is on his way home from Paris, Eustacia Vye finds relief from her boredom in fantasy: "That five minutes of overhearing furnished Eustacia with visions enough to fill the whole blank afternoon. Such sudden alterations from mental vacuity do sometimes occur thus quietly. She could never have believed in the morning that her colourless inner world would before night become as animated as water under a microscope" (*RN* 108). Though real Victorian women certainly scrutinized animalcules in the water, Eustacia is no naturalist: these words belong to Hardy's narrator. He provides an elaborate analogy for the change in Eustacia's mental state, from quiescence and emptiness to animation and fullness, as he generalizes about the contents of her mind.

Even the most sympathetic readers find Eustacia impulsive and enigmatic: she characteristically acts before she thinks. What drives her self-destructive behavior? At the time Hardy was writing *The Return of the Native,* many Victorians examined the fascinating world of water droplets, aided by the popularizing works of Philip Henry Gosse. They found them teeming with creatures.[34] They wondered how that animation under the lens might act in their real world. The germ theory of disease had just been conclusively demonstrated in 1875 by Robert Koch, but the idea that contagion spread from microorganisms had been in circulation for at least thirty years. The link between these curious creatures of the water droplet and consequences for individuals and unknowing populations of people was just beginning to take hold in the period.

Hardy's metaphor for Eustacia's mind diagnoses an infection, with germ-like thoughts animating her brain and behavior. She scarcely realizes what has happened to her, like a person who has unwittingly been exposed to an infectious disease. The narrator knows and reports her condition, though Eustacia only experiences the time-loss of fantasizing and

---

34. An 1859 American edition of Philip Henry Gosse's *Evenings at the Microscope* was in Hardy's personal library at the time of his death. See Michael Millgate, "Thomas Hardy's Library at Max Gate: Catalogue of an Attempted Reconstruction."

the spontaneous wandering that takes her ("why should she not go that way?") to spy on the Yeobrights' house. Her "colourless inner world" is transformed, active with impulsions that initiate her destruction. Hardy's fascination with the behavior of individuals who do not know their own minds meshes with his view of the universe, driven by the stimuli of the unconscious Immanent Will. As we have seen, in *The Dynasts,* he figures the Will as a network of neurons discharging its energy across the cosmos. Much earlier, in the poem "Hap," he figures human agents as the unacknowledged victims of "purblind Doomsters" (*WP,* v. 1, 10, l. 13). Hardy understands the evolved human condition as dramatizing a cruel conundrum. He intuitively coalesces imagery from neurology and psychology to figure forth his central paradox, a cosmic Theory of Mind consisting of an unfeeling, unwitting but motive universe inhabited by human creatures tragically evolved to feel.

CHAPTER 1

Psychological Influences on Hardy

Hardy the Reader

When readers enter imaginatively into a poem, a story, or a novel by Thomas Hardy, they meet a reader there. Man of Dorset, lover of music and art, architect, too, but always Hardy as reader obtrudes upon his fictional worlds. He knows his Bible, chapter and verse, and his liturgy and hymnody.[1] We can see his effort to link his representations to the Greek and Roman classics through allusions that may seem awkward or stretched now but at one time laid claim to the allusion-maker's hard won gentleman-like education.[2] We register his literary historical interest in the older genres, especially tragedy, and in honored precursors such as Shakespeare.[3] A poet himself, he is an inveterate quoter of poetry: an early novel takes its title from a poem by Thomas Gray.[4] Readers attuned to the alternatives for Victorian writers will note his pastorals and satires, his sensation fiction, his serials, his flirtation with French models, and his

---

1. See Mary Rimmer, "'My Scripture Manner': Reading Hardy's Biblical and Liturgical Allusion" (2006).

2. See William R. Rutland, *Thomas Hardy: A Study of His Writings and Their Background* (1962); Marlene Springer, *Hardy's Use of Allusion* (1983); and more recently, Mary Rimmer, "A Feast of Language: Hardy's Allusions" (2000).

3. See Dennis Taylor, "Hardy and Hamlet" (2006).

4. See Barbara Hardy, "Literary Allusion: Hardy and Other Poets" (2006).

ambition to achieve the career-capping goal of epic. He was alert to the capacities and limitations of the available genres, which he studied with a craftsman's interest.[5] Even Hardy's stories and poems about the least bookish sorts are permeated by a readerly mind, belonging to a man who raised himself by his own autodidactic reading programs from the high end of the artisan class to the lofty position of late Victorian sage. This chapter wends its way through Hardy's reading in psychology, following a path blazed by Lennart A. Björk, who edited Hardy's *Literary Notebooks* and wrote an important monograph about the influence of Hardy's reading on his psychological vision.[6]

The traces of Hardy's reading point backward, revealing the imprints of traditional curricula, vocational training, and theological disputation. His early reading owes a great deal to the encouragement of his bookish mother, Jemima, whose own mother Betty Swetman was also a great reader (*Life and Work* 11–12). Hardy claimed to have learned to read almost before learning to walk (19) and when he was young he formed the habit of rising early to read before work began (32). He referred to the "peculiarities of his inner life" when he was a young man, so intensely devoted to scholarship that it "might almost have been called academic" (36). The traces of Hardy's reading radiate outward, to the stacks of newspapers he combed through, the reference books he used and the periodicals he read, and the contemporary thinkers he absorbed: Auguste Comte, Charles Darwin, Charles Fourier, T. H. Huxley, George Henry Lewes, John Stuart Mill, Herbert Spencer, Schopenhauer, and Spinoza. Whether through play with imagery, direct allusion (Hardy twice mentions the philosopher Spinoza by name in his published work), imitative phrases (Comte, Fourier, and Spencer come in through these verbal echoes, which Hardy's contemporaries were primed to notice), dedications (especially to fellow authors), or even direct homage, Hardy leaves his readers in no doubt that he is a reader himself, a self-proclaimed reader of advanced literature (such as the poetry of Swinburne), the most demanding philosophers, and the cutting-edge thinkers of his day. These included scientists: as a young man he read Darwin; he met and liked T. H. Huxley (125), and in his eighties Hardy read Einstein's Theory of

---

5. See Richard Nemesvari, "'Genres Are Not to Be Mixed. . . . I Will Not Mix Them': Discourse, Ideology, and Generic Hybridity in Hardy's Fiction" (2009).

6. Björk, in *Psychological Vision and Social Criticism,* emphasizes Hardy's antirationalist stance and his interest in inter-social emotions over purposeful commitments to social change, and he sees Charles Fourier, Auguste Comte, other utopian Positivists, and Matthew Arnold as especially important influences.

General Relativity, which he took as confirming the views he had already formed about the universe—that neither chance nor purpose governs its workings (364).

Because he never stopped reading, Hardy the reader is a moving target, more likely to be assessed by a critic coming to his work looking for traces of particular strands of interest than to be seen as a whole, complicated, contradictory fellow with eclectic tastes in books. Though his reading journals understandably emphasize his deliberate reading programs on the one hand (as his biographer Robert Gittings noticed), and his project-based research on the other, he had a restless intelligence that was spurred on by intellectual curiosity, by fascination with the weird, by his social aspirations, and by chance associations. Hardy's brain was a rattle-bag of knowledge from different phases of life and spheres of reading. He somewhat misleadingly insisted on several occasions that he had no coherent philosophy, and it is true that he adhered to no school. He was especially annoyed by critics' insistence that he was a pessimist, which he denied.[7] Not an atheist, but an agnostic, he asserted that he was no scientist, and complained with some exasperation that it was his misfortune "that people will treat all my mood-dictated writing as a single scientific theory" (*Life and Work* 441). However, a focus on his career-long interest in human psychology reveals persistent strands in Hardy's thought: his commitment to affective psychology, his materialism, his Darwinian convictions about origins and evolution, his speculations about human consciousness (lamentably aware of feelings but not self-determining), his observations that social structures thwarted human fulfillment, and his certainty that the Prime Mover, Will or Cause was both indifferent and unconscious. One appetite of Hardy's reading, for large-scale organizing philosophies or systems (satisfied by Fourier and Comte), combined with his desire to know more about peculiar incidents, strange behavior, or quirky coincidences like the ones he noticed, and made note of, from personal observations or from his reading in old newspapers. Thus Hardy's notes about curious incidents in his *"Facts" Notebook* include entries on altruism and revenge; love-at-first-sight and suicide; fervent patriotism and fear of Bonaparte; draconian punishments and remarkable acts of mercy; escapees from lunatic asylums and pugnacious clergymen:[8] all indicate his broad interests in human psychology. The familiarity of this

---

7. See *Complete Poetical Works* v. 3, 166; and the excerpted correspondence with critic Alfred Noyes in *Life and Work* 438, 441.

8. See William Greenslade, ed., *Thomas Hardy's "Facts" Notebook: A Critical Edition* (2004).

Hardy, the folk-psychologist perennially fascinated by character-revealing behavior, has occluded a more learned, book-informed Hardy, who possessed up-to-date knowledge of the psychology of his day.

This chapter reviews the likely sources of Hardy's discipline-specific knowledge about human brains and behavior, nerves and their diseases, cognition and emotion. Though there is good evidence of psychological science responding to Hardy's representations,[9] in what Gillian Beer has theorized as the two-way traffic of ideas,[10] I focus here on documenting the influence of Victorian psychology on Hardy. In addition to discussing well-known influences, I emphasize sources of knowledge that have been noted before (not least by Hardy himself) but underestimated, and I place them in the context of the developing disciplines of psychology and neurology. I redirect critical attention to monist Eduard von Hartmann, anti-supernaturalist medical psychologist Henry Maudsley, evolutionary biologist George Romanes, as well as medical writers such as Robson Roose. In this my interest differs from earlier emphases on Hardy's knowledge of philosophy[11] and more recent accounts of Hardy's study of science,[12] though I am indebted to both. In the nineteenth

---

9. See James Crichton Browne, "Dreamy Mental States" (1895), an essay that cites Hardy's fiction, and 84 below, on Freud's response to *Tess*. Just three years after Hardy's death, his fiction was already being subjected to scrutiny by psychoanalytic practitioners. See S. M. Coleman, "'Two on a Tower': An Analytical Study", which was published in *Psychology in* 1931. Articles on Hardy's fiction have appeared in *Comprehensive Psychiatry, The International Journal of Psychoanalysis, The Journal of Evolutionary Psychology, and Modern Psychoanalysis*. Typically these essays treat Hardy's fictional characters as clinical case studies, though occasionally they reach through the representations to interpret Hardy's own psyche.

10. On the interpenetration of shared stories of nineteenth-century culture and the scientific presentation of new discoveries, see Gillian Beer, *Open Fields: Science in Cultural Encounter* (1996).

11. See, for example, Phillip Mallett, "Hardy and Philosophy" (2009), which argues for the importance of Comte, Darwin, Mill, and Schopenhauer. Early debate about philosophical influences centered on how well Hardy knew Schopenhauer and to what degree he adhered to pessimism. See, for example, Helen Garwood, *Thomas Hardy: An Illustration of the Philosophy of Schopenhauer* (1911) and the rejoinder by Harvey Curtis Webster, *On a Darkling Plain: The Art and Thought of Thomas Hardy* (1947). More recently, Hardy's influence by monist philosophers has been studied by G. Glen Wickens, *Thomas Hardy, Monism, and the Carnival Tradition: The One and the Many in* The Dynasts (2002), and his metaphysics by Mark Asquith, *Hardy, Metaphysics and Music* (2005).

12. See Robert Schweik, "The Influence of Religion, Science, and Philosophy on Hardy's Writings" (1999) and Angelique Richardson, "Hardy and Science" (2004). Though Darwin's influence on Hardy has long been acknowledged, more recent work emphasizes astronomy and geology. Canonically, see Gillian Beer, *Darwin's Plots: Evolutionary Narrative in Darwin, George Eliot, and Nineteenth-Century Fiction* (1983); on astronomy, see Pamela Gossin, *Thomas Hardy's Novel Universe: Astronomy, Cosmology, and Gender in*

century contributions to psychology came from both philosophers and scientists, experimentalists and theorists. Subsequent chapters bring the interests highlighted by this source recovery to bear on Hardy's poetry and fiction, including *The Dynasts,* but I proceed by suggesting first what Hardy gleaned from his reading and how we can verify his interests. (I also note what Hardy seems not to have read—Freud—not that this has deterred earlier psychoanalytic critics.)

Fortunately, Hardy took detailed notes on his reading and his *Literary Notebooks* survived the bonfire he made of more private papers. We can take this to mean not only that he preserved working materials for his second wife, Florence, to consult while she prepared his self-ghosted biography, but that he took some pride in transcribing the record of his intellectual journey, which opens with an 1863 drawing schematizing his study of Fourier's system and closes with an excerpt from a 1927 article on man's place in the universe and the impossibility of self-determination. We can imagine Hardy copying out with some satisfaction the pertinent quotation from a 1927 issue of *The Journal of Philosophical Studies,* into the notebook in which he had collected nuggets from a half century of reading:

> It is impossible that a man should be determined purely by himself; he is always determined by others . . . he is they, & they are he. . . . He derives from the whole universe, & *is* in a way the whole universe. He is an expression, a moment of the whole universe; but since he is this he may be regarded as being with one life with the universe, & therefore also, its other expressions. (*Literary Notebooks* v. 2, 249)

Hardy's reading had created the mental universe in which he in turn wrought fictional worlds, but that did not make him their arch-determiner, rather, in an echo of the creed, "as being with one life with the universe," an expression among other expressions.

For all his assiduous professionalism as a writer, he remarked at the end of his life that his only ambition "was to have some poem or poems in a good anthology like the *Golden Treasury*" (*Life and Work* 478), an image of a writer who wants not to stand alone, but to be read in the company of other writers. Hardy's intersubjectivity as much as his introspection makes him a fascinating subject for an historicist cognitivist study.

---

the *Post-Darwinian World* (2007); on geology, archaeology, and anthropology, see Andrew D. Radford, *Thomas Hardy and the Survivals of Time* (2003).

The literary-historical cognitivism I practice in this chapter by means of source study is not just a route back to context. It follows Hardy's lead in tracing how a self-aware writer's mind operates in one of its matrices, the environment of reading, created by our human habit of distributing our ideas, knowledge, wishes, and opinions in locations outside ourselves. We neither know, nor learn, on our own. For Hardy the recommendations of two friends and mentors, Horace Moule and Leslie Stephen, were to prove especially influential; Moule's recommendations are among the first works excerpted in Hardy's *Literary Notebooks,* and we often find Hardy learning from Stephen's articles on important thinkers.

The notes Hardy took from a variety of sources show him following leads, consulting books, periodical articles, encyclopedias, and book reviews. We may also speculate about reading he might have done in those sources, without making a surviving note, and such an exercise helps to form a sense of the emergent popular awareness of the materialist science of the period, such as he might have picked up in conversation with educated interlocutors. He wrote in his memoranda on the 30th of April, 1870, about the feeling of prescience that arises when ideas are in the air: "Thoughts seem to be epidemic. No sooner is a conviction come to than it appears in print" (*Personal Notebooks* 4). The print sources in which Hardy may have observed his convictions on record or acquired the elements of ideas were diverse: secondary sources read for a different reason; articles in the periodicals of the day; parodic cartoons in *Punch;* review essays; and reference books. For instance, the scholarly ninth edition of the *Encyclopedia Britannica,* published between 1875 and 1889, came out during the years when Hardy was building a career as a professional writer. It includes up-to-date and thorough illustrated entries on the physiology of brains and nerves. We know that Hardy consulted the *Encyclopedia* for an article on Schopenhauer (*Literary Notebooks* v. 1, 203). He took no notes on the articles on neuroanatomy, but his poem *The Dynasts* shows vividly that he had picked up that contemporary knowledge somewhere.

The Availability of Psychological Science

Victorian readers had ready access to specialist information about neurology and psychology, not only in medical journals. Periodicals for general readerships routinely discussed scientific topics. For instance, just during the 1874 run of *Far from the Madding Crowd* in the *Cornhill* magazine, articles on dreams, artificial memory, and brains appeared. During Hardy's career as a working writer, the *Fortnightly Review* ran articles on biology and animal automatism by T. H. Huxley, on brain science by G. H. Lewes, on neurology by George Romanes, on Positivism by Frederic Harrison, on materialism by Henry Maudsley, on mental imagery by Francis Galton, on disinfection by Robson Roose, on automatism by Herbert Spencer, on feelings and the will by Alexander Bain, on human personality by F. W. H. Myers, and on the education of the emotions by Frances Power Cobbe. This magazine of the advanced thinking of the day was the place Hardy chose to publish "The Midnight Baptism," a scene from *Tess of the D'Urbervilles* too scandalous to appear with the rest of the bowdlerdized novel in the *Graphic*.[13] Like the *Fortnightly*, the *Contemporary Review* often appears in Hardy's literary notes. Here, too, the philosophy, psychology and science that interest Hardy, from Comtean Positivism, to human automatism, to essays on hereditary defects and the psychology of art appear. Hardy's 1886 notes on George Romanes's "The World as an Eject," published in the *Contemporary Review,* record the first impact of imagery that he will reconfigure in *The Dynasts:* "unless we can show in the disposition of the heavenly bodies some morphological resemblance to the structure of the human brain, we are precluded from rationally entertaining any probability that self-conscious volition belongs to the universe" (*Literary Notebooks* v. 1, 174). Hardy would represent the universe as a brain and the Will as a neural network, but he understood that the analogy between human brain and universal source of volition could emphasize the unconsciousness (or nescience) of both, and he told a tale of "*Life's impulsion by Incognizance*" in *The Dynasts* (*Dynasts* v. 4, 58). This early-twentieth-century expression of an astronomical context for human psychology was built on solidly Victorian foundations. Between the late 1870s and 1900, the *Nineteenth Century* (another magazine frequently extracted by Hardy) runs wrap-up essays on recent science and individual articles on cosmic emotion, historical psychology and the new psychology, multiplex personality, mutual aid among animals, wireless telegraphy and brain-waves, brain function, and brain structure.

Whether Hardy regularly saw research on brain science and neurology as it came out in more specialized medical periodicals such as *The Lancet* (he cites the journal once in his notes [*Literary Notebooks* v. 2, 78]),

---

13. Thomas Hardy, "The Midnight Baptism." (1891).

or psychological work in *Mind* (founded by Alexander Bain), is a matter for conjecture, but he certainly had access to these journals through the library at the British Museum, where he habitually read, as well as at his club libraries. The Athenaeum, where he was a member from 1891, had a well-stocked library with journals, including *The Lancet* and *Mind*.[14] The Club's library catalogs indicate their holdings in science, psychology, and philosophy, and they also had magazine subscriptions that were available to members, but not preserved in the permanent collection. Books in a library may be read or left on a shelf, however, and absence of a book from a collection does not prove that a reader missed it.

For instance, no work by Charles Darwin was recorded in Hardy's Max Gate personal library at the time of his death,[15] yet we have his direct testimony that he was an early and convinced reader of Darwin's *On the Origin of Species* (1859),[16] and in 1888 he recommended the "recently published Life of Charles Darwin" to a correspondent (*Letters* v. 1, 174). A complex of words used by Darwin and his precursors entered Hardy's working vocabulary: in Hardy's published works the word heredity appears thrice, evolution four times, evolve five times, trait thirteen times, compete and competition thirty times, species sixty-four times. Still, the record of Hardy's annotations of Darwin's work remains frustratingly scanty, and the fact that many of the terms predate Darwin does little to support Hardy's direct indebtedness. Hardy's knowledge of Darwin may not have extended to the most psychological book, *The Expression of the Emotions in Man and Animals* (1872), but redactions of Darwin's argument for continuities of human emotions with those of the lower animals appear in works by later writers that Hardy did read, early on in John Stuart Mill and T. H. Huxley and later in the work of French Darwinian psychologist Théodule Ribot and Darwin's biographer G. T. Bettany.[17] As early as *Far from the Madding Crowd* (1874), Hardy's anti-supernaturalist view of the human species combines with representation of the impulsive emotions and motives of dogs, which could have been derived from direct observation, but might also have received sup-

---

14. Personal correspondence of the author with Anton Kirchhofer, on his incidental notes taken from the minutes of the Athenaeum Club library sub-committee (volumes for 1865–78 and 1878–1906). See VICTORIA Archives, "Re: Periodicals in London Athenaeum Club Library?"

15. See Michael Millgate, "Thomas Hardy's Library at Max Gate."

16. On 26 April 1882, Hardy attended Darwin's funeral in Westminster Abbey. "As a young man he had been among the earliest acclaimers of *The Origin of Species*" (*Life and Work* 158).

17. G. T. Bettany, *The Life of Charles Darwin* (1887), 126–35.

port from Darwin's *Expression,* a bestseller in 1872 which was widely discussed in English periodical essays and reviews (Ekman xxix). Philip Mallett points out that the 1873 novel *A Pair of Blue Eyes* contains a "virtual typology of the male and female blush," a topic theorized by Darwin just a year earlier (Mallett, "Hardy and Philosophy" 34). Even though in 1884 Hardy records his sister Mary's opinion that "Face-expressions have fashions like clothes" (*Life and Work* 175), his writing typically endorses a view of human behavior driven by instinct, rather than by intellectual reasoning, and inexorably shaped by heredity. Thus in the poem "Heredity," Hardy writes:

> I am the family face;
> Flesh perishes, I live on
> Projecting trait and trace
> Through time to times anon
> (*MV*, v. 2, 166–67, ll. 1–4)

This long view of the survival of a "projecting trait" certainly accords with Darwin's argument that facial expressions of emotions are universal (innate, not learned) and the product of natural selection. Hardy was also interested in weirder commonalities between animals and humans, such as his note on "*Fascination,*" in which he records the idea that "Basilisk & opoblepa—kill other animals by staring at them. Mouse running round open-mouthed snake, crying; at last as if forced, leapt in. Same effect from eye of setter on partridge. *Human eyes also* ("*Facts*" Notebook 268, emphasis in original). Together this patchwork of evidence encourages but does not verify the critical assumption that Hardy knew all of Darwin's work as well as he knew *The Origin of Species.* Yet I will maintain in this study that Hardy's subsequent notes on psychology and philosophy show, at the very least, his preference for ideas that can be squared with Darwin's theory of evolution.

John Stuart Mill

Without recourse to speculation, it is still possible to affirm that Hardy read a number of thinkers who contributed to the emergent studies of mind and behavior that would become psychology and sociology. An early important influence was the philosopher, radical, and social theorist John Stuart Mill (1806–1873), as Hardy's extracts and comments in his *Literary Notebooks* show (v. 1, xxvii, 368).[18] Mill does not usually loom large in standard histories of psychology, though his credentials are impressive. Grandson of a couple who ran a private lunatic asylum, son of James Mill (strict elementist author of *An Analysis of the Phenomena of the Human Mind* [1829]), John Stuart Mill spent the first twenty years of his life as an experimental subject in his father's application of associationist psychology to his education. His mental crisis of 1826–1827, with the cure he found in reading poetry for pleasure, forms the centerpiece of Mill's *Autobiography* (1873), an exercise in psychological introspection and self-diagnosis.[19] Mill's study of cognition, or what he called mental chemistry, emphasized the potentially transformative power of combination (in contrast to his father's view of mental compounds). John Stuart Mill's ideas about human psychology are diffused throughout his works, including notes on his father's associationist philosophy of mind.

Hardy especially admired several works and ideas of Mill. From an article written by Leslie Stephen, Hardy notes Mill's doctrine "Not a single fixed element anywhere—a general flux of things." Mill departed from associationist doctrine by contending that a compound may differ in its properties from the qualities of its component parts, and this resonated with Hardy's hope that ideas can form new wholes, an important aspect of his later hopes for cosmic evolution. Hardy made a note on Mill's concern that belief in innate human characteristics (over differences produced by circumstances) was "one of the greatest stumbling blocks to human improvements" (*Literary Notebooks* v. 1, 132). Later on he records a remark by Mill, under the heading *Statement of the Case of the Evolutionists, Materialists, Pessimists &c:* "nearly all the things which men are hanged or imprisoned for doing to one another, are nature's everyday performances" (152–53). That is, Hardy read Mill as holding out hope that "general flux" could allow individuals to break free from inborn constraints (though Hardy seems to agree with Darwin about the continuities between animal and human behavior). Mill's suggestions about improvements to social structures also mattered to him. Mill's *On Liberty* (1859), especially the section "Of Individuality," and

---

18. Early commentators on Hardy's sources discussed the influence of Mill on *The Dynasts*. See for example William R. Rutland, *Thomas Hardy: A Study of His Writings and Their Background* (1938), 20–45. In the 1960s Mill's radical social philosophy and Hardy's treatment of destructive conventions resonated: see William J. Hyde, "Theoretic and Practical Unconventionality in *Jude the Obscure*" (1965) and Björk, *Psychological Vision and Social Criticism in the Novels of Thomas Hardy (1987)* 123.

19. Jose Harris, "Mill, John Stuart (1806–1873), Philosopher, Economist, and Advocate of Women's Rights."

Utilitarianism (1861) were important to Hardy. *On Liberty* he claimed to know almost by heart when a young student (*Life and Work* 355), a claim supported by the thorough annotations he made in his own copy (F. E. Hardy, *The Early Life* 68–70) and the arguments he gave to Sue Bridehead as she seeks to break with Phillotson (*Jude* 215). "Of Individuality" Hardy recommended as a cure for despair after a time of depression in 1868 (*Life and Work* 59); as for *Utilitarianism,* he has his character Ethelberta read it over as she makes a decision about an expedient offer of marriage.

This bequeathing of his own reading to one of his fictional characters provides a good opportunity to see Hardy's processing of the implications of intellectual influences, as well as his nascent psychology of fictional character, which had already developed by 1876 from the cruder representations of his sensation fiction, *Desperate Remedies* (1871), where motive passions drive the plot without much interference from reflection,[20] and brains operate hydraulically. But just because his characters are better educated (exposed to the current thinking in Paris, for instance), does not mean that their reading informs their decisions. It can work the other way round. Ideas gleaned from characters' reading do not always serve innocent or desirable ends in Hardy's fiction, and in the wrong hands they can be abused. Justifications out of books come after the original impulsive desire, on characters' parts, to do what they want even if it will harm them. In Hardy's character-psychology, unconscious wishes guide behavior, deliberate actions bring unintended consequences, and overtly ethical reflections often reveal the traces of blind self-interest. In *The Hand of Ethelberta* (1896), the eponymous heroine, deciding on the advantage to herself and the private utility of her decision to bring happiness to at least a few, bends Mill's words to her wishes "By a sorry but unconscious misapplication of sound and wide reasoning did the active mind of Ethelberta thus find itself a solace. At about the midnight hour she felt more fortified on the expediency of marriage with Lord Mountclere than she had done at all since musing on it" *(HE* 296).[21]

---

20. As Björk has argued, the influence of Charles Fourier's ideas about emotions can be seen in *Desperate Remedies*. See Lennart A. Björk, "Psychological Vision and Social Criticism in *Desperate Remedies* and *Jude the Obscure*" (1976).

21. In lieu of an Oxford paperback of this novel, I employ references to the New Wessex Edition of *The Hand of Ethelberta*, general editor P. N. Furbank (1975). Like the Oxford editions, the New Wessex Editions are based on the 1912 Wessex edition, which Hardy edited and approved. In this case, Hardy revised the quoted passage, playing up Ethelberta's deliberate misapplication of Mill's ideas, for an interim edition, The Osgood McIlvaine version (1896), which was subsequently incorporated into the 1912 Wessex Edition. Cf. Thomas

Ethelberta goes on to consult casuists who justify her concealing information from her suitor. Considering that in 1906 Hardy publicly testified to Mill's impact (in a letter to *The Times* on the occasion of the 100th anniversary of Mill's birth), we might expect a more flattering depiction of the "luminous moralist" (*HE* 296) in this novel of 1876. Unlike Sue Bridehead, Ethelberta does not consult *On Liberty,* where she might have encountered Mill's argument with Christian self-denial, but Ethelberta is attempting to conform, not to break with convention. Reading can ennoble, it can mislead, and it can be bent to expedient purposes.

Here Hardy represents Ethelberta's reading career as instigating a moral change that can as easily be understood as degradation as improvement:

> She had begun as a poet of the Satanic school in a sweetened form; she was ending as a *pseudo*-utilitarian. Was there ever such a transmutation effected before by the action of a hard environment? It was not without a qualm of regret that she discerned how the last infirmity of a noble mind had at length nearly departed from her. She wondered if her early notes had had the genuine ring in them, or whether a poet who could be thrust by realities to a distance beyond recognition as such was a true poet at all. Yet Ethelberta's gradient had been regular: emotional poetry, light verse, romance as an object, romance as a means, thoughts of marriage as an aid to her pursuits, a vow to marry for the good of her family; in other words, from soft and playful Romanticism to distorted Benthamism. Was the moral incline upward or down? (*HE* 297)

Hardy was always interested in the impact of environment on the expression of character in the immediate generation of an organism (as has often been noted, many of his major characters fail to produce offspring that live). One of the categories he created retrospectively to sort out his fiction for the Wessex Edition was "Novels of Character and Environment," and the shaping influence of circumstances and contexts, here named as a "hard environment," pressures the temperament of Ethelberta. She is a survivor who jettisons her "soft and playful Romanticism" to become a self-aware abuser of the ideas of Utilitarianism. It works for her and suits her desires. Just as Sue Bridehead later employs Mill's arguments to seek her freedom from Phillotson, Ethelberta's citations from philosophy

---

Hardy, *The Hand of Ethelberta,* ed. Tim Dolin (1997) 287. The Penguin is based on the first book edition, published by Smith & Elder. See Tim Dolin, "A History of the Text" (1997) 413 and 453n1.

justify her impulses by back-formation, reaching for authoritative sanction of decisions she has already taken. The arguments from authority are
not meant to convince, but rather to reveal the anxious dispositions of
characters using them. In *Jude,* Phillotson sees this clearly when he moans
in response to Sue Bridehead's *argumentum ad verecundiam,* "What do I
care about J. S. Mill! . . . I only want to lead a quiet life! (*Jude* 215).

What we do not find when we read Hardy's character-psychology in
light of his psychological influences are characters representing psychological ideas as in allegorical tableaux of the passions, updated to demonstrate modern schools of thought. As Terry Eagleton has observed,
Hardy's characters do not represent singular types (Eagleton 14). Argu-
ably, only Hardy's late and last-published novel, *The Well-Beloved*
(1897), embodies a fixed idea in his characters. They are typically more
complex in their constitutions and circumstances. An early note on Fourier refers to "character a conglomeration or pudding stone" made out
of many ingredients (*Literary Notebooks* v. 1, 3). Even if his fictional
characters have shown themselves to be susceptible to diagnostic label-
ing (e.g., Farmer Boldwood suffers from monomania; Sue Bridehead is
sexually repressed; Angel Clare's sleepwalking and talking reveal his
neurosis), Hardy does not employ psychological principles or temperamental models as cookie cutters to shape his fictional characters. Though
some of his contemporaries pursued Ethology, a science of character that
sought to deduce the general laws of human nature, Hardy gravitated
instead towards the delineation of characters with conglomerate temperaments, worked on by oppressive customs and social conventions,
tyrannical public opinion, unquestioned patriarchal authority, and the
bossy religiosity of the pious. Though he consistently represented family
traits as recurrent characteristics, Hardy also recognized that the *idea* of
an inescapable heredity could act more powerfully than the trait itself, as
he shows in *Tess,* and he was acutely aware of the impact of altered circumstances, such as access to a national school, on attitudes and expectations. Certainly bodily and temperamental endowments play a role in
Hardy's characterization, but no sooner does he introduce a recognizable "type" than he conjures up a set of circumstances to poke and prod
the type into action.

Some characters fare better than others in this pressure-cooker of environment: women suffer more than men; children and animals are especially vulnerable. In this Hardy largely agreed with the ideas of John
Stuart Mill (and Harriet Taylor). Hardy's fiction often describes the suffering of animals, children and woman, and even depicts cross-species

altruism. In *Far from the Madding Crowd,* a dog helps the fainting and heavily pregnant Fanny Robin drag herself to Casterbridge (*FFMC* 261–62). Yet Hardy's commitment to affective psychology goes beyond sympathy for victims or illustrations of their specific forms of suffering. For sources of Hardy's commitment to emotionality as both a core trait and a central vulnerability of human beings, we must look to several other thinkers from which he extracted elements of an affective psychology. Two of them, Fourier and Comte, were known as social theorists rather than psychologists, but Hardy mined them for ideas about human development that conformed to his observations of real people. Hardy wrote in 1876 "there is more to read outside books than in them" (*Life and Work* 110), and he would discard psychological ideas, such as phrenology, that did not jibe with his experiences of people, including himself. His early processing of Fourier's ideas shows him testing them introspectively.

Fourier and Comte

That the French utopian socialist thinker Francois Marie Charles Fourier (1772–1837) was important to Hardy, we infer from his distillation of Fourier's system in an elaborate set of drawings of 1863 that Hardy preserved and later pasted into his *Literary Notebooks* under the heading "Diagrams shewing Human Passion, Mind, and Character—Designed by Thomas Hardy" (*Literary Notebooks* v. 1, 4). As Björk has demonstrated in his edited versions of Hardy's *Literary Notebooks* (xxvi–xxvii), Hardy especially valued Fourier's affective psychology and his emphasis on inter-subjective feeling that would ideally develop into what Fourier called "unityism" (3), a communitarian vision of the future. Hardy's drawings emphasize the shapes of individual lives over social developments, however. One chart lists the affective outcomes of "Friendship, Love, Familism, and Ambition"; another integrates Intellect, Passions, and Will in a drawing of an intertwining set of vines (Intellect and Will) winding around the trunk of the Passions (4). This 1863 drawing anticipates the strangling imagery of "The Ivy Wife" in a psychological, rather than Darwinian context. A second tree trunk on the same page shows the same three elements, possibly envisioned as roots, fusing as they cross a boundary marked "Amalgam," where Hardy re-labels the trunk "Moral Harmony." Its subsequent separation into four branches suggests continued competition among these expressions of affective life (Friendship, Love, Familism, and Ambition), as all four are unlikely to dominate in any one person. That Hardy associated Fourier's ideas with individual lives shows in his delineation of the life cycle on the same sheet, showing a peak in energy at 19 that begins to slope down after age 26, and is abruptly boxed off at 40 (Hardy was 23 when he drew this page).

The implication seems to be that there will not be infinite time in which to achieve the fusion required to reach "Moral Harmony," from whence the four affective qualities can reach "dominant" phases. For Hardy we may speculate Love and Ambition were to dominate, though as yet unmarried, he adorns "Familism dominant" with eight daisy-like offshoots. Hardy was to remain childless, but he was productive in his thirties. In 1876, with five published novels to his name, Hardy wrote a gloss on "all that a man learns between 20 and 40," in terms that suggest the endurance of his reading of Fourier (and Darwin): "all things merge in one another—good into evil, generosity into justice, religion into politics, the year into the ages, the world into the universe. With this in view the evolution of the species seems but a minute process in the same movement" (*Life and Work* 114). This is an optimistic vision of what a serious course of reading and growth towards moral harmony can achieve in the short life of a man.

The twenty-first-century reader of Hardy's notes on Fourier's *The Passions of the Human Soul* (English translation, 1851) observes the emphasis on affect as a combination of passions, will, and intellect, naturally but not inevitably growing towards moral harmony unless the strangling vines of will and intellect kill the central trunk of undifferentiated passions. The diagram also inks in the "Impossible Monsters" of all three components, suggestive of characters in later novels: Knight, an impossible monster of the intellect; Boldwood, an impossible monster of the passions; Bathsheba, impossible monster of the will. (The term is Hardy's own extrapolation from Fourier and does not appear in the book he consulted.[22]) On the notes that appear on the reverse of the drawings I have been describing, we can extract from Hardy's jottings phrases suggestive of his writerly interest in Fourier's psychology: "Emotion of Pursuit— Plot interest / Sympathy / The fine art Emotions" all point to varieties of emotion that will concern Hardy in later writings (*Literary Notebooks* v. 1, 3), though he will usually opt for cultivating sympathy over race-and-chase romance plot interest. Twenty years later finds Hardy the novelist still emphasizing character over plot: approving of Trollope's insistence

---

22. Charles Fourier, *The Passions of the Human Soul* (1851). Björk establishes that this was Hardy's source in "Psychological Vision and Social Criticism" 89.

on eliciting readers' sympathy with a novel's characters (Hardy triple underlines the word sympathise); wondering at the incidents of story Dickens calls up to eventuate the states of feeling "he foreshadowed in his mind" for his characters; and admiring Meredith's call to his fellow-authors to "produce real pictures of human life in its environment" through philosophy that eschews sentimentalism (164–65). Hardy's own commitments to the representation of human character always circle back to the emotions. In 1882 he identified his "ample theme: the intense interests, passions, and strategy that throb through the commonest lives" (*Life and Work,* 158) and in 1888 he differentiated his interest in novels of psychical sensation from the action-driven physical sensationalism popular at the time: "in the psychical the casualty or the adventure is held to be of no intrinsic interest, but the effect upon the faculties is the important matter to be considered" (213). Hardy's drawings from Fourier suggest an early commitment to a variant of faculty psychology, in which the separate modules of passion, will, and intellect compete, have the potential to produce their own impossible monsters, and even after fusion into the state of moral harmony, may still erupt into behaviors in which one or another affective style dominates.

While Hardy's debt to Fourier is well-documented in his own hand, his relation to Auguste Comte's thinking should be approached with care, for there was much to slough off from once-fashionable Positivism. His contemporaries and subsequent critics noticed the impact of Comte and Positivism on Thomas Hardy, which was not unusual for an intellectual of the period: in Britain Harriet Martineau, John Stuart Mill, G. H. Lewes, and George Eliot were also deeply engaged with Comte's ideas. Hardy acknowledged in a 1903 letter that "no person of serious thought in those times could be said to stand aloof from Positivist teaching & ideals" (*Letters* v. 3, 53), and although he insisted in the same letter that he was not a Positivist, Hardy certainly read Comte's work and read about him.[23] Moule gave him a copy of *A General View of Positivism* and the book survives with Hardy's (and Moule's) annotations (*Literary Notebooks* v. 1, 311). Phillip Mallett summarizes the critical consensus: "Certainly Hardy

---

23. When Hardy read Comte in May 1870 (as he declares in *Life and Work* 79), the text he was likely to have consulted was *A General View of Positivism,* translated into English by J. H. Bridges (1865), whom he later met (*Life and Work* 178). This book was in his Max Gate library at the time of his death, with Comte's *Catechism of Positivist Religion,* translated by Richard Congreve, 3rd ed. (1891). Hardy also took notes from Comte's *Social Dynamics* (*Literary Notebooks* 311–12). On Hardy's influence by Comte, see T. R. Wright, *The Religion of Humanity: The Impact of Comtean Positivism on Victorian Britain* (1986).

engaged closely with [Comte's] ideas. . . . He acknowledged ti
ence of Comte's writing on *Far from the Madding Crowd*, took e.
notes on his *Social Dynamics*, attended Positivist lectures at Newtc
and kept up a long friendship with Frederic Harrison, Comte's leading
British advocate" (Mallett, "Hardy and Philosophy" 22). Comte's social
theory of three stages, the theological, metaphysical, and positivist, is an
early sociological model of human progress not usually understood as an
aspect of emergent psychology, in part because Comte did not include
psychology in his system of the sciences (an incremental model starting
with arithmetic, leading to the physical sciences, and extending to sociology). Hardy was skeptical of Whiggish narratives of political progress
on the part of societies. Yet Comte himself argued that the three stages
applied not just to societies, developing over time, but also to individual
lives, and this insight can be seen as anticipating some ideas of developmental psychology. A child was theological, a youth metaphysical, and a
mature adult a scientist, capable of judgments based in empirical observations of sensory data, the foundation of positivist philosophy.

Like many of Hardy's sources for ideas about human understanding,
however, Comte's system offered theories rather than empirical investigations of their own, which leaves Hardy open to make his own applications in novels. Hardy's descriptions of imagined lives do not accord with
Comte's equation of maturity and unemotional objectivity. Yet the English
Positivist Frederic Harrison thought *Tess* was like "a Positivist allegory or
sermon" (*Literary Notebooks* v. 1, 312), and this points to the techniques
of Hardy's narrator. The words "allegory or sermon" are well chosen to
suggest Hardy's narrator's glosses on his characters' actions: the narrator
injects the interpretive frame around illustrations from characters' behavior. Comte eschewed introspection as a methodology, and his insistence
on employing objective observations was to become the fundamental
assumption of twentieth-century behaviorist psychology. While this connection does not make Hardy a behaviorist, it surely supports his habit of
narratorial generalization about characters' minds (a topic I address in the
next chapter). Yet it is likely that Hardy drew more direct support from
Comte's precept that "In human nature, and therefore in the Positive system, Affection is the preponderating element" (Comte, *General View* vii)
than from his commitment to objective observation. For Hardy Comte's
belief that "The proper function of the Intellect is in the service of the
Social Sympathies" would have been appealing (vii). In his extensive notes
from Comte's *Social Dynamics*, the following stands out: "*Feeling*—the
great motor force of human life" (*Literary Notebooks* v. 1, 68).

We must take care to disentangle the legacy of a thinker from the impact on one contemporary reader. The relationship of Positivism to twentieth-century Behaviorism provides a case in point. Rosemary Sumner sees Hardy as anticipating some aspects of Behaviorism, especially operant conditioning (Sumner 23–26). Rather than lauding Hardy for presciently inventing elements of Behaviorism, a science he did not know, we should instead restore Comte as a common influence on both the imaginative writer and the later social sciences, for Positivism contributes to the development of empiricism in the social sciences, including cognitive psychology. This does not make Hardy a cognitivist before his time. Indeed, his commitments were always more affective. The most lasting impacts of Comtean thought on Hardy were these: a muted version of Comte's idea of society's future progress, observable in Hardy's evolutionary meliorism and his visionary predictions in *The Dynasts;* and a robust ideal of affective human relations embodied in the term altruism. I argue in the conclusion of this study that Hardy understood his own empathetic disposition in Comtean terms, as altruism, a word Comte coined and advanced as an important goal of his humanist Positivist religion. Even though Hardy shed his Positivist associations, he hung onto altruism as a right description of his mode of systematic perspective taking in his life and art.

Lewes, Huxley, and Spencer

A trio of contemporary scientific writers, G. H. Lewes, T. H. Huxley, and Herbert Spencer, contributed to Hardy's knowledge of human psychology and provided a materialist, biological foundation for Hardy's view of the centrality of the emotions. G. H. Lewes was the author of both *Comte's Philosophy of the Sciences* (1853) and psychological studies such as *The Physical Basis of Mind: The Second Series of Problems of Life and Mind* (1877). Hardy read Lewes on Goethe, physiology, evolution (*Literary Notebooks* v. 1, 14–15, 92, 152), and he jotted a note on Spinoza from Lewes's *History of Philosophy from Thales to Comte* (1880) (v. 2, 519), a book that was in his library at the time of his death. Hardy found in Lewes's writings further justification for his own agnosticism and materialism, copying out the observation, "Physiology began to disclose that all mental processes were (mathematically speaking) *functions* of physical processes, i.e.—varying with the variations of bodily states; & this was declared enough to banish for ever the conception of a Soul, except as a term simply expressing certain functions" (v. 1, 92). From T. H. Huxley, author of *Lessons in Elementary Physiology* (1866), Hardy drew arguments in favor of brisk scientific inquiry over irrationally held truths. He made a long extract from a *Fortnightly Review* essay by Huxley on materialism (177). He approvingly noted Huxley's recommendation of rigorous argumentation that would make theories struggle for existence (146); that is, he noticed Huxley applying the notion of the survival of the fittest to ideas as well as to animal species. He admired Huxley's spirited argument with Wilberforce, the Bishop of Oxford (205) on the side of evolutionary theory, and he copied Huxley's views on "Intoxication with Ideas" into his *"Facts" Notebook:* "Men can intoxicate themselves with ideas as effectually as with alcohol or bang, and produce, by dint of intense thinking, mental conditions hardly distinguishable from monomania" (267). The most highly prized material of cognition—ideas—and its most honored practice—intense thinking—here take on an emotional coloration.

One of Hardy's notes links Huxley with Spencer (*Literary Notebooks* v. 1, 184). Through this association Hardy's specific interest in materialist affective psychology comes into focus (208–9). When Hardy was reading up on psychology in the 1880s, he studied the materialist context for Huxley's ideas in an article in French by the psychologist Pierre Janet:

> *"Psychologie,* (une chair de)." R. *Deux Mondes,* April 1:Mr Huxley considers Descartes to be the true creator of modern physiology, & notably as having opened the way by his automatism to the famous theory of reflex actions. . . . Malebranche, mystic that he was, continued on this point the tradition of Descartes . . . proclaiming, before H. Spencer, that every time there are changes in the part of the brain to which the nerves tend, there will happen also changes in the soul, & that the soul can neither feel nor imagine anything without change in the fibres in the same part of the brain. (208–9)

Hardy was fascinated by the idea of automatism, and took several notes in French and English on its theorists. He regarded most men as sleepwalkers in their own lives, unaware of the cause of their actions (*Life and Work* 190, 192), and he was persuaded by materialist explanations that saw impulsions of nerve and brain as simultaneous with actions. Uncontrollable and unknown emotions could push human behavior past even habitual bounds or the limits of temperament. Extracting from Spencer, Hardy notes, "The fact that even an inveterate habit may be broken by a gust of passion or a permanent mood of profound emotion, has given a semblance of rationality to the doctrine of free-will. Sometimes the snapped chains of habit are prevented by love, veneration for Xt, &c, from being welded together again. But . . . apt to be transitory—Cyclones, violent but short" (*Literary Notebooks* v. 1, 191). Hardy was to visit such transitory cyclones of feeling on characters such as Michael Henchard in the *Mayor of Casterbridge,* where Hardy exposes the irrationality of behavior in a fateful universe.

Hardy knew Spencer as both a biologist and a social theorist.[24] He took notes on Herbert Spencer's *Principles of Biology* (1864–67) and *The Principles of Psychology* (1855), in which Spencer advanced the biological basis of mind, in interaction with the environment. (Spencer never repudiated elements of Lamarckianism, but he was strongly associated by Darwin and his contemporaries with evolutionism.) Hardy read Spencer's political essays in the *Fortnightly Review* and the *Contemporary Review.* In Hardy's Max Gate Library at the time of his death were a number of editions of Spencer's works: *An Autobiography* (1904), *Essays: Scientific, Political and Speculative* (1868–78), *First Principles,* 4th edition (1880); and a book belonging to his second wife, Florence, *Education: Intellectual, Moral and Physical* (1905). Two editions of *First Principles* belonging to Hardy are now held by the Harry Ransom collection at the University of Texas (*"Poetical" Notebook* 95). Of these two books, Hardy's copy of the 4th edition of Spencer's *First Principles* is heavily marked and lightly annotated, with special attention given to the pages on evolution.[25] We may infer that this book was an important source for Hardy's knowledge of the physiology of feeling. In this work Spencer repeatedly describes emotions and sensations as causing muscular contractions and other bodily changes such as secretions. He treats emotions as causing actions even when undirected by volitions. Emotions vary according to the supply of the blood to the brain, according to Spencer, and their outcomes also vary in the degree of muscle tension produced—in respiratory and vocal muscles as well as the muscles of the face, trunk, and limbs. All these effects, in Spencer's account, arise from nerve discharges in turn provoked by chemical changes in the brain (Spencer also accounts for inhibitory responses, in terms of forces to be overcome). All this Spencer regarded (and reported) as the commonplaces of the science of the day.

Spencer's synthesizing in *The Principles of Psychology* was probably an important source for Hardy's ideas about human and animal instincts.

---

24. For Hardy's testimony to Spencer's impact, see his letter to Lena Milman (*Letters* v. 2, 24–25).

25. Herbert Spencer, *First Principles,* 4th edition (1880) 278–82, Harry Ransom Research Library, The University of Texas, Austin, TX.

For Hardy, instinct and reflex action were qualities of animal nature shared by human beings, but that did not mean higher instincts, such as altruism, were impossible. Indeed, Hardy would have known that George Eliot linked reflex action and sympathetic responses, as Vanessa Ryan points out (Ryan 70). Spencer attempted to account for both biological drives (instincts of self-preservation) and socially beneficial impulses (such as maternal and parental instincts). Instinct, because biological, does not cease to function in the face of experiential knowledge: the nutritive instinct to seek nourishment, the sexual instinct to mate and reproduce carry on regardless of the rebuffs of experience. Comte believed that cultivation of sympathetic instincts could encourage positive developments in human character and society. Darwin thought that natural selection could preserve and continually accumulate variations of instinct, and he theorized that sequences of small changes could produce complex instincts such as the cell-building behavior of bees. Darwin's emphasis on competition displaced sympathy as a human instinct, but Herbert Spencer continued to theorize the roots of altruism in the parental instinct interacting with tender feelings (*Principles of Psychology*, 3rd ed. 626). Since instinct competed with consciousness in determining behavior, Hardy often associated it (as did Spencer) with the emotions. Hardy's characters' instincts are typically emotional: writing about his character Henry Knight in *A Pair of Blue Eyes*, whose impulse to claim Elfride conflicts with his scruples, Hardy links the key terms: "His instinct, emotion, affectiveness—or whatever it may be called—urged him to stand forward, seize upon Elfride, and be her cherisher" (*PBE* 317). In *The Return of the Native*, Hardy's narrator characterizes Egdon Heath as calling upon "a subtler and scarcer instinct, to a more recently learnt emotion" than to the aesthetic appeal to charm (*RN* 10). Characteristic in political theories of the day as motivating the behavior of savage others, instinct in Hardy's representations moves all human beings (as well as animals), though two thirds of his uses of the word refer to female characters. Of those that refer to male characters, most pertain to courtship. Hardy could have found in Spencer the notion that instinct precedes reason (indeed that the dividing line between them is hard to fix).

Spencer's most original contribution was to apply general laws from biology to societies. Specifically, Spencer saw analogies between the workings of forces on nerves in the body and the energy of aggregates expressed in society, viewed as an organism. Although today Spencer is remembered for his application of Darwinian evolution to human groups or societies, for coining the phrase "survival of the fittest," and for his contribution to Social Darwinism (a label applied to him retrospectively), Hardy noticed in Spencer the ethical thinking that emphasized mutual aid and altruism, noting "The highest life [is] reached only when, besides helping to complete one another's lives by specified reciprocities of aid, men otherwise help to complete one another's lives" (*Literary Notebooks* v. 1, 163). Like Hardy, Spencer gleaned Comte's altruism from the mixed ingredients of Positivism, discarding most of what remained (in the end Spencer would also jettison altruism itself from his system). Hardy agreed with Spencer that an outcome of the Darwinian conception of life was that all life was inter-related, and he found in Spencer support for one of his core beliefs: "The Sympathetic, generous heart, which recognizes the rights & claims of others, wh. is pained by their suffering, & rejoices in their joy, is declared [by Spencer] to be the only trustworthy source of that social morality on wh. general well-being depends" (191).

Human beings would have to accomplish this without the divine intervention of a sympathetic deity, however. In *First Principles,* Spencer writes of an unknowable Ultimate Cause, a power to whom no emotion can be ascribed, which Hardy glossed as "Persistence or the Persister" (*"Poetical" Notebook* 27). As Hardy noted, *"Spencer's* Unknowable closely resembles the Noumenon or Thing-in-itself conceived by Kant as underlying all phenomena, which is also closely allied to the sublime idea of an impersonal Diety" (*Literary Notebooks* v. 2, 153). Hardy was to figure this cause variously as a brain-dead Creator, a Prime Mover without feelings, and a Will that differed fundamentally from the emotional beings his impulses pushed around on the world stage. From Spencer's *Autobiography* Hardy extracted Spencer's "paralyzing thought": "what if, of all that is thus incomprehensible to us [the Universe] there exists no comprehension anywhere?" (163). Hardy would worry this bone in many poems and narratorial asides.

A major commonality between Hardy and Spencer was their agnosticism, expressed by Spencer in terms of scientific materialism. Hardy found a friend and mentor on this intellectual path in Leslie Stephen, man of letters and editor of *Cornhill Magazine.* Stephen was an early appreciator of Hardy's literary talent, praising and publishing his breakthrough novel *Far from the Madding Crowd* in his *Cornhill* (*Life and Work* 100). Stephen's books, *Essays on Freethinking and Plainspeaking* (1873), *History of English Thought in the Eighteenth-Century* (1876), *The Science of Ethics* (1882), and *An Agnostic's Apology and Other Essays* (1893), as well as his articles in magazines, commanded Hardy's attention, as his extracts in the *Literary Notebooks* demonstrate. In this case, however, the personal connection, especially the long conversations Hardy enjoyed having with Stephen, were to make a deeper impress than reading alone. Hardy testified that once he got to know Stephen in the early 1870s, he was "mentally influenced by him so deeply" (*Life and Work* 42), and it is hard to underestimate the range of subjects where Stephen's lead encouraged Hardy's subsequent reading and thinking. In just one conversation in 1875, Hardy discussed with Stephen "theologies decayed and defunct, the origin of things, the constitution of matter, the unreality of time, and kindred subjects." Later Hardy testified that he had been "much influenced by his philosophy, and also by his criticism" (131), and he was terribly pained when Stephen (growing deaf and unwell, as Hardy later realized) spoke to him caustically and antipathetically rather than in the sympathetic, constructively critical manner that Hardy valued so dearly (188, 178).

Clubs and Connections

One of the kindest turns that Stephen did for Hardy was to bring him into contact with like-minded professionals and intellectuals. In 1878, Hardy was elected to the Savile Club (*Savile Club* 124), of which Leslie Stephen was one of the early members, elected in 1870 (*Savile Club* 102). The Savile was an artistic, literary club with some scientists and medical men among the members: F. W. H. Myers, founder of the Society for Psychical Research and popularizer of the unconscious mind was a member (11). A little more than a decade later, Hardy was to be elected to a more prestigious group, The Athenaeum. Hardy's personal connection to the Athenaeum Club was also Stephen, the person whom he cited as having most influenced him more than any other contemporary (*Life and Work* 102). Stephen's patronage may have had some social limits, for while Stephen was a member of the Athenaeum from 1877, Hardy was not admitted until 1891 (Hardy's biography shows some signs of his attempting to secure a patron to nominate him earlier [238]). By that time Hardy had amassed considerable knowledge of psychology, and was in a good position to learn about advances in neurology. Through the Athenaeum Hardy could have conversed with scientists and medical men who made up a significant portion of the membership: the naturalist George James Allman; physician George Fielding Blandford; surgeon Sir Francis Seymour Haden, elected in the same year as Hardy; and the linguist and polymath Thomas Spencer Baynes, editor of the *Encyclopedia Britannica*.

The intellectual contacts made possible by Hardy's club memberships, though often undocumented in notes, should not be underestimated, and his socializing, though easy to disparage as tuft-hunting, yielded interesting conversations. Hardy's biography occasionally records a dialogue such as one in 1893 with James Crichton Browne, a medical psychiatrist and co-founder of the journal *Brain*. They discussed gender and brain size, and differed on the question as to whether men choose less passionate women for mates in civilized society (*Life and Work* 275). Interdisciplinary cross-pollination occurred by means of these discussions. Browne later cited Hardy's fiction in a *Lancet* article on "Dreamy Mental States" (Browne 1–5, 73–75). As Hardy's fame grew, purely literary connections also made fortuitous contact with neurologists possible. Late in life, Hardy got to know the neurologist Henry Head through Head's wife, Ruth Mayhew Head, who was the editor of little anthologies. Both Ruth and Henry Head loved Hardy's poetry.[26] These personal connections do not prove that Hardy would have read the issues of *Brain* edited by Head (1910–25) in the years of their acquaintance or earlier (when Head was publishing on sensation and aphasia), but if he did, Hardy would have been exposed to the cutting edge of late-Victorian and early-twentieth-century neurology.[27] In the pages of *Brain*, Hardy could have observed hopeful possibilities of discovering the cures of nervous diseases to balance out his grim vision of an Unconscious Will, brain and nervous system writ large over an unfeeling universe.

The years of Hardy's serious reading, from 1859, when Darwin's *Origin of the Species* and Bain's *Emotions and the Will* came out, through 1927, when he made the last extracts in his *Literary Notebooks,* coincided with an explosion of discoveries in psychology and neurology. A selection from "Milestones in Neuroscience Research" suggests the range of these advances, in neuroanatomy, techniques of investigation, diagnosis of diseases, and development of effective medicines.[28] In 1860, Karl L. Kahlbaum described the psychological disorder catatonia and in 1861 Paul Broca discussed cortical localization by showing that a brain lesion causes speech loss. John Hughlings Jackson showed how brain injuries

---

26. Hardy later consulted Head about Florence's health. *Collected Letters* v. 6, 95–96. The couples became friendly, and Head moved into Hardy's neighborhood in Dorset; Hardy trusted Head's advice in his last illness (*Life and Work* 480).

27. For more about Head and Hardy, see L. S. Jacyna's *Medicine and Modernism: A Biography of Sir Henry Head* (2008).

28. E. H. Chudler, "Milestones in Neuroscience Research," supplemented by items from Marcos Emanoel Pereira, "History of Psychology Timeline."

could cause loss of speech in 1864. In 1866, John Langdon Haydon Down discussed congenital idiots, in 1867 Henry Maudsley published *Physiology and Pathology of the Mind,* and in 1868 Julius Bernstein timed the action potential. 1869 saw the publication of Francis Galton's *Hereditary Genius,* and in 1876 Galton used the terms nature and nurture to explain the effects of heredity and environment. Meanwhile, in 1871 Weir Mitchell described phantom limb syndrome, in 1872 Darwin published *The Expression of the Emotions in Man and Animals,* and Camillo Golgi published the first work on the silver nitrate method of staining tissue in 1873. In 1875 Richard Caton recorded electrical activity from the brain and Wilhelm Heinrich Erb and Carl Friedrich Otto Westphal documented the knee jerk reflex. In 1876 Bain founded the journal *Mind,* dedicated to psychological research. David Ferrier published *The Functions of the Brain* and in 1879 Wilhelm Wundt set up his laboratory at Leipzig, initiating European experimental psychology. Jean Baptiste Edouard Gelineau coined the term narcolepsy in 1881 and two years later, Emil Kraepelin first used the words *neuroses* and *psychoses.* George Romanes published *Animal Intelligence* in 1882, an anecdotal rather than experimental study, while F. W. H. Myers and William Barrett founded the Society for Psychical Research, which sought to investigate the psychic phenomena of spiritualism in a scientific spirit. James Spence's 1882 *Lectures on Surgery,* a book in Hardy's personal library, included advice on brain surgery and the treatment of head injuries.[29] In 1884 Karl Koller discovered that cocaine could work as an anesthetic; Georges Gilles de la Tourette described movement disorders that would later be known by his name; Theodor Meynert published *A Clinical Treatise on the Diseases of the Forebrain;* and William James published *What is an Emotion?* In 1887 Alfred Binet and C. Fere published *Animal Magnetism,* a study on hypnosis. In 1890 William James published *Principles of Psychology.* Wilhelm von Waldeyer named neurons in 1891 and three years later Franz Nissl stained them with dahlia violet. In 1896 John Dewey theorized the reflex arc. In 1897 Felix Hoffmann synthesized aspirin. Two years later Bayer AG marketed it commercially, but not until 1915 was it available without a prescription. Freud published *The Interpretation of Dreams* in 1900. In 1903 Ivan Pavlov demonstrated conditioned reflexes. Golgi and Cajal shared the 1906 Nobel Prize for their work on the structure of the nervous system. Emil Kraepelin named Alzheimer's disease in 1910 and a year later, Eugen Bleuler

---

29. See Millgate, "Thomas Hardy's Library at Max Gate."

added schizophrenia to the psychologist's lexicon. In 1920 Hardy's friend Henry Head published *Studies in Neurology*.

Monists and Materialists: The Evolution of Feeling Minds

From this wealth of available knowledge, Hardy zeroed in on reading from monists and Darwinian psychologists. His note taking shows a preference for anecdotal studies and theoretical speculations over analysis of experiments, while the books he owned demonstrate an interest in medical applications. The experimental methods used by neurologists in the nineteenth century included chemical analyses, dissection of the brain, comparative anatomy, observations of diseases and injuries, microscopy, observations of fetal development, phrenology, and experiments on living animals (Clarke and Jacyna 9–10). As an anti-vivisectionist who read Darwin as confirming the family relationship of all life, he may have shied away from medical neurology that experimented on animals while they were alive, and his notes on F. W. H. Myers's work record his awareness that even "the single cell of protoplasm" is "endowed with reflex irritability" (*Literary Notebooks* v. 1, 167). Hardy was skeptical about the examination of cranial bumps as revealing character (*Life and Work* 43). His work depicts an anatomist with a microscope, but most of the evidence of Hardy's psychological observations takes the form of behavioral records. As a student of human nature, Hardy was aware of current theories of reflex action that put free will in question. We can see this in the glosses he appended to his notes, as for instance in these remarks on Myers: "[The drift of the article is that beings have a multiplex nature, human as other; that what we suppose to be choice is reflex action only—that by implanting impulses in hypnotic states they can be made part of the character . . .]" (*Literary Notebooks* v. 1, 168). He was aware of theories of the evolution of the brains of more sophisticated animals and of their "higher centres of cerebration" where abstract ideas and memories could be stored and coordinated (167).

Hardy gleaned support for monist ideas even from sources not obviously by or about scientific materialism. From an article in *The Spectator*, Hardy copied "the history of our inward life can prove that the introduction of a spiritual germ into the mind of man can . . . make his life & death totally differ' things . . . ," adding his own gloss "[Thus thought shapes the very world: matter creates thought: reciprocal action]" (*Literary Notebooks* v. 1, 147) and he recorded alternative hypotheses, as for instance considering mental life as an epiphenomenon of physical events, "at best representing a mere inner aspect of the outward frame of things—a sort of backwater from the stream of physical forces" (148). Hardy's notes on monist writers such as W. K. Clifford emphasize his interest in squaring their theories with Darwin without closing off opportunity for future developments, a ground for optimism:

> Clifford's theory of the intellectual growth of mankind: "as the physical senses [e.g. the eyes of the first animals with eyes] have been gradually developed out of confused & uncertain impressions, so a set of intellectual senses or *insights* are still in course of development, the operation of which may ultimately be expected to be as certain & immed.ᵗᵉ as our ordinary sense-perceptions. (186–87)

That is, while Hardy remained fascinated by the apparently supernatural possibilities of telepathy and what we would call extra sensory perception, he excerpted writers who proposed an eventual material explanation for them, whether as emanating from Clifford's "mind-stuff," the molecular source of consciousness, from Bain's "double-faced unity" of substance with both physical and mental properties, or from Spinoza's unthinking "universal substance" (*Literary Notebooks* v. 2, 108).

Hardy found support for his materialist views about paranormal aspects of the human mind in the works of Théodule Ribot. Hardy took notes from two works by the French Darwinian psychologist. From Ribot's *Heredity: A Psychological Study of Its Phenomenon* (1875), Hardy extracted the following anecdote:

> I know a man who has been all his life subject to hallucination. This disposition is of such a nature that if he meets a friend in the street he cannot tell at once whether it is an actual person or a phantasm. By dint of attention he can make out a difference between the two. Usually he connects the visual impressions by touch, or by listening for the footfalls. This man is in the flower of his age, of sound mind, in good health, & engaged in business. Another member of his family has had the same affection [affliction], though in a less degree. (*"Facts" Notebook* 288)

This extract shows not only Hardy the craftsman collecting anecdotes from a rich source, for he notes "(Other instances follow in the same book)" (288), but it also demonstrates the novelist's awareness of the heritability of nervous disorders and the curious disposition of afflicted man, which combines a tendency to hallucinate with an empirical temperament: he patiently tests his visual phantasms with the evidence of the other senses. From this same book of Ribot's Hardy drew the observation that "Mind has two parallel modes of activity, the one conscious, the other unconscious" (*Literary Notebooks* v. 2, 130), but he was clearly interested in the ways that the conscious mind could keep tabs on the unpredictable projections and impulsions emerging from the unconscious. He took notes from Henry Maudsley's *Natural Causes and Supernatural Seemings* (1886) about the likely sources of hallucinations, excerpting "In hallucinations & illusions a certain tract of the brain has taken on a morbid function. In brains with a predisposition to insanity the confederate centres are more loosely bound together, more apt to act separately. . . . Then a slight cause may suffice to produce delirium . . . fever, emotion, overwork . . . wh. w.[d] have had no serious effect upon a strong brain" (*Literary Notebooks* v. 1, 199). Hardy owned a copy of Charles Creighton's *Illustrations of Unconscious Memory in Disease* (1886) and Robson Roose presented a copy of *Nerve Prostration and Other Functional Disorders of Daily Life,* 2nd ed. (1891) to Hardy.[30] Without knowing Freud's work on dream interpretation, the return of the repressed or neuroses,[31] Hardy had access through Maudsley and Ribot to the idea of the unconscious mind as the source of hallucinations and even ghosts, through Havelock Ellis to current dream theory,[32] and through Creighton and Roose to the notion that unconscious promptings could cause illness and pain.

In his 1905 poem "The Noble Lady's Tale," one of Hardy's personas offers what sounds like a Freudian explanation of a ghost as the return of the repressed, a wraith projected "Thither, by my tense brain at home aggrieved" (*TL* v. 1, 354). However, there is no evidence that Hardy ever became aware of the work of his contemporary, Sigmund Freud. Though he was aware of John Dewey and William James in the United States and

---

30. See Millgate, "Thomas Hardy's Library at Max Gate."

31. Though Freud's *On the Interpretation of Dreams* was available in German from 1900 (English translation of the 3rd edition, 1913) and *The Psychopathology of Everyday Life* from 1901 (English translation, 1914), Hardy's reading records show no direct evidence of his knowledge of the books. A. A. Brill's earliest translation of Freud appeared in 1909; after 1910 English redactions of and commentaries on Freud's theories became more common. See G. G. Meynell, "Freud Translated: An Historical and Bibliographical Note" (1981).

32. Havelock Ellis, "The Logic of Dreams" (1910), an essay that calls upon Binet, Ribot, and Wundt as authorities, not Freud. Ellis's *The World of Dreams* (1911) respectfully disagrees with Freud's dream-theory and could have attracted Hardy's notice (but if it did, Hardy left no records of it).

Pierre Janet and Théodule Ribot in France, Hardy never mentions, quotes, or refers to Freud in his published works, notebooks, or letters. As I have earlier suggested, writers publishing in journals such as the *Fortnightly Review* or the *Contemporary Review,* or, in French, the *Review des deux Mondes* were more likely to be read by Hardy. So, for instance, Hardy may have seen Havelock Ellis's 1910 essay, "The Logic of Dreams," in *The Contemporary Review.* Because Hardy's German was less strong than his French, he was unlikely to have encountered Freud in the original. The availability of Freud in English began in 1909 with the earliest of A. A. Brill's translations (Meynell 306). Hardy's Bloomsbury connections through Leslie Stephen's children and their associates might suggest a conduit for Freud's ideas. Though James Strachey began analysis with Freud in 1920 in Vienna, he did not begin translating Freud's essays in English until 1927. By then Hardy was in retirement at Max Gate, where he was still a serious reader and active note-taker. In any case, the first volumes of *The Standard Edition of the Complete Psychological Works of Sigmund Freud* did not come out until 1953, long after Hardy's death. Freud arrived in London in 1938, too late to meet Hardy among the literary and scientific luminaries of the day. All of these factors militate against Hardy's possible knowledge of Freud.

Just as psychoanalytic literary critics have borrowed Freud's concepts and vocabulary to analyze Shakespeare and other writers from periods long before the late nineteenth century, Hardyans have at times considered his work through the lens of psychoanalysis. The best of these studies, such as Rosemary Sumner's *Thomas Hardy: Psychological Novelist* (1981), show Hardy anticipating Freud in his depiction of neurotic characters or those who struggle against inhibition. As Sumner writes,

> The use of these Freudian terms . . . is appropriate because Hardy is here anticipating Freud's diagnosis of some of the problems facing "civilised" man. This is not to suggest that the correspondence with Freud necessarily gives extra validity to Hardy's perceptions, but we can see from this parallel that even Hardy's very early thoughts about human nature, an in particular about the psychological problems of his contemporaries, were developing on very similar lines to those expressed by Freud some 50 years later. (Sumner 125)

The recognition of Hardy's prescience, anticipating not only Freud but also Jung and aspects of Behaviorism, has to a great degree occluded his knowledge of the psychological science out of which those later developments arose. Discovering just how deeply Hardy studied psychology, especially in the 1880s, shows him acquiring the groundwork that makes such displays of forward thinking possible. Though it is not the subject of this study, Hardy's incipient Freudianism has struck many twentieth-century readers and critics. No less an authority than Freud himself recognized Hardy's insights into the behavior of human creatures rendered in fiction. Freud was a reader of Hardy's *Tess,* and found in him—post-humously—a kindred spirit. In August 1929 Clarence Oberndorf visited Freud in Bechtesgaden. Suffering from a plate in his mouth and grumpy about American resistance to his therapeutic ideas, Freud hardly said a word to Oberndorf. After lunch, Freud invited his visitor into his study to see what he was reading. Obderndorf reports, "on his desk lay open Thomas Hardy's *Tess of the d'Urbervilles."* When Obendorf showed surprise and pleasure at seeing one of his favorite novels, Freud "smiled and said, 'He knew psychoanalysis'" (Oberndorf 181–82). If he did, it was through earlier sources on the unconscious mind.

F. W. H. Myers, a fellow member of the Savile Club with Hardy, also advanced the idea of a subliminal self that might be tapped through hypnosis, telepathy, or automatic writing. Myers was the first English writer on psychical phenomena to redact the work of Pierre Janet and Sigmund Freud for English readers.[33] As we have seen, Hardy read both Janet and Myers in journals. From Ribot Hardy might have also become familiar with the ideas of Alexander Bain (from which he makes only one brief extract in his *Literary Notebooks* [v. 2, 108]). Robert Schweik believed that Hardy acquired knowledge about the ideas of Alexander Bain secondhand through John Stuart Mill's fifth chapter of *Utilitarianism,* a book Hardy knew well.[34] Through Ribot Hardy could have also read about William James's theories of the emotions, particularly in Ribot's *The Psychology of the Emotions* (1897), from which he made a lengthy extract (*Literary Notebooks* v. 2, 63). Hardy excerpted notes from James's *A Pluralistic Universe* (1909) and *The Meaning of Truth* (1909), and he had a book by James, *Human Immortality: Two Supposed Objections to the Doctrine* (1898), a work on psychic survival, in his Max Gate Library.[35] Though Hardy does not make extracts from James's psychology of the emotions, he tantalizingly quotes Florence Gay on James: "He asks us to think of our brains as thin & transp.ᵗ places in this material veil,

---

33. Alan Gauld, "Myers, Frederic William Henry, 1843–1901."

34. Robert Schweik, "Mill's Images of Justice in Utilitarianism: The Influence of Bain and Darwin" (c. 2005).

35. See Millgate, "Thomas Hardy's Library at Max Gate."

permitting the Infinite Thought to pierce them as white light pierces glass" (240). Here Hardy entertains the notion that thought could be transmissive through the instrument of the brain. As in this extract, though, Hardy's reading notes often show him questioning what he read: "He asks us to think . . . " suggests that Hardy demurs. Sometimes he makes his convictions explicit, as in his sarcastic late poem, "Our Old Friend Dualism," whose persistence he remarked in a comic verse:

> All hail to him, the Protean! A tough old chap is he:
> Spinoza and the Monists cannot make him cease to be.
> We pound him with our "Truth, Sir, please!" and quite appear to still
>   him:
> He laughs; holds Bergson up, and James; and swears we cannot kill him.
> We argue them pragmatic cheats. "Aye," says he. "They're deceiving:
> But I must live, for flamens plead I am all that's worth believing!"(*WW*
>   v. 3, 233, ll. 1–6)

Naming Bergson and James as the reanimators of an outdated, deceptive dualism that is the creed of priests (flamens), Hardy allies himself with Spinoza and the monists. Their explanations for human behavior and sensations lay not in the promptings of disembodied infinite thoughts, but in the living self's own impulses. As we will see in a later discussion of the poetry of Hardy, he constructed a loop running from the human mind, creator of such projections as God or the Immanent Will, back to human beings, motivated by impulsions emanating (unbeknownst to them) from the mind.

Though he was to move away from Fourier and discard most of what he learned from Comte, Hardy was most interested in grand unifying theories that brought the individual mind of man into alignment with the universe. He noted from Eduard von Hartmann's *The Philosophy of the Unconscious* (1869), a book in his personal library at his death,[36] the following observation on the logic of "*The principle of the Uncons.*[s] {[Unconscious Force?]}":

> There is a general tendency of thought towards this single principle. In each succeeding chapter one piece more of the world *crystallizes,* as it were, around this *nucleus,* until, expanded to all-unity, it embraces the

---

36. Hardy owned the 1893 edition in translation. See Millgate, "Thomas Hardy's Library at Max Gate."

Cosmos, & at last is suddenly revealed as that wh. has formed the core of all great philosophies, the Substance of Spinoza, the Absolute Ego of Fichte, Schelling's Absolute Subject-Object, the Absolute Idea of Plato & Hegel, Schopenhauer's Will &c. (*Literary Notebooks* v. 1, 185)

Material correlates of the mind anchor monist explanations of the universe's matter in motion. George John Romanes's 1886 essay "The World as an Eject" in the *Contemporary Review* expressed ideas that he had shared in 1885 lectures and were to be expanded in *Mind and Motion and Monism* (1895). Hardy recognizes these ideas from the work of W. K. Clifford, as his notes demonstrate:

> *The World as an Eject.* Prof. Clifford s.ᵈ that unless we can show in the disposition of the heavenly bodies some morphological resemblance to the structure of the human brain, we are precluded from rationally entertaining any probability that self-conscious volition belongs to the universe. . . . This is . . . illogical . . . {*The Theory of Monism,* wh. supposes matter in motion to be substantially identical with mind . . . } But . . . Although all conscious volition is matter in motion . . . it does not follow that all matter in motion is conscious volition . . . elaborated consciousness. (*Literary Notebooks* v. 1, 174)

Hardy adds his own question, referring to his reading of Clifford: "[Qy. How much complication is necessary to produce consciousness.]" (174). Clifford was a mathematician and philosopher who died young, and whose works were collected and edited by none other than Leslie Stephen, Hardy's first and most influential literary patron.[37] An evolutionary biologist and author of *Mental Evolution in Man* (1888), Romanes was characteristic of the post-Darwinian scientist who struggled to maintain Christian faith despite his commitments to scientific reason. *Thoughts on Religion,* 4th ed. (1895) was in Hardy's Max Gate library.[38] Romanes believed that his own loss of faith was in part due to the over-emphasis on reason and the neglect of emotion as a source of truth, a view that might well have appealed to Hardy's sense of human psychology driven by affective impulses.

The medical psychologist Henry Maudsley contributed most substantially to Hardy's understanding of the material basis of mind, including

---

37. See W. K. Clifford, *Lectures and Essays,* ed. Leslie Stephen and Frederick Pollack (1879).

38. See Millgate, "Thomas Hardy's Library at Max Gate."

the emotions. Important works include Maudsley's *The Physiology and Pathology of Mind* (1867), *Body and Mind* (1870), and *Natural Causes and Supernatural Seemings* (1886). Hardy took extensive notes on Maudsley's *Natural Causes and Supernatural Seemings* (*Literary Notebooks* v. 1, 195–97, 198–201) and also recorded Maudsley's views on human automatism from an article in French (184). Unlike most of the other sources of Hardy's psychological knowledge, Maudsley was a practicing alienist. He was unusual in his own community of medico-psychological practitioners because he was an agnostic and a convinced Darwinian,[39] both of which factors would have appealed to Hardy, though they contributed to Maudsley's unpopularity in general. As Sally Shuttleworth has recently discussed, Maudsley's gloomy account of degenerate traits passing down from parent to child could justify a pessimistic view of child suicide (Shuttleworth, *Mind* 335, 343–45). Hardy's depiction of congenital mental ailments such as those afflicting the Fawley family in *Jude the Obscure* nearly match Maudsley's treatment of the topic of pathological development of inherited disease in *Natural Causes and Supernatural Seemings* (Maudsley 237–38).

Maudsley's materialist views on the physical aspects of mental states meant that he saw the essential unity of body and mind as a prerequisite of a physician's practice. This included the emotions:

> The mental suffering or psychical pain of a sad emotion testifies to actual wear and tear of nerve-element, to disintegration of some kind; it is the exponent of a *physical* change. What the change is we know not; but we may take it to be beyond question that, when a shock imparted to the mind through the senses causes a violent emotion, it produces a real commotion in the molecules of the brain. It is not that an intangible something flashes inward and mysteriously affects an intangible metaphysical entity; but that an impression made on the sense is conveyed along nervous paths of communication, and produces a definite physical effect in physically-constituted mind-centres; and that the mental effect, which is the exponent of the physical change, may be then transferred by molecular motion to the muscles, thus getting muscular expression, or to the processes of nutrition and secretion, getting expression in modifications of them. (Maudsley, *Body and Mind* 107–8)

While negative emotions might then cause mental illnesses (rather than

---

39. T. H. Turner, "Maudsley, Henry (1835–1918)."

moral failings), positive emotions, for Maudsley, also play a role in mental development.

Hardy was attracted to Maudsley's affirmative comments about how new ideas, emotional responses, and mental habits combined, possibly because they described the potential for change to occur. He extracts from *Natural Causes and Supernatural Seemings* a set of related passages: "The new conception is reached tentatively & by degrees, by modifications of old notions through impressions made by altered facts & relations, much of the modifying impression being unconscious in the first instance. The increments of experience saturate the mind silently, until they crystallize consciously into a new conception of things"; "Wonder wins assent . . . because wonder, like other emotions, craves for & embraces gladly that wh. is agreeable to it & fitted to increase it"; "habit is acquired faculty, wh. means function-made structure—structural knowledge, in fact—& therefore the automatic & easy performance of acts wh. were performed at first only with conscious labour" (*Literary Notebooks* v. 1, 196–97). Together these passages could describe the effects of imaginative work on a novelist—and not least his readers—opening their minds through careful, curious observation and what twentieth-century literary theorists would re-label defamiliarization. "The difficulty," Hardy quotes from Maudsley, "is to break the enthralling chain of unheeding habit" (197).

Evoking emotions from readers would be a part of a successful argumentative effort: "It is always a far more effective way of persuasion to awaken sympathetic feeling for the weakest argument than to present an irrefutable argument to an unsympathethic mind. . . . The emotion {attracts the congenial & reinforcing, repels the uncongenial & opposing ideas. . . . } The natural effect of an emotion {is} to attract to itself congenial ideas, getting strength & support from them" (*Literary Notebooks* v. 1, 199). This practical application of the emotions at work in the act of persuasion was not only an ingredient of classical rhetoric, familiar to Hardy from his reading of Aristotle, but it also contributed to a hopeful possibility of changing minds. Hardy noted from Maudsley, "The force of originality needed to break through traditional routine of thought, feeling, & conduct & to give freedom of expansion to impulses of variation, is not so great . . . most of the resistance . . . being convention" (200). Thus, though most of Maudsley's contemporaries read him as grimly pessimistic, Hardy's notes show a more optimistic view. Yet he also found in Maudsley support for his thinking on the limits of cognition: "Consciousness tells him indeed that he is a self-sufficing individual with infinite potentialities of freewill; it tells him also that the sun goes round the earth" (201). Whether readers in this condition could be educable remained a point of skepticism for Hardy, but he had has own experience of extraordinary intellectual growth as an example of what reading makes possible.

For Hardy, whose life with books opened a way to a writing career even as it deprived him of his childhood faith, reading was a core strategy of intellectual development. Evolved to develop in interaction with its surrounding culture, the human brain realizes its cognitive potential in dynamic relation to a distributed communication network. In literate cultures this network includes the reading materials that are valued enough to be kept, taught, referenced, and responded to. Historical study of sources and interpretation of the intellectual response to the distributed materials of culture comprise the environment in which any writer's cognition, perception and feeling operate. Every person's mind is adapted to function in a complex symbolic network, but not every person spends a lifetime acquiring, studying, making notes upon, and alluding to the wide range of materials that we humans find it convenient to distribute in the relatively stable format of print language. Hardy did. Thomas Hardy had a lifelong commitment to developing his personal knowledge, deepening his understanding of the past, extending his awareness of current discoveries in a wide array of sciences, including the science of mind. He used his brain in interaction with the distributed materials of a culture that was engaged in rapid revision of its understanding of the material world and cosmos. Because he was a writer, Hardy left an extraordinary record of his own evolving understanding of what he labeled, in the early drawings tipped into his *Literary Notebooks,* "Diagrams shewing Human Passions, Mind and Character."

Combined with a Darwinian sense of shaping environment, his elucidation of these concerns in his fictional worlds, introspective lyrics, and in a panoramic historical epic can be regarded as thought experiments, staged over a half century. Chapter 2 and chapter 3 show how Hardy's knowledge of psychology, and later, neurology, entered his imagistic schemas in his poetry and conditioned the narrative techniques he employed to represent sentient characters who do not control their own fates. Because he used his writing to think, not just to earn a living, and because he never stopped inquiring through reading, his views developed, as I discuss in more detail in chapter 4, "The Neurological Turn." Hardy the biological man could not evolve by himself in a changing environment, but his mind could respond—intuitive, alert to others, and persistently attentive to scientific advances. He marked a passage in his copy of Spencer's *First Principles* that identifies opinions and ideas as markers of a man in time:

> It is not for nothing that he has in him these sympathies with some prin-
> ciples and repugnance to others. He, with all his capacities, and aspira-
> tions, and beliefs, is not an accident, but a product of the time. He must
> remember that while he is a descendent of the past, he is a parent of the
> future; and that his thoughts are as children born to him, which he may
> not carelessly let die. (*First Principles,* 4th ed. 123)

Early mastery of the ideas in Darwin primed Hardy to think of his own species and the universe it inhabited as one that would inevitably change, not necessarily for the better. Paradoxically for a novelist who only rarely told a story that spanned more than a generation (*The Well-Beloved* is an important exception), Hardy possessed a vivid sense of deep time and extensive space. He did not expect sudden improvements in the lot of human creatures, but he hoped for change over the long run. In the end of *The Dynasts* Hardy imagines the Will evolving to consciousness as human beings already have: "Men gained cognition with the flux of time, / And wherefore not the force informing them" (*Dynasts* v. 5, 252). As for the poor benighted "sentient subjects" (255) of the "Inadvertent Mind" (252), at best they can recognize the injustices generated by this situation and not over-rate their good fortune, if they get any. Mostly Hardy's characters proceed unaware of the rigged system that has made them feeling beings in a universe of action they cannot control. Although in *The Mayor of Casterbridge* he grants Elizabeth-Jane the insight that in spite of her current tranquility, "happiness was but the occasional episode in a general drama of pain" (*MC* 310), Hardy's narrators ordinarily occupy a privileged position in their fictional universes, knowing what characters do not. They may not control the actions, but the narrators feelingly and knowledgably relate them. By the time Hardy wrote *The Dynasts,* he had practiced many times the depiction of unconscious motive forces at work in fictional worlds overseen by a privileged knower. In Hardy's scheme, a narrator is not God-like, but the Immanent Will might come to resemble a good narrator. How Hardy's fictional narrators handle the curious predicament of characters driven by impulsions they scarcely recognize requires a detailed look at his narrative technique, which is the subject of the next chapter.

CHAPTER 2

The Minds of Hardy's Characters

Hardy's Distinctive Narrative Techniques

Considering his own habits of introspection, documented in his verse, in his studious literary notes, and in his self-ghosted biography, Thomas Hardy was remarkably chary about exposing the interior workings of his characters' minds in the mode of free indirect discourse.[1] This narrative technique for the representation of the character's mind stuff in the tense and person of the narration, commonly associated with the development of psychological realism, appears far less in Hardy's work than in the fiction of Jane Austen, George Eliot, or Henry James. Though he knew how to use it, he employed it with restraint. This was not an accident. Hardy's favored representational technique, *thought report* (also known as *psycho-narration*), demonstrates and underscores his embodied, affective theory of mind of beings driven to actions they do not understand by emotional impulses or innate dispositions.[2] As Vanessa Ryan establishes, "Victorian psychologists and novelists alike show how much of our inner life remains obscure, even opaque, to our conscious minds: they

---

1. A search of the MLA Bibliography for any of the keywords that name "free indirect discourse" and "Thomas Hardy" yields no entries (in contrast to dozens of citations for "free indirect discourse" and "Jane Austen").

2. On embodied consciousness in Hardy, see Elaine Scarry "Work and the Body in Hardy and Other Nineteenth-Century Novelists" (1983).

question the conception of interiority, calling attention to the physiological, reflexive, and automatic aspects of mind and action" (Ryan 165). I argue here that what has sometimes been seen as Hardy's old-fashioned narrative technique for representing minds actually reveals his up-to-date psychological insight. Hardy was as interested in human consciousness as a problem as in its formal rendering as a matter of craft, and his conviction that most human beings were sleep-walkers or automata clearly posed a challenge to narrative fiction's easy entry into other minds (*Life and Work* 158, 175, 190, 192). This chapter is concerned less with the contents of Hardy's characters' minds than with the methods he used to represent them, but, as I hope to show, his techniques suited his views about consciousness, nescience, and communal judgments (whether right or wrong) about characters' behavior.

As a craftsman Hardy had mastered the techniques involved in what later theorists would distinguish as three modes for representation of fictional thoughts, *narrated monologue, quoted monologue,* and *psycho-narration.*[3] Though Victorians lacked this terminology, reviewers certainly responded to what they perceived as unusual in Hardy's methods for representing characters' thoughts and states of mind.[4] Their comments, accompanied by the illustrative extracts they embedded in their reviews, show the ways they saw Hardy departing from Victorian norms which tended to emphasize narrated monologue (free indirect discourse, *Erlebte Rede*). They saw that Hardy's discourse about characters' minds often used language the characters themselves would never employ, and many found this jarring. They also noticed that Hardy sometimes used external descriptions of settings and circumstances to imply states of mind or moods, rather than taking the reader inside the characters' heads.

Though a chapter of this length cannot provide the contrasting analysis of his contemporaries' narrative strategies that would prove the assertions I have just made, it rests on the assumption that Hardy's techniques differed sufficiently from the third person fiction of novelists such as Eliot, Trollope, Dickens, Thackeray, Collins, Charlotte Brontë,

---

3. Dorrit Cohn, *Transparent Minds: Narrative Modes for Presenting Consciousness in Fiction* (1983) 14. I employ Cohn's terms with supplements from cognitive narratologists. Key sources for the narratology in this chapter are Alan Palmer's *Fictional Minds* (2004) and *Social Minds in the Novel* (2010).

4. R. G. Cox, *Thomas Hardy: The Critical Heritage* (1979). Unless otherwise noted, references to contemporary reviews cite this compilation of early responses to Hardy's works as they were published.

and the earlier, highly influential Jane Austen,[5] to attract notice in reviews of his fiction. I thus begin by considering these early comments on Hardy's minds, written in the critical vocabulary of the day. Extracts from Hardy's fiction provide materials for case studies of his technique, described by me in today's narratological terminology. In addition to demonstrating how his contemporaries registered Hardy's distinctiveness, I engage here with cognitive narratology's debates. Though it is not at all surprising that cognitive narratology has closely examined fictional minds, the representation of consciousness constituting one of the defining features of fictionality (in the view of Monika Fludernik [*Fictions of Language* 3–6]), the categories and functions of these narrative techniques have recently undergone extension. This chapter thus participates in the rehabilitation of thought report as a sophisticated and flexible technique for the representation of fictional consciousness, including intermental thought, as described by cognitive narratologist Alan Palmer. Hardy used *psycho-narration,* also called *thought report,* to provide by far the majority of his narrators' generalizations about the inner feeling states, thoughts, desires, private responses, and most importantly, their lack of awareness of their own motivations. That he did so as a way of working out in his formal choices his understanding of human psychology, especially his paradoxical belief in species-wide shared feeling and individual nescience, I argue here.[6]

---

5. For accounts of the narrative techniques of other nineteenth-century novelists, see essays by Dames and Herman in David Herman, ed., *The Emergence of Mind: Representations of Consciousness in Narrative Discourse in English* (2011). Richard Menke's doctoral dissertation, "Victorian Interiors: The Embodiment of Subjectivity in English Fiction, 1836–1901" (Stanford University, 1999), usefully discusses the embodied subjectivity of Victorian novelists in light of narrative theories for representation of consciousness. Austen's techniques are much studied, most recently by Alan Richardson in *The Neural Sublime* 79–96. Among those who have discussed Austen's free indirect thought, see especially Joe Bray, "The Source of 'Dramatized Consciousness': Richardson, Austen, and Stylistic Influence" (2001); Helen Dry, "Syntax and Point of View in Jane Austen's *Emma*" (1977); Frances Ferguson, "Jane Austen, Emma, and the Impact of Form" (2000); Louise Flavin, "Mansfield Park: Free Indirect Discourse and the Psychological Novel" (1987); Daniel P. Gunn, "Free Indirect Discourse and Narrative Authority in *Emma*" (2004); and Anne Waldron Neumann, "Characterization and Comment in *Pride and Prejudice*: Free Indirect Discourse and 'Double-Voiced' Verbs of Speaking, Thinking, and Feeling" (1986). On an aspect of Eliot's representation of consciousness, see Kay Young, "Middlemarch and the Problem of Other Minds Heard" (2003).

6. Christine Brooke-Rose judges this technique more negatively, writing "the blurred and empty use of old ironic devices is not simply an error of taste but the inevitable result of a world-view in which . . . someone controls things, but indifferently and unfairly" in "Ill Wit and Sick Tragedy: *Jude the Obscure*" (1989) 46.

It is quite true, as cognitive narratologist Alan Palmer has recently demonstrated in his *Fictional Minds,* that the canonical exhibits of modernist stream-of-consciousness and Victorian free indirect discourse actually include a great deal of thought report as well. This mode, so habitual to Hardy's narrative art, divulges characters' states of mind through the better-informed observations of an authorial narrator *about* his characters, and it can seem both controlling and antiquated. It certainly struck his contemporaries as odd. The time has come, however, to break the habit of interpreting a progressive development in formal strategies. The familiar story goes like this: representations of mind develop from old-fashioned thought report (characteristic of ancient epic and narratives before the novel) into the psychologically revealing free indirect discourse that flowers with realism until the flow of interior monologue begins, by which high modernism sweeps away the controlling channels of a narrator's omniscient perspective. Abandoning this simplifying narrative of formal progress helps us first to observe how many nineteenth-century novelists incorporated all three modes in their handling of characters' internal states of mind. Despite the wide diffusion of the technique often called free indirect discourse, few novelists could do without thought report, and the two modes blend nicely in third person past tense narration. I concur with Alan Palmer that more accurate assessments of the proportional deployment of the techniques of psycho-narration, narrated monologue, and quoted monologue will reveal that in third-person fiction, thought-report dominates well into the twentieth century: Virginia Woolf, for example, plants psycho-analogies to bloom all around her winding paths of quoted monologue. The modern interiority of Woolf is to a great extent anchored in passages of image-rich thought report. Departing from an implicitly developmental scheme of narrative form also permits re-evaluation of writers whose techniques set them apart from their peers: are they really so old-fashioned, or innovative, as they have appeared to critics who weigh formal choices by merit? We may discard some of the ideological baggage that has been bundled with discussions of form.[7] This helps us to recognize that *many* Victorian novelists told *about* their characters' minds some of the time rather than presenting their inner discourse item by item all the time. To suggest that Hardy relies more heavily on thought report than his peers indicates his choices among available modes and downplays the eccentricity of his techniques.

---

7. For a cautionary treatment of the implicit ideology of formal devices, see Meir Sternberg, "Proteus in Quotation-Land: Mimesis and the Forms of Reported Discourse" (1982).

However, Hardy's way of telling about his characters' minds did seem different to his contemporaries. His friend Horace Moule, writing in an unsigned review of *Under the Greenwood Tree,* complained in 1872 that Hardy's country folk "express themselves in the language of the author's thought" ([Moule] 417–18), but that refers to dialogue, not representation of consciousness. Indeed, Moule concedes that cottagers can think with "subtle distinction" . . . more completely than the well-dressed world are apt to suppose (418). R. H. Hutton was among the earliest to describe what he saw as a fault in Hardy's writing, in a *Spectator* review of *Far from the Madding Crowd* (19 December 1874). He complains, "George Eliot never confuses her own ideas with those of her dramatic figures, as Mr Hardy seem to us so often to do" (Cox 24). In contrast to Eliot's technique, which clearly flags narratorial commentary on characters and marks the center of consciousness by using discourse appropriate to the character, "Mr Hardy seems to us, while using first-rate materials derived from real observation, constantly to be shuffling his own words or tone of thought with those of the people he is describing" (25). For Hutton, this "is the main fault of drawing in a most amusing book. But it is a great one" (25). In the same season, Andrew Lang identified a possible source of Hardy's discomforting discourse about characters, in an *Academy* review of 2 January 1875: "He contemplates his shepherds and rural people with the eye of a philosopher who understands all about them, though he is not of them, and who can express their dim efforts at rendering what they think and feel in language like that of Mr Herbert Spencer" (Cox 36). Spencer's psychology proposed a somatic, materialist basis for mind and a vocabulary that would be familiar to intellectuals but not to the subjects of Hardy's rural stories, Lang thought: "this way of writing and thinking . . . gives the book its peculiar tone" (36). A few years later, an anonymous reviewer in the *Saturday Review* (18 November 1882), writing about *Two on a Tower,* disapproves: "Again, Mr Hardy has fallen too much in this book into the trick of attempting analytical discussion of mental processes—a trick which is but too apt to lead the way to dullness" (Cox 98). The extract that follows consists of the narrator's observations about Swithin's and Lady Constantine's states of mind, rendered entirely in the mode of thought report. Reviewers did not inevitably disapprove; an unsigned review of *The Mayor of Casterbridge* in the *Athenaeum* (29 May 1886) admiringly commented, "He has a wonderful knowledge of the minds of men and women, particularly those belonging to a class which better-educated people are often disposed to imagine has no mind" (Cox 133).

While he was admired as a psychologist (see Minto in Cox 174), Hardy's psychological diction attracted negative attention. Coventry Patmore exclaimed in *St. James's Gazette* (2 April 1887), "Why such a master of language should . . . have repeatedly indulged in such hateful modern slang as 'emotional,' and 'phenomenal' . . . and in the equally detestable lingo of the drawing-room 'scientist,' seems quite inexplicable" (Cox 149). William Watson, writing in the *Academy* (6 February 1892), agrees: "Mr Herbert Spencer's diction is no doubt very accurate, but probably not more so than Lord Tennyson's" (Cox 199). Though Victorian reviewers consistently equated the narrative voice of third person fiction with the author, attributing what we would call the narrator's discourse to the real person (and equally frequently referred to the author's creations as people), the examples they provide show that what disturbed them derived from the authorial narrator's psycho-narration or thought. The incursion of erudite and specifically scientific diction into generalizations about fictional characters' minds seemed to them a deviation from the usual practice, as Hutton opines: "George Eliot never confuses her own ideas with that of her dramatic figures" (Cox 24).[8]

A second feature of Hardy's narration also struck his contemporaries as unusual: looking back at the century from the vantage point of 1896, in the *National Review,* A. J. Butler remarks on Hardy's faculty for correlating external description with "an aspect of the human mind" (Cox 285). Not unknown in other novelists (Butler remarks that Dickens and the Brontës do the same thing), the application of external details "to arouse the desired emotion in the reader" is a technique easier to detect than describe according to Butler (285). That it is a technique especially noticeable in Hardy depends in part on the difference from other novelists: "It is not very conspicuous in Sir Walter Scott . . . Thackeray . . . George Eliot had little or none of it" (286). Victorian reviewers saw the components of the technique as description of physical scenes and presentation of dialogue. From these a reader derives a sense of mental states and feelings (Cox 5). Sometimes the authorial voice of the narrator seems to emanate not from a person but from the external world itself, offering observations on the human creatures inhabiting the scene. In 1892 William Watson admired this as poetic, praising Hardy's "manner of sometimes using external Nature not simply as a background

---

8. George Eliot does use psycho-narration, most famously in her striking analogies for characters' mental states, but she slides into *narrated monologue,* transcribing individual character's thought-stream word for word. The matching tense and person of narrated monologue and psycho-narration make them especially compatible to blending.

or setting, but as a sort of superior spectator and chorus, that makes strangely unconcerned comments from the vantage-ground of a sublime aloofness upon the ludicrous tragedy of the human lot" (Cox 201). The narrator's capacity to offer descriptions of settings that imply vantage points on the human beings inhabiting the scene points to an unusual combination: an external and apparently omniscient narrative voice that deigns not to show the insides of human beings' heads, but offers wry observations about their behavior. Later narrative theorists would name this technique behaviorist or externalized narration.

As these brief excerpts suggest, Hardy's handling of fictional consciousness, whether through narratorial generalization, attribution of thoughts and feelings in language unsuited to the characters' own voices, or in externalized implications of mood and motive, appeared unusual to his original reviewers. It still seems exceptional today, but it is an aspect of Hardy's art that has attracted more general commentary and less sustained analysis. Though often characterized by critics, Hardy's techniques for the representation of fictional consciousness have not been studied comprehensively. J. Hillis Miller's influential account of Hardy's distancing tactics (*Distance and Desire* 1), with his analysis of the "advance and retreat of the narrator's consciousness," pointed the way for subsequent narratological analysis (57), but very little in fact followed.[9] Christine Brooke-Rose asserts in a reading of *Jude the Obscure* that Hardy's "peculiar" identifying structure "is achieved through: (1) a skillful use of dialogue to conceal what is suggests; (2) a heavy-handed use of narration; (3) a blurred use of free in direct discourse" (Brooke-Rose 35). By blurring she means the movement between narrated monologue and psycho-narration, or narrator's thought report (38–41). The few narratological discussions of representation of consciousness in Hardy's fiction that do exist have been limited in scope, treating just single texts.[10] This

---

9. Among the subsequent critics who have noticed Hardy's objectifying characterization and deviations from normative Victorian narrative techniques are William A. Cohen, "Faciality and Sensation in Hardy's *The Return of the Native*" (2006); Michael Irwin, *Reading Hardy's Landscapes* (2000); Elaine Scarry, "Work and Body in Hardy and Other Nineteenth-Century Novelists"; John Paterson, "Lawrence's Vital Source: Nature and Character in Thomas Hardy" (1977), especially 465; and Robert Kiely, "Vision and Viewpoint in *The Mayor of Casterbridge*" (1968), especially 189–91. Though each of these critics notes Hardy's materialist emphases on externalities of character and his shifting viewpoints, none brings a narratological approach to Hardy's representation of characters' inner lives.

10. Kay Young treats mood and nonintrospective consciousness in *Jude* and *Tess* in her *Imagining Minds: The Neuro-Aesthetics of Austen, Eliot, and Hardy* (2010) 127–83. Linda Shires treats the multiple perspectives and fractured characters of *Tess* as demonstrating Hardy's radical aesthetic of alienated consciousness, influenced by Victorian poetic techniques, in

chapter goes further than any prior narratological consideration of Hardy's representation of consciousness, treating four novels and charting some of the range of ways that Hardy uses thought report: objective or behaviorist narration; intermental thought; and the techniques that preoccupy most narratology on the topic, narrated monologue (free indirect discourse) and quoted monologue. It establishes his difference from his contemporaries, recognized early in his career by Havelock Ellis. It suggests that the experiments and developments of technique between the 1874 novel *Far from the Madding Crowd* and the 1891 novel *Tess of the d'Urbervilles* correlate with Hardy's emerging sense of human psychology in an indifferent universe, presented most fully in *The Dynasts*. However, it only opens the conversation. It is to be hoped that a more thorough investigation of Hardy's narrative techniques for representing minds can soon be undertaken, without sliding back into the zone of generalizations that place Hardy as awkwardly combining modern themes and old-fashioned narratorial habits.

Three Modes for Representing Fictional Minds

NARRATED MONOLOGUE

A celebrated quality of nineteenth-century novels lies in their wide-spread adoption of this double-voiced discourse that enables a narrator smoothly to move from presentation of externals of action and situation to glosses of the thought-stream of the character(s) involved, preserving the tense and person of the narration (usually 3rd person and past tense), but conveying the words of the character's mind. The technique variously named narrated monologue, free indirect discourse (FID), empathetic narration, or *Erlebte Rede,* carries the past tense and third person narration of the outer scene while reporting inwardly. This technique, by any of its theoretical labels, enjoys precedence as one of the most characteristic features of nineteenth-century narrative fiction. One can easily find examples of it

---

"The Radical Aesthetic of *Tess of the d'Urbervilles*" (1999). Also treating *Tess,* Jakob Lothe takes a Stanzelian approach to Hardy's authorial narration, noticing narrated and quoted monologue but inexplicably omitting the ubiquitous psycho-narration entirely, in "Hardy's Authorial Narrative Method in *Tess of the D'Urbervilles*" (1986). Christine Brooke-Rose treats thought report (as Genettian narrativized discourse) in her nuanced discussion of *Jude.* Brooke-Rose also notices that Hardy deploys internal focalization strategically, allowing access to Jude's mind but rarely to Sue's (40, 43).

in the third-person fiction of every major Victorian novelist, and its variations (spread out among many characters, as in Trollope, or limited to
a single center of consciousness, as in Henry James) have been detailed
and examined by narrative theorists and literary historians of the form
of the novel.[11] It is a dominant technique in the rendering of interiority, but Hardy used it less frequently than his contemporaries. Like most
novelists, Hardy blends the modes for representation of consciousness,
however, and we may find in his stories many passages in which narrated
monologue and psycho-narration coexist. His short story "An Imaginative Woman" seems a good place to start, since it tells the story of an
obsession, and its main events are perceptions and misunderstandings
rather than traditional plot actions. Drafted in the 1880s for the volume
Wessex Tales (1888), the story later appeared in the volume *Life's Little
Ironies* (1894), and it has a few passages of narrated monologue, in which
the character's mental discourse appears in the guise of the narration. The
story reveals Hardy's psychological interests of the 1880s, especially his
convictions about embodied affectively charged consciousness, the little-
understood force that drives characters' behavior. One of the rare happen-
ings of the story occurs when the main character Ella transgressively dons
the mackintosh and waterproof cap that belong to the poet Robert Trewe,
object of her remote affections. She imagines them as the inspirational
"mantle of Elijah" (*LLI* 15), and Hardy reports her feeling states in alter-
nating sentences of generalized thought-report (psycho-narration) and
narrated monologue: "Her eyes always grew wet when she thought like
that [*psycho-narration: a generalization about the nature of her physiological response to thinking*], and she turned to look at herself in the glass
[*narration*]. *His* heart had beat inside that coat, and *his* brain had worked

---

11. Critics of the novel after Percy Lubbock have often marked the development of
techniques for the representation of consciousness as formal advances. See Erich Auerbach,
Mimesis: The Representation of Reality in Western Literature (1953); Wayne C. Booth,
The Rhetoric of Fiction (1983); Roy Pascal, *The Dual Voice: Free Indirect Speech and Its
Functioning in the Nineteenth-Century European Novel* (1977); and Ian Watt, *The Rise of
the Novel: Studies in Defoe, Richardson and Fielding* (1957). The narratological literature
on the subject is too vast to contain in a single note, but, beyond Cohn, *Transparent Minds,*
see Monika Fludernik's magisterial *The Fictions of Language and the Languages of Fiction.*
See also Susan Erlich, *Point of View: A Linguistic Analysis of Literary Style* (1990); Manfred
Jahn, "Contextualizing Represented Speech and Thought" (1992). Notable earlier studies
include Melvin Friedman, *Stream of Consciousness: A Study in Literary Method* (1955);
Paul Hernadi, "Dual Perspective: Free Indirect Discourse and Related Techniques" (1972);
and Brian McHale's useful survey, "Free Indirect Discourse: A Survey of Recent Accounts"
(1978). For a dissenting voice on the dual nature of free indirect discourse, see Ann Banfield,
Unspeakable Sentences: Narration and Representation in the Language of Fiction (1982).

under that hat at levels of thought she would never reach [*narrated mono-logue: the words track with Ella's thoughts*]. The consciousness of her weakness beside him made her feel quite sick [*psycho-narration; report of a physiological response to a thought*]" (*LLI* 15, emphasis in original; my commentary in brackets). Many passages in the story follow this pat-tern, interjecting short bursts of Ella's thoughts into a matrix of the nar-rator's reports on her increasingly over-wrought, aroused state of mind and body. This highly conventional blend of narration, psycho-narration, and narrated monologue enables the Victorian narrator to move smoothly from external events to internal states without the abrupt jump into the first person, present-tense distinctiveness of quoted monologue.

QUOTED MONOLOGUE

Thought transcripts of first person, present tense discourse that could be spoken aloud with no adjustment of tense and person comprise quoted or interior monologue. This mode of representation of consciousness also exists in English fiction as early as the work of Aphra Behn, but it is rela-tively rare in nineteenth-century fiction and appears more frequently in modern and contemporary fiction, with celebrated instances in Dorothy Richardson, James Joyce, and Virginia Woolf. It presents the thought-stream of the character's mind in the present tense and implicit first person, just like dialogue, from which it is sometimes distinguished by tagging "She thought," rather than "She said." To some degree, identifi-cation of the different modes demands interpretive judgments, and these interpretations are inevitably conditioned by the received literary history of forms.

Probably because of its use by major modernist innovators, quoted monologue is often regarded as the most immediate, least filtered, and most authentic kind of representation of fictional thoughts, and it is often the technique in use when critics gesture towards a writer's stream-of-con-sciousness (though not invariably). To spot it, a reader of traditional third person, past tense narration looks for unspoken discourse belonging to a character that swerves into present tense and first person. Tagging makes it easier to locate, as in this rare occurrence of quoted monologue from Hardy's *A Pair of Blue Eyes* (1873): "'She will never come again; she *has been gone* ten minutes,' he said to himself. . . . 'As many more minutes will be my end,' he thought" (*PBE* 202, emphasis added). In passages of quoted monologue, any past tense verbs that remain are the words that could also be used in speech about something that has happened in the *characters'* past—"she has been gone ten minutes"—, since the entire thought can plausibly be spoken aloud without alteration. By Cohn's nomenclature, this sort of thought is "quoted," not told, as differentiated from narrated monologue. In later fiction quoted monologue without tagging is often italicized to indicate its difference from dialogue, and in this form it is ubiquitous in contemporary fiction.

Thus, a critic intent on demonstrating a late Victorian novelist's incipient modernity could do so by singling out passages of quoted monologue in fiction antedating *Mrs. Dalloway* (1925), the "Penelope" episode of *Ulysses* (1922), or the early installments of Dorothy Richardson's *Pilgrimage* (1915–67). Indeed, Hardy occasionally writes a line or two in which an introspective character speaks to herself, as in the short story "An Imaginative Woman," mentioned above. The protagonist Ella Marchmill, a poet and a married woman pregnant with her third child, becomes obsessed with a rival poet, Robert Trewe, in whose rooms she and her husband find themselves temporarily lodging. Provided an opportunity to go out yachting with her husband, Ella prefers to stay in the poet Trewe's rooms, where she has been poring over his shelves and putting on his clothing: "'I don't want to go!' she said to herself. 'I can't bear to be away. And I won't go'" (*LLI* 16). This is tagged quoted monologue of inner speech. More often, Hardy makes his characters speak their private thoughts aloud, in the mode of dramatic soliloquy. Later, after news of his suicide reaches her, Ella effuses in her grief:

> "O if he had only known of me—known of me—me! . . . O if I had only met him—only once; and put my hand on his hot forehead—kissed him—let him know how I loved him—that I would have suffered shame and scorn, would have lived and died for him! Perhaps it would have saved his dear life!. . . . But no—it was not allowed! God is a jealous God; and that happiness was not for him and me!" (27)

Here Hardy is less clear that the quoted monologue transcribes a private thought-stream, however, since he characterizes this outburst as at least occasionally voiced: "Broken words came every now and then from her quivering lips" (27). This leaves to the reader the decision to take the passage as spoken aloud, partly voiced, or mostly interior, with just occasional "broken words" escaping Ella in her "frenzy of sorrow" (27).

THOUGHT REPORT/PSYCHO-NARRATION

In comparison with his contemporaries, Hardy relies more heavily on thought report employed by itself, in passages of psycho-narration. As Cohn describes it, psycho-narration permits not only a narrator's characterization of states of mind ("Ella was blithe and buoyant" [*LLI* 24]), but also admits generalizations about feeling-states of long duration: "Ella seemed to be only too frequently in a sad and listless mood which might almost have been called pining" (30). Psycho-narration often features imagistic analogies or metaphors for inner feelings, using words to catch subverbal aspects of inner experience, what Cohn calls psycho-analogies: "she was sleeping on a poet's lips, immersed in the very essence of him, permeated by his spirit as by an ether" (20). It certainly cedes authority to the narrator over the character, as psycho-narration can report conditions of the mind of which the character remains unaware: "The author's thoughts were diverted to another groove just then by the discovery that she was going to have a third child, and the collapse of her poetical venture had perhaps less effect upon her mind than it might have done if she had been domestically unoccupied" (12). That Ella thinks less about her vocational disappointment than she might have, due to her pregnancy, we readers owe to the narrator's over-arching knowledge of the character. There is no evidence that she shares his insight into her own mind's behavior, "diverted to another groove."

In Hardy's hands, psycho-narration as often reports conditions of not knowing—in his word *nescience*—as of overt consciousness:

> The personal element in the magnetic attraction exercised by this circum-ambient, unapproachable master of hers was so much stronger than the intellectual and abstract that she could not understand it. To be sure, she was surrounded noon and night by his customary environment, which literally whispered of him to her at every moment; but he was a man she had never seen: and that all that moved her was the instinct to specialize a waiting emotion on the first fit thing that came to hand, did not, of course, suggest itself to Ella. (*LLI* 14)

Only Hardy's narrator knows what's going on in this peculiar story, in which a pregnant woman out-of-love with her husband and father of her children becomes obsessively attached to a fellow writer whom she never meets in person. She doesn't know; her remote beloved doesn't know; and her husband, widowed when she dies in childbirth, doesn't know.

He mistakenly assumes that his own child belongs to his wife's "Trewe" lover because of a chance resemblance of the child's hair color. Hardy writes, "By a known but inexplicable trick of Nature there were undoubtedly strong traces of resemblance to the man Ella had never seen" (32), and these cause the natural father to reject his own child in the closing words of the story: "'Get away, you poor little brat! You are nothing to me!'" (32).

Gaps in characters' knowledge underwrite many of the ironic effects in Hardy's stories, especially in the volume *Life's Little Ironies*. As I have earlier noted, Hardy closes the minds of characters to one another in his early pastoral novel *Under the Greenwood Tree* (1872), a strategy that introduces an element of unease to the apparently happy union that concludes the tale. Some of Hardy's characters, such as Fancy Day, deliberately keep secrets from one another, and others, like Ella Marchmont, act under impulsions about which they know nothing. These uncalculating impulses arise from characters' biological nature, from what Kay Young has called their "nonintrospective consciousness" (Young 127–30). We might identify hormones as the source; Hardy observes the behavior and attributes it to instinct. Hardy's narrator coolly remarks, "that all that moved her was the instinct to specialize a waiting emotion on the first fit thing that came to hand, did not, of course, suggest itself to Ella" (*LLI* 14), implying that her obsession with the absent Trewe could have settled naturally on any other object, driven as it is by her pregnant condition. "The instinct to specialize a waiting emotion" indicates a force beyond Ella's ken or control. The same Nature who interferes with her unborn child's appearance, by a "known but inexplicable" method (32), has already set Ella up for her disaster by making her fertile, pregnant, moody, and (as we would know, armed with *What to Expect While You're Expecting*) primed with oxytocin to bond with an unknown stranger. Within the bounds of the story world, no individual character can grasp any of this: Trewe commits suicide, Ella dies in childbirth, and her widowed husband confidently acts on his misinterpretation of compared hair samples, rejecting his own child as a result. Only Nature, the narrator, and the privileged reader could possibly know what's going on.

The ironic conclusion (tragic for the unnamed toddler) comes about through a procedure that looks a bit like observational natural science. Marchmill finds the labeled and dated lock of hair, compares it to his child's, calculates the dates from the stay in the poet's lodging at Solentsea, and comes to his unfair conclusion. Yet he gets it all wrong and responds emotionally, with cruel rejection of an innocent. This adds a cautionary level to Hardy's depiction of selves unknowing, which tends to shift importance to empirical evidence: observation of external behavior and physical evidence is just as fallible as the incomplete self-understandings that come from inside characters. Nicholas Dames calls this an "interiority function" of Victorian narration: "fictional selves are signaled as psychologically real to the extent that they are incapable of accurate introspection" (Herman 227). Blind to their own motivations, prone to keep secrets from one another, self-deceived as often as deceiving, pushed around by their emotions, Hardy's characters nonetheless trust in their own rationality, ennoble their desires, and justify their rash responses to the evidence of their senses. Though Hardy's characters need to be able to read others effectively, they often misinterpret the clues. Perhaps for this reason, Hardy does not invest in a purely externalized narrative technique that would leave the interpretation of motives and hidden intentions to the reader. This would be a different formal choice, a more austere strategy that avoids representation of consciousness altogether.[12]

EXTERNALIZED NARRATION

Behaviorist, or objective narrative, as it is sometimes labeled, eschews representation of characters' inner states and thoughts, hewing closely to the conventions of dramatic scene and relying heavily on dialogue. In the modern period, Ivy Compton-Burnett's fiction provides a rich corpus of examples, and several stories by Ernest Hemingway, "Hills Like White Elephants" (1927) and "The Killers" (1927) are the canonical examples cited in narrative theory. Alan Palmer extends the roster to include Evelyn Waugh's *Vile Bodies* (1930) in his discussion in *Fictional Minds* (206 ff). In objective narration, characters know more than the narrator reveals, which shifts the "knowing" function from the narrator to the implied author and the actively decoding reader. Though rarely sustained to the length of a whole story or novel, this dramatic technique of representing

---

12. Alan Palmer is correct that even the most celebrated examples of objective narration contain moments of thought report (*Fictional Minds* 206–7). For example, Ivy Compton-Burnett's *Manservant and Maidservant* (1947), a brilliant book about the psychology of a dysfunctional family oppressed by the *pater familias* Horace, operates through dialogue in nearly pure scene. Yet at climactic moments Compton-Burnett deploys thought report: "He missed his cousin in a measure he could not confront or confess. His sense of wrong was sunk in the depth of his need. This was where his bitterness had its real source" (216) and "He hoped it would fade from their minds, knew it was rooted there, and left it to the future, at once a threat to his ease and a basis for his life with them" (299).

minds indirectly through pure scene does occur on some pages of many nineteenth-century novels. Though the publishing circumstances of the nineteenth century encouraged expansion and even pauses for lengthy passages of description (stretching to make the length required to fill a triple-decker novel), novelists were also familiar with dramatic conventions of dialogue and group conversation. They could and did interpolate passages of objective narrative to imply qualities of mind that could be verified or enriched using narrated monologue and psycho-narration. In a review of *Far from the Madding Crowd* in the *Nation* (24 December 1874), Henry James singled out Hardy's extensive passages of dialogue as unwieldy tools for narration: "to tell a story almost exclusively by reporting people's talks is the most difficult art in the world, and really leads, logically, to a severe economy in the use of rejoinder and repartee, and not to a lavish expenditure of them" (Cox 28). James was to develop an alternative mode for lavish expenditure of words in his own characters' narrated monologue. But for James the individual perspective, the center of consciousness, took priority over communal thought.

INTERMENTAL OR COMMUNAL THOUGHT

Hardy rarely keeps his reader in the dark for longer than a few pages, but he does often employ behaviorist dialogue, especially among groups of secondary characters, to convey the essence of communal thought. For instance, in *Under the Greenwood Tree,* the members of the instrumental church choir gather to talk over the new pastor, who has brought unwelcome innovations to Sunday services:

> They talked with deliberate gesticulations to Mr Penny enthroned in the shadow of the interior.
>
> "I do like a man to stick to men who be in the same line o' life—o' Sundays, anyway—that I do so."
>
> "Tis like all the doings of folk who don't know what a day's work is—that's what I say."
>
> "My belief is the man's not to blame: 'tis *she:* she's the bitter weed."
>
> "No—not altogether. He's a poor gawkhammer. Look at his sermon yesterday."
>
> "His sermon was well enough—a very good guessable sermon, only he couldn't put it into words and speak it. That's all was the matter wi' the sermon. He hadn't been able to get it past his pen."

"Well—ay: the sermon might have been good; for 'tis true, the sermon of Old Eccl'iastes himself lay in Eccl'iastes inkbottle afore he got it out."

Mr Penny being in the act of drawing the last stitch tight, could afford time to look up and throw in a word at this point. "He's no spouter—that must be said 'a b'lieve."

"Tis a terrible muddle sometimes with the man, as far as spout do go," said Spinks.

"Well, we'll say nothing about that," the tranter answered; for I don't believe 'twill make a pennorth o' difference to we poor martels here or hereafter whether his sermons be good or bad, my sonnies."

Mr Penny made another hole with his awl, pushed in the thread, and looked up and spoke again at the extension of arms. "Tis his goings-on, souls, that's what it is." He clenched his features for an Herculean addition to the ordinary pull, and continued. "The first thing he done when he came here was to be hot and strong about church business."

"True," said Spinks. "That was the very first thing he done."

Mr Penny having now been offered the ear of the assembly, accepted it, ceased stitching, swallowed an unimportant quantity of air as if it were a pill, and continued. "The next thing he do do is to think about altering the church until he found it 'twould be a matter o' cost and what not, and then not to think no more about it."

"True: that was the next thing he done."

"And the next thing was to tell the young chaps that they were not on no account to put their hats in the christening font during service."

"True."

"And then 'twas this, and then 'twas that, and now 'tis——" Words were not forcible enough to conclude the sentence, and Mr Penny gave a huge pull to signify the concluding word. (*UGT* 71–72)

The indictment of the new pastor by recitation of his failings as a preacher and his tactless corrections of local customs rings true to any reader who has worked in an organization with a new manager, in a university with a new dean, or indeed belongs to a congregation blessed with a new minister. Much appears right on the surface, punctuated by signifying gestures. The pastor lacks fluency; he has new ideas about the respect due to articles of church furniture. On one level, the negative judgment of the community emerges from Hardy's ink-bottle in plain increments of dialogue. As an example of his behaviorist narrative technique, it demonstrates the flow of attention and the authority centered in the shoemaker

Mr. Penny, even as it documents a highly recognizable gripe-session. Hardy does not have to generalize through his narrator, specifying the group's dissatisfaction with the sequence of small changes, and he does not need to spell out their fears about what's next. Readers see plainly enough what the group of men anticipate—the end of a musical tradition. (Hardy had himself witnessed and lamented such a change, when instrumental church choirs underwent replacement by organists.)

Another level of representation of consciousness inheres in this passage, though it is reticent about private thoughts. The conversation reveals that the community comfortably intuits the meanings of the pastor without his uttering them. He has delivered "a very good guessable sermon" which the congregation gets even though "he couldn't put it into words and speak it." Equipped with the familiar readings from scripture and memory of past sermons, they can still understand the "gawkhammer" who has left his homily in his inkbottle. The metaphor of the inkbottle that contains the thoughts of homilists and prophets even when they cannot release them through writing implies a world in which characters assume that other minds possess contents even if they cannot communicate them effectively. They are still "guessable." Equally guessable are intentions divined from a sequence of actions, even trivial seeming reprimands, and in this case the church musicians are absolutely correct that they are about to be given the shove. The conversation admits the possibility that "she," the organ-playing Fancy Day, has inspired the pastor's demotion of the instrumentalists, though the influence of "the bitter weed" may operate without the pastor's knowledge. That remains debatable, and they go on to speculate about her motives as well. All this evidences Hardy's awareness that people believe that other people's minds are readable, even in the case of a tongue-tied individual who is "no spouter." This observation about Hardy's technique, that he often represents the embedded, easily understood, but only implicit perspective of a character within a community, points to a painful paradox in his representation of consciousness. Hardy shows how individuals fail to understand their own motives and simultaneously vouches for the community's easy habit of mind-reading. If minds are so easy for community members to read from the outside, then why can't individuals know themselves better? Hardy poses this question again and again, and many of his major novels stage thought-experiments around variants of the problem.

Why does intermental thought, shared or communal thinking (Palmer, *Fictional Minds* 218; *Social Minds* 4) possess powers that intramental thought, individual thinking, cannot achieve? In Hardy's major fiction, the intermental thinking of groups represents social norms distributed among minor characters, observers of the action, nosy neighbors, and members of his rural choruses. It is as hard for individual characters to keep secrets from these groups as it is for them to divulge the contents of their own minds to their closest companions. Hardy's pervasive imagery of figures glimpsed through windows or observed by passers-by coexists with his plot devices of private miscommunication such as failed disclosures and lost letters. His self-unknowing protagonists exist in fictional worlds where their behavior nearly never stays private, and many of the coincidences in Hardy's fiction operate to reveal what might otherwise have remained unknown. All of these features of Hardy's world-making conspire to suggest a universe run along the lines of the Panopticon, without an eye of God in the central watchtower. One of the immediate consequences of Hardy's Darwinian convictions and Spencerian influences shows not only in his agnosticism about an all-knowing God, but also in his persistent representation of the groups arrayed around his individuals. Someone is still watching. He renders the social worlds and the pressures they bring to bear on his protagonists as consequential elements of environment: the Hardy protagonist, no matter how obscure, can never entirely escape the tribe.

Elaine Scarry notices this preoccupation of Hardy's in a discussion of the problem of imagining others. For Hardy, she points out, it isn't that people fail to imagine others, but that they do, with inevitably incomplete evidence: "The British novelist Thomas Hardy is a brilliant explicator of this problem. He places before our eyes the dense interior of a man or a woman. He then juxtaposes the ontological robustness with the inevitable subtractions, the flattenings, the emptyings out that occur in other people's vision of the person" (Scarry, "Difficulty" 48). Under these circumstances, the judgment of the tribe may be unjust, peremptory, inflected by prejudice, or out-and-out misinformed, but in Hardy's presentation, the tribe retains its power to judge and punish—on rare occasions, to show mercy and urge clemency. Even when shown to be dead wrong, intermental thought loses little of its force in Hardy's fictional worlds. Many of his ironic effects depend upon the readers' knowledge of the gap between the protagonist's perspective and the communal perspective, darker still when the authorial generalizations condemn the community's punitive enforcement of social norms and still show the hapless protagonists victimized by their own impulses. Like the Spirits of *The Dynasts,* Hardy's readers enjoy understanding without possessing powers of intervention.

Hardy employs a variety of techniques to represent intermental, communal thought in his fiction: the behaviorist or objective version analyzed above in the passage from *Under the Greenwood Tree,* in which the group's interests, concerns, and conclusions emerge from details of speech and action; the double-cognitive implication of what a group of others *must* be thinking, conveyed through a character's certainty about social disapproval or suspicion (the certainty does not equate with correctness; right or wrong, it gains force through the character's belief in the others' attitudes); and overt thought report by the narrator about the community's opinions, ideas, and responses. Hardy represents intramental, *individual* thought most often through psycho-narration, and collects groups of thoughts residing in collections of characters to suggest a crowd's view. There are other forms of information about the insides of characters' minds, however. One character can intuit what another's mind contains. This is an example of what Alan Palmer describes as a double cognitive narrative,[13] in which one character in a fictional world gathers, from her knowledge of his disposition and the situation, what a second character must be thinking.

The next section of this chapter details through a series of exhibits from four of the major novels Hardy's thought experiments concerning the intersections of communal knowledge and individual states of mind. While space does not permit thorough study of every Hardy novel, representative passages from *Far from the Madding Crowd, The Return of the Native, The Mayor of Casterbridge,* and *Tess of the d'Urbervilles* demonstrate how Hardy's narrative techniques support his demonstration of human psychology, an affective embodied psychology evolved to feel, often incapable of knowing its own mind, but endowed with certainty about the likely thoughts of others. In Alan Palmer's astute narratology of intermental thought, the content of communal knowledge about one individual's thoughts need not be accurate (it can indeed be warped by prejudice and error). Wrong certainties about others can be as influential as right ones, Hardy demonstrates. Hardy makes no simple equations:

---

13. In *Fictional Minds,* Palmer uses the term "embedded narrative" in a specialized sense excluding its usual meaning of a story level within a story, an interpolated document, or a text presented within a text (*Fictional Minds* 15). He has since altered his terminology, replacing "embedded" with "cognitive," to avoid confusion with the usage of embedded narrative that means interpolated text. For an explanation of the shift in terms, see *Social Minds in the Novel* 12–13. Whether labelled "double embedded narratives" or "double cognitive narratives," the terms describe how "versions of characters exist within the minds of other characters and . . . the relationships between these versions determine to a great extent the teleology of the plot" (*Social Minds* 12).

accurate communal insights can result in merciful outcomes (Boldwood's life is spared when the community realizes his monomania) or in tragedy (Henchard is ruined when the town learns his secret); inaccurate communal beliefs (Eustacia is a witch; Lucetta is a proper lady) can also exert influence when they are trusted or debunked. Hardy's art interrogates the painful intersection of individual minds subject to blindness to their own motives with social minds that judge by appearances.

'The Disease of Feeling': Mental Breakdown and Communal Knowledge

In Hardy's 1874 novel *Far from the Madding Crowd*, his technique of representing intermental thought frames an episode in which impulsive action on Bathsheba Everdene's part begins a process that will drive Farmer Boldwood out of his mind. Having perceived that he does not notice her at the Corn Exchange, Bathsheba sends a teasing, anonymous valentine to the bachelor farmer. Within just a few pages of the novel, Hardy charts an inward-moving path from a communal perspective to Bathsheba's mind, then following the path of the "idly and unreflectingly" sent valentine (*FFMC* 98), dips into to Boldwood's tormented perspective. Hardy traces this trajectory through increments of narrator's thought report. Dabbing in a line or two of narrated monologue for Boldwood's obsessional imaginings, Hardy then shows the force of embedded consciousness. Handling the valentine, Boldwood imagines the unidentified woman in whose brain his own person must have been imagined. He does not need to know her identity to be ignited by the awareness that she has thought of him. He does not realize how lightly.

Upon her entrance to the Corn Exchange, intent upon managing her affairs "in her own person" (*FFMC* 90), Bathsheba immediately attracts the attention of all the farmers. Hardy describes her passage through the hall, her behavior as she bargains, and asserts that these externally available cues evoke a group response from the men:

> It would be ungallant to suggest that the novelty of her engagement in such an occupation had almost as much to do with the magnetism as had the beauty of her face and movements. However the interest was general, and this Saturday's debut in the forum, whatever it may have been to Bathsheba as the buying and selling farmer, was unquestionably a triumph to her as the maiden. (91)

Here Hardy employs a generalizing thought report to explain the communal reaction to the attractive Bathsheba's appearance. Magnetized by her assumption of a selling role normally played by a man, the farmers understand her as advertising herself, not just her grain, and one speaks for the group, saying "she'll soon get picked up" (91).

Hardy does not give the reader direct access to Bathsheba's intentions at this point, but he reports on her "instinct" as she responds to the attention: "Indeed the sensation was so pronounced that her instinct on two or three occasions was merely to walk as a queen among these gods of the fallow, like a little sister of a little Jove, and to neglect closing prices altogether" (*FFMC* 91–92). Hardy's sense of "instinct" derives from two major sources: Herbert Spencer's description of the selfish instincts of personal rights, "a feeling that leads him to claim as great a share of natural privilege as is claimed by others" as the individual moves through an atmosphere of attraction and repulsion (Spencer, *Social Statics* 110); and Auguste Comte's account of the interaction of social and biological dispositions. In Spencer's theorizing, sympathetic affection for others is a reflex action of selfish personal instincts (116); in Comte the altruistic and egoistic instincts, including the sexual, are at odds with one another (Comte, *Catechism* 185). Hardy's emphasis on the egoism inherent in the sexual instinct that makes Bathsheba parade among the men sets up her subsequent selfish, impulsive action as natural if also destructive. Comte saw the sexual and destructive instincts as companions (186), but he casts females as the victims of male sexual desire. Hardy saw that female desire could also be destructive to males, perhaps especially if the woman experiencing it acts in ignorance of the cause of her feelings.

Psycho-narration gives Hardy's narrator the brief to say what the young woman does by instinct, to provide a classical allusion illuminating her demeanor, and to specify what she omits to think about: closing prices for the grain. Attracting her attention instead is the one man, "a black sheep among the flock" (*FFMC* 92) who notices her not at all:

> The numerous evidences of her power to attract were only thrown into greater relief by a marked exception. Women seem to have eyes in their ribbons for such matters as these. . . . It perplexed her first. If there had been a respectable minority on either side, the case would have been most natural. If nobody had regarded her, she would have taken the matter indifferently: such cases had occurred. If everybody, this man included, she would have taken it as a matter of course: People had done so before. But the smallness of the exception made the mystery. (92)

By this point the reader knows two additional things about Bathsheba's thoughts (her self-regard having been dramatized in the opening pages of the novel). One, she is interested in Boldwood because he does not notice her (this much she knows, too); two, she will make him pay attention simply because he has set himself apart from the general admiring crowd.

When her maid Liddy capriciously suggests sending the valentine to "stupid old Boldwood" (*FFMC* 97), Bathsheba's motives receive elaboration through a lengthy passage of thought report:

> Bathsheba paused to regard the idea at full length. Boldwood's had begun to be a troublesome image—a species of Daniel in her kingdom who persisted in kneeling eastward when reason and common sense said that he might just as well follow suit with the rest and afford her the official glance of admiration which cost nothing at all. She was far from being seriously concerned about his non-conformity. Still it was faintly depressing that the most dignified and valuable man in the parish should withhold his eyes, and that a girl like Liddy should talk about it. So Liddy's idea was at first rather harassing than piquant. (97)

Thus Bathsheba "frolicsomely" seals the valentine with a stamp that imprints "MARRY ME" on the envelope. As far as we can tell, a mixture of mischief and pique drives Bathsheba's behavior, not attraction, and Hardy's narrator brings the point home: "Of love as a spectacle Bathsheba had a fair knowledge; but of love subjectively she knew nothing" (97).

Bathsheba's "pert injunction" (*FFMC* 99) imprinted in the wax seal unleashes a remarkable change in its recipient, and Hardy lavishes thought report on the seismic shift in Boldwood's mental and emotional state:

> Since the receipt of the missive in the morning, Boldwood had felt the symmetry of his existence to be slowly getting distorted in the direction of an ideal passion. [*Thought report: concerns a period of time*] The disturbance was as the first floating weed to Columbus—the contemptibly little suggesting possibilities of the infinitely great. [*Thought report: psycho-analogy*]
>
> The letter must have had an origin and a motive. [*Possibly narrated monologue of Boldwood's thought-stream*] That the latter was of the smallest magnitude compatible with its existence at all Boldwood of course did not know. [*Thought report of nescience*] It is foreign to a mystified condition of mind to realize of the mystifier that the processes of approving a course suggested by circumstance, and of striking out a

course from inner impulse, would look the same in the result. [*Thought report: narrator's generalization about human failings in reasoning generally*] The vast difference between starting a train of events and directing into a particular groove a series already started, is rarely apparent to the person confounded by the issue. [*Thought report: mismatch of Bathsheba's insouciance and Boldwood's imputation of motives*] (99, with my interpolations in brackets)

Curiously, the governing scene under the chapter heading "The Effect of the Letter" does not confine the narrator to representation of Boldwood's consciousness alone. To initiate Boldwood's descent into monomaniacal obsession, Hardy's narrator establishes the ignorance of the confounded, mystified Boldwood at the same time conveying his mistaken certainty of the sender's motives. To do so the narrator reminds us of Bathsheba's impulsive state of mind. He shuttles back and forth between Boldwood's increasingly heated fantasies and Bathsheba's obliviousness.

Not Bathsheba but a projection of Boldwood's mind emerges from the writing on the envelope, and here scraps of Boldwood's erotic thought-transcript glimmer through the matrix of thought report:

> Somebody's—some *woman's*—hand had traveled softly over the paper bearing his name: her unrevealed eyes had watched every curve as she formed it: her brain had seen him in imagination the while. Why should she have imagined him? Her mouth—were the lips red or pale, plump or creased?—had curved itself to a certain expression as the pen went on— the corners had moved with all their natural tremulousness: what had been the expression? (*FFMC* 100)

At least half of the phrases in this brief passage can be read as narrated monologue, the words of Boldwood's autoerotic mental stroking of the valentine. But Hardy's narrator briskly dispenses of this phantom with a return to no-nonsense thought report: "The vision of the woman writing, as a supplement to the words written, had no individuality. She was a misty shape, and well she might be, considering that her original was at that moment sound asleep and oblivious of all love and letter-writing under the sky" (100). So while this passage vouches for the ability of characters within the fictional world to form estimates of the minds of others in that world, these projections are revealed as insubstantial fantasies. The projection of a cognitive narrative of consciousness on Boldwood's part is the first step in his progress towards madness.

Hardy maintains a special form of nescience for the delusional and self-deceived: they literally cannot see straight because of the failings of their perception. The last time Boldwood's mind receives the narrator's thought report occurs as he cheerfully invites Troy into the house, unaware of the stranger's identity: "Boldwood was among those who did not notice that he was Troy" (*FFMC* 366). When Troy stares into Boldwood's face, "Even then Boldwood did not recognize that the impersonator of Heaven's persistent irony towards him, who had once before broken in upon his bliss, scourged him, and snatched his delight away, had come to do these things a second time" (366). Only when Troy laughs does the penny drop: "Boldwood recognized him now" (366). By the time Boldwood's monomania has brought him to his ultimate crisis, in which he turns murderer and attempted suicide, Hardy has made what we will increasingly realize is a characteristic withdrawal from direct transcription of inner thoughts. He draws the veil over despairing or shocked minds, and not only Boldwood's: "The truth was that Bathsheba was beyond the pale of activity—and not yet in a swoon. She was in a state of mental *gutta serena*; her mind was for the minute totally deprived of light at the same time that no obscuration was apparent from without" (366). (*Gutta serena* is blindness without organic fault in the eye, suggesting a psychological rather than physical reason for the blanking out of thought.) Speech and action, facial expressions and body language, Hardy's narrator reports from an externalized perspective available to Troy and Bathsheba and thence to the reader: "Boldwood's face of gnashing despair had changed. The veins had swollen and a frenzied look had gleamed in his eye" (367). With this expression of rage as the sole warning, Boldwood explodes into violence and shoots Troy dead on the spot. About his internal motives as he rapidly moves to kill himself Hardy's narrator is silent. By now "the general horror" has frozen everyone in the room except for the servant Samway, who prevents the suicide. Boldwood escapes into the night because "Nobody [is] thinking of preventing him" (367). The disease of not-thinking spreads even to the witnesses as shock blanks out light, bewildering the men and sending the women into a huddled flock "like sheep in a storm" (368). A "temporary coma" of nescience takes over the community until Oak arrives.

Communal, intermental thought soon flows in with its perfect hindsight and shared certainties, as the condemned killer's private obsession with Bathsheba is exposed to general comment. The discovery in a locked closet Boldwood's collection of expensive garments in Bathsheba's size provide "somewhat pathetic evidences of a mind crazed with care and love," as the people gathered at Warren's Malthouse agree (*FFMC* 373). Though just a bit earlier, "nobody imagined that there had shown in him unequivocal symptoms of . . . mental derangement" (373), the community quickly corrects its failure to notice:

> The conviction that Boldwood had not been morally responsible for his later acts now became general. Facts elicited previous to the trial had pointed strongly in the same direction, but they had not been of sufficient weight to lead to an order for an examination into the state of Boldwood's mind. It was astonishing now that a presumption of insanity was raised how many collateral circumstances were remembered, to which a condition of mental disease seemed to afford the only explanation— among others, the unprecedented neglect of his cornstacks in the previous summer. (373–74)

Thus the intermental conclusions of the community exonerate themselves for their earlier failings in attentiveness. Just in the nick of time they reform their narrative to affirm he must have been out of his mind to kill Troy, a petition is made, and Boldwood receives a last-minute commutation of his death sentence. Hardy does not report Boldwood's thoughts about the reprieve.

Though a few passages of narrated monologue do occur in *Far from the Madding Crowd*, the dominant mode of representation of consciousness in the novel is thought report. As the preceding analysis suggests, psycho-narration is not a simple business of a narrator's straightforward description of characters' thoughts. The psycho-narration delivered by the narrator as often reports the conditions of ignorance, unknowing, or failure to apprehend of major characters, as it clarifies mood states and recognized motives. Individual, intramental thought is often blind and sometimes delusional. To say that Bathsheba does not know her own mind as she considers the various attractions and shortcomings of her three suitors is only to emphasize how representative a character she is for Hardy. While Hardy's version of internal thought (the zone of introspection, private desires, and individual memory) vouches for characters' unwitting responses to the impulses of the feelings and whims of the moment, his representation of external thought posits a working intersubjectivity that embodies the public mind. Group intermental thought more often arrives at shared opinions, but the community also receives the gentle mockery of the narrator for not noticing at first opportunity what it will later decide was obvious all along.

Emotion Infused into Externals: Crisis on the Heath

In *The Return of the Native* (1878), Hardy reconsiders the powers and limitations of the social mind of the community. Though still very much a presence and a force in the novel, the communal judgment represented through intermental thought report operates around the edges of Egdon Heath, a narrative space devised to isolate and separate his human characters, and possessing a dark consciousness of its own. Critics have often noticed Hardy's prosopopoeia in his introductory description (*RN* 9), representing the heath with a face, but attention to the narrator's thought report reveals its mind, as well. The following phrases of description indicate the waste ground's personality, best observed at twilight: "Its complete effect and *explanation* lay in this and the succeeding hours before the next dawn: then and only then *did it tell its true tale*. . . . The somber stretch of rounds and hollows seemed to rise and meet the evening gloom *in pure sympathy*. . . . The place became full of a *watchful intentness* now. . . . The heath appeared slowly *to awake and listen*" (9–10, emphases added). These terms of cognitive and affective qualities are not sinister, and they may appeal, says Hardy's narrator, to "the moods of the more thinking among mankind" (10). Formally, there is no difference (saving the impersonal pronoun) between a narrator's thought report about a human figure and its assertion about the heath, "solitude seemed to look out of its countenance. It had a lonely face, suggesting tragical possibilities" (11). This affective imagery links the potential for crisis with solitude or loneliness.

In *The Return of the Native* Hardy experiments with a limit case featuring relatively few central characters, deployed in a large and empty space, mostly out of view of a supervising community. The artistic consequence is a remarkable evocation of the impossibility of avoiding human contact and the force of social judgment, which lends its affective coloration to the landscape itself. In 1878, regarding a painting by Boldoni, Hardy wrote of the technique of "infusing emotion into the baldest external objects either by the presence of a human figure among them, or by mark of some human connection with them" (*Life and Work* 124). *The Return of the Native* was his canvas for emotional infusion into externals. Such a technique might be thought to flatten out differences between and among characters depicted, or at least to emphasize physical traits over internal qualities of personality. In a full-length critical essay published on Hardy's fiction through *Two on a Tower* (1882), Havelock Ellis offered in 1883 the opinion that Hardy's female characters were all variations on a single model ("Thomas Hardy's Novels" 165). In Hardy's hands, the externalization of emotion, handled largely through narrator's thought report, in fact distinguishes characters by qualities of mind that show on the outside. A comparison of the mental and emotional characteristics of Eustacia Vye and Thomasin Yeobright reveals Hardy's contrasting technique.

In the same year that Hardy published *The Return of the Native,* he made a craftsman's note on the art of tragedy: "A Plot, or Tragedy, should arise from the gradual closing in of a situation that comes of ordinary human passions, prejudices, and ambitions, by reason of the characters taking no trouble to ward off the disastrous events produced by the said passions, prejudices, and ambitions" (*Life and Work* 123). While not as insistent on the characters' lack of access to their own mental processes than in *Under the Greenwood Tree* and *Far from the Madding Crowd,* *Return of the Native* reflects Hardy's explanation of the inevitable entanglement of emotional beings, their impulses, and events set in motion by these impulsions. The claustrophobic consequence, "the gradual closing in of a situation," works even when the characters move with relative freedom across a large outdoors space. They move about as a result of emotional impulsions: "passions, prejudices, and ambitions." As Hardy was shortly to note in an early plan for the work that would become *The Dynasts* three decades later, "Mode for a historical Drama. Action mostly automatic, reflex movement, etc. Not the result of what is called motive, though always ostensibly so, even to the actors' own consciousness" (152). Movement in space, towards objects of desire and away from antagonists, operates through "reflex movement," already a foundational concept of experimental psychology by the mid-1860s.[14] The persons involved may not grasp what drives them, although they may possess cover stories as to their ostensible motives. This is a key quality of characters who "take no trouble to ward off . . . disastrous events": failures in self-understanding lead straight to tragic consequences. Additionally, in *The Return of the Native,* characters have less privacy than they realize, subject as they are to eavesdropping, accidental overhearing, observation, misunderstanding, and gossip. These help to facilitate development of "disastrous events," and preserve the matrix of communal intermental judgment that is to provide Hardy with a career-long source of tribulation to his characters.

---

14. Wilhelm Wundt's two-volume *Vorlesungen über die Menschen- und Thierseele* (1863) treats experimental investigations of reflex movements among other topics.

Dispositional variations among characters do make differences in their outcomes—disastrous or not—, in the degree to which their emotional states bleed into the environment around them, and in their potential for successful integration into an accepting community. The contrast between Eustacia Vye's and Thomasin's mental and emotional response to fraught circumstances catches Hardy's analysis of these differences. Eustacia is the more passionate, prejudiced, and ambitious of the two, to adopt the terms of Hardy's definition of tragedy. Out at night on Black-barrow in an attempt at escape from Egdon, Eustacia's mind is as open to the reader as Hardy can render it, in a blend of thought report and a few phrases of narrated monologue:

> Never was harmony more perfect than that between the chaos of her mind and the chaos of the world without. A sudden recollection had flashed on her this moment: she had not money enough for undertaking a long journey. Amid the fluctuating sentiments of the day her unpractical mind had not dwelt on the necessity of being well-provided, and now that she had thoroughly realized the conditions she sighed bitterly, and ceased to stand erect, gradually crouching down under the umbrella as if she were drawn into the barrow by a hand from beneath. Could it be that she was to remain a captive still? (*RN* 340–41)

Using externalized details ratchets up the sense of Eustacia's misery, which is reflected in the condition of the landscape and foul weather surrounding her, rendered in pure thought report:

> Anyone who had stood by now would have pitied her, not so much on account of her exposure to weather, and isolation from all humanity except the mouldered remains inside the barrow; but for that other form of misery which was denoted by the slightly rocking movement that her feelings imparted to her person. Extreme unhappiness weighed visibly upon here. Between the drippings of the rain from her umbrella to her mantle, from her mantle to the heather, from the heather to the earth, very similar sounds could be heard coming from her lips; and the tearfulness of the outer scene was repeated on her face. (341)

Not quite an instance of pathetic fallacy (where the earth mourns as a response to personal grief), the passage of thought report links the chain of physical impulses that goes from feelings to embodied expressions to matching drippings of tears and rain. Eustacia makes her own weather.

Characteristically, Hardy renders his character's most intense bitterness and grief not through thought report but through speech. Since there is no one there to hear it, the narrator's choice stands out, and Hardy justifies the awkward soliloquy: "She uttered words aloud. When a woman in such a situation, neither old, deaf, crazed, nor whimsical, takes upon herself to sob and soliloquize aloud there is something grievous in the matter" (341). Though she is alone and unobserved, Hardy establishes, Eustacia's position in the storm, her circumstances, her posture, her outward expressions, and her moaning speech reveal her mind. The fact that her old enemy Susan Nonesuch is even at that moment melting a voodoo doll image of Eustacia seems a nearly gratuitous contribution to her imminent death: Hardy shows how she has already turned her surroundings into a lethal projection of her own emotional state. She will drown in a tumult of water, having let flow an outburst of grievous feelings.

Out on the very same stormy night on the heath, Thomasin experiences an entirely different and significantly less threatening environment: "Thomasin's imagination being so actively engaged elsewhere, the night and the weather had for her no terror beyond that of their actual discomfort and difficulty" (RN 349). Where Eustacia is egotistical in her misery, Thomasin is other-directed in her concern, and the distinction marks a fundamental contrast in the two characters' dispositions. The weather is equally miserable and the hazards of the heath, especially concealed pools, just as dangerous:

> Yet in spite of all this Thomasin was not sorry that she had started. To her there were not, as to Eustacia, demons in the air, and malice in every bush and bough. The drops which lashed her face were not scorpions, but prosy rain; Egdon in the mass was no monster whatever, but impersonal open ground. Her fears of the place were rational, her dislikes of its worst moods reasonable. At this time it was in her view a windy wet place, in which a person might experience much discomfort, lose the path without care and possibly catch cold. (349)

Even though she has braved the night and soaking rain with her infant, she comes to no harm even when she loses the path, finding a rescuer in the reddleman's van rather than a death like Eustacia's in the ten-hatch weir pool. Hardy makes it plain that Thomasin's attitude affords her a fundamental protection from dangers that originate inside the mind, compounding the hazards of the heath. Nature by itself certainly poses risks, but the disposition of the creature navigating the natural world possesses a greater power to predict peril or survival. In his notebook Hardy wrote late in 1877, "An object or mark raised or made by man on a scene is worth ten times any such formed by unconscious Nature" (*Life and Work* 120), and his emotional plotting in *The Return of the Native* bears out this insight. The unconscious heath cannot be held to blame for its shapes, its traps, or its weather. Human actions make it lethal. Appropriately, Eustacia drowns in the wier pool, a dammed part of the stream that has been subject to human alteration.

Given that Hardy so often insists on the unconsciousness of his characters, on their lack of awareness of the emotional impulsions that drive their actions, it might seem likely that introspective habits could be a guard against disaster. The handling of the consciousness of characters in crisis in *The Return of the Native* suggests otherwise. Introspection that leads to selfish indulgence of whims and justification of egotistical desires. Carelessness for the wellbeing of others turns out to be as dangerous as nescience. Hardy holds out Thomasin's other-directed concern as an ethically attractive alternative. He does so in part by making a habit of thinking of others look like a survival advantage. The novel's other survivors, Clym Yeobright and Diggory Venn, share this quality. Thomasin cannot marry both of them, but all three are reintegrated into the relative warmth of community by the novel's end. Of Clym, taken to itinerant nonsectarian preaching, Hardy comments, "everywhere he was kindly received, for the story of his life had become generally known" (*RN* 390). The omniscience of intermental knowledge is once again affirmed in Hardy's closing sentence.

Critical Interlude:
What a Victorian Psychologist Saw in Hardy's Fiction

Between the publication on *Two on a Tower* (1882) and *The Mayor of Casterbridge,* Hardy's fictional *oeuvre* was subjected to extensive discussion in a full-length periodical review essay. The Victorian psychologist and sexologist Havelock Ellis examined the short stories and novels that had been published through 1883 in an essay published in the April 1883 *Westminster Review.* The essay is of interest not only because it recognizes Hardy as a major talent prior to the publication of his acknowledged masterworks (*The Mayor of Casterbridge, Tess of the d'Urbervilles,* and *Jude the Obscure*), but also because it frames an evaluation of Hardy's evolving craft in psychological terms. Ellis had not yet embarked in 1883 on his magisterial *Studies in the Psychology of Sex* (1897–1928), but he had begun his medical training, which was to provide a foundation for his subsequent scientific investigations. He was convinced that human behavior was driven by innate characteristics, and perhaps for that reason he found Hardy an admirable psychologist of character. Hardy's female characters, Ellis judged, formed a series of "instinct-led women" who "can hardly be matched" ("Thomas Hardy's Novels" 164). Ellis admired Hardy's depiction of "young healthy creatures, chiefly instinct-led, in their reaction with circumstance, circumstance mostly against them, but which they are rarely wishful, very rarely able, to break through. . . . What we see in them, then, is the individual and egotistic instincts in a reaction with circumstances which is only faintly coloured by an elementary altruistic consciousness" (165). In terms that come straight out of Comte, Spencer, and the biological materialist psychology of his time, Ellis congratulates Hardy for representing women as creatures motivated by desire.

Ellis sees clearly that Hardy sets aside the language of morality in favor of what appears to Ellis a more truthful account of female behavior than that available in the fiction of Charlotte Brontë and George Eliot:

> [W]ith Mr. Hardy the individual self with its desires is neither *per se,* a devil to be resisted, nor a soul to receive its due heritage in the fellowship of souls. It is an untamed instinctive creature, eager and yet shy, which is compelled to satisfy its own moderate desires for happiness before it can reflect its joyousness on others. It is instinct only that saves so egoistic and primitive a moral conception—if it can be so termed—from becoming utterly evil. In so far as it is a guide to conduct, it stands at the opposite pole to Charlotte Brontë's. Mr. Hardy is not concerned, as George Eliot is, with the bearing of moral problems on human action. ("Thomas Hardy's Novels" 165)

In addition to the notable gesture of inclusion that places Hardy as a novelist in a tradition that includes Jane Austen, Brontë and Eliot (164), a better psychologist than Dickens or Thackeray (164), Ellis's insight is to identify the inchoate motivations that drive Hardy's characters. Ellis also notices Hardy's departure from the conventional *bildungsroman* narrative of development, even when telling stories of education, as in *A Pair of Blue Eyes*. Ellis sees Hardy as rejecting the model bequeathed to English fiction by redactors of Goethe's *Wilhelm Meister*: "Mr. Hardy, however, is mostly indifferent to these things; his hero passes through no such process of development one way or another. In general he is a sensitive being, gentle and pure as a woman, characterized by nothing so much as his receptivity" (167–68). These fictive versions of men and women, acted upon by environment but settled in fixed dispositions, provide Hardy's work with a "freshness of insight into certain aspects of Nature and human character" that is both "intensely original" and "altogether impersonal" (171). For Ellis, who was in his mature sexological writing committed to the description of human beings as biologically determined to behave in natural, but not necessarily socially acceptable manners, Hardy's "microscopical minuteness of vision" was preferable both to moralizing and to progressive narratives of development. The one flaw, to Ellis's mind, in the "absolute fixity" of Hardy's characters is the mystery of their biological origins: "One wonders, indeed how the characters of these people had a genesis at all; there are no children in Mr. Hardy's novels" (176). Considering Hardy's commitment to writing love stories, upon which Ellis also remarked, the absence of offspring may point to Hardy's commitment to description. If social norms prevented direct representation of the process of procreation, procreation itself would be omitted.

Ellis also noticed something else that was missing from Hardy's art: direct representation of the consciousness of his characters. Congratulating Hardy for not making his female characters mouthpieces for morality, Ellis notices Hardy's impersonal method of narration: "Generally, he is only willing to recognize the psychical element in its physical correlative. This dislike to use the subjective method or to deal directly with mental phenomena is a feature in Mr. Hardy's psychology which has left a strong mark on his art" ("Thomas Hardy's Novels" 175). External observation of speech, behavior, posture, and expressions substitutes for direct revelation of internal mind-states. Ellis praises Hardy for the greater realism of such a commitment to external details: "The interest here is an interest of drama, certainly, but, above all, of character, of psychology. And Mr. Hardy seems to feel that the problems thus raised, fascinating as they are, much as the novelist has to do with them, are, after all, infinitely difficult of adequate presentation, that the utmost possible is by the exercise of a fine and suggestive observation to indicate them" (175). Though we do not have Hardy's response to this perceptive review, we do have the evidence of his subsequent fiction, which may be seen as responding to some of Ellis's remarks as challenges (for instance, Tess and Jude have babies). Hardy also makes notes in his *Literary Notebooks* from later pieces by Ellis. A similar pattern prevails with his other reviewers: no notes on the actual review followed by attentive reading of subsequent pieces run across in the periodicals Hardy habitually studied. Thus while the demonstration of a direct influence is debarred by the form of Hardy's attention, the evidence of his correspondence and later art suggests an impact. Dennis Taylor has persuasively documented the dynamic process with respect to Hardy's responses to reviews of his poetry[15]; indeed, an important part of Hardy's personal account of his turn from novel writing to poetry has to do with chafing against critical strictures (*Life and Work* 255–57, 302). Certainly Hardy approvingly copied out a correlative passage from John Addington Symonds' *Essays Speculative and Suggestive* (1890):

> The range of human thoughts & emotions greatly transcends the range of such symbols as man has invented to express the; & it becomes therefore the business of Art to use these symbols in a double way. They must be used for the direct repres.^{n} of thought & feeling; but they must also be combined by so subtle an imagination as to suggest much which there is no means of directly expressing. (*Literary Notebooks* v. 2, 43)

A close look at the techniques employed in two novels that Hardy wrote after Ellis's 1883 review suggests his increased deliberateness in the deployment of what Ellis called psychical elements and physical correlatives ("Thomas Hardy's Novels" 175). Because Hardy's narrative technique for representation of the consciousness of fictional minds has been so little studied, scant critical discussion of the specific impact of Ellis's observations on Hardy's craft exists. I posit here a marked advance in Hardy's strategy for deploying external reports followed by internal psycho-narration, especially noticeable in his handling of the minds of Henchard and Tess. Hardy also juxtaposes representation of intermental, communal judgment with passages of quoted (interior) monologue of rejected and alienated characters, to suggest the excruciating experience of severance from the realm of good opinion. He seems to take up as a direct challenge Ellis's observation regarding the lack of development in his male protagonists, answering the traditional *bildungsroman* model with a strong statement of dispositional psychology. Like psychoanalysis afterwards, Hardy's psychology recognized the Greek tragic models that resonated with late Victorian accounts of enduring human dispositions. We can see Henchard's fate as a strong restatement of Hardy's convictions about characters' immutable qualities, affirmed by Havelock

---

15. See Dennis Taylor, *Hardy's Literary Language and Victorian Philology* (1993).

Ellis's sympathetic criticism. Yet Hardy's reading of Darwin meant that he hoped for development over time, so the contrast between the doomed and reproductively unsuccessful Henchard with the fate of the novel's survivor deserves attention. Hardy's depiction of Elizabeth-Jane answers Ellis's observations about the sameness of Hardy's instinctual women with a character who develops in thoughtfulness through her experiences: unlike her stepfather, she grows intellectually and exhibits reproductive fitness.

"The Instinct of a Perverse Character"

Hardy's fiction offers a rich array of external details, often reported by observers about their fellows, and supported by behaviorist narration, from which readers may recognize characters' psychological conditions. In his short fiction, Rosemary Sumner reports, aberrations such as obsessions, delusions, and hysteria appear (*Psychological Novelist* 29). Working within a psychoanalytic diagnostic schema that would have been unfamiliar to Hardy, other critics have identified in Hardy's characters neuroses,[16] sublimation, regression, narcissism, and the repetition compulsion.[17] Without possessing a post-Freudian vocabulary, Hardy could still observe signs of unusual behavior that indicated ailments, while preserving his strong commitment to the realism of every day life. In 1881, Hardy wrote "the writer's problem is, how to strike the balance between the uncommon and the ordinary so as on the one hand to give interest, on the other to give reality. . . . In working out this problem, human nature must never be made abnormal, which is introducing incredibility" (*Life and Work* 154). Human nature, for Hardy, extended to a range of uncommon but not unlikely behaviors that would be labeled medically today. Thus, in his novels, without using the precise diagnostic language, Hardy depicts characters suffering from depression, obsessions (such as Farmer Boldwood's monomania), suicidal crises,[18] cognitive impairment, sexual anxieties,[19] sleep paralysis, tinnitus, and even Tourette's syndrome.

16. See Albert Guerard, *Thomas Hardy: The Novels and Stories* (1949). Guerard sorts Hardy's protagonists into categories: "neurotic voyagers" and "impotent spectators."

17. See Peter Alan Dale, *In Pursuit of a Scientific Culture: Science, Art, and Society in the Victorian Age* (1989) 262, 264–67, 271.

18. On Hardy's suicidal characters, see Frank Giordano, Jr., *"I'll Have My Life Unbe": Thomas Hardy's Self-destructive Characters* (1984).

19. On Hardy's character's sexual anxieties, see Annette Federico, *Masculine Identity in Hardy and Gissing* (1991).

To take the last and perhaps the most surprising of these, consider Hardy's depiction of a character suffering from Tourette's syndrome. A spectrum of disorders probably caused by a hereditary neurobiological disease, Tourette's syndrome is characterized by motor and vocal tics, sometimes including copralalia, the spontaneous speaking of taboo words. It was not formally identified until 1885, in Gilles de la Tourette's *Study of a Nervous Affliction,* though its symptoms had been observed as early as 1825 by a French physician. Afflicting as few as one in a thousand individuals, Tourette's syndrome is an uncommon disorder, but it seems likely that Thomas Hardy knew of someone who had it. He described a character with its symptoms in 1874. Andrew Randle in *Far from the Madding Crowd* stammers and has great difficulty bringing out conventional phrases in ordinary conversation. Another of Bathsheba's farm-workers, Henery Fray, reports that Randle is "a stammering man," who has lost his last job because of his blasphemous outbursts: "the only time he ever did speak plain he said his soul was his own and other iniquities, to the squire. 'A can cuss, mem, as well as you or I, but 'a can't speak a common speech to save his life'" (*FFMC* 80). Only fleetingly present in the story world, the Touretter Andrew Randle receives Hardy's attention as a token of individuality. The farm workers that Bathsheba Everdene meets and pays cannot blend into one another in a faceless mass when one of them has such a striking trait.

Hardy associated readers' pleasure in fiction with the opportunity to recognize distinctive persons, writing in 1881: "The real, if unavowed, purpose of fiction is to give pleasure by gratifying the love of the uncommon in human experience mental or corporeal. . . . This is done all the more perfectly in proportion as the reader is illuded to believe the personages true and real like himself" (*Life and Work* 154). At the same time that Hardy's differentiation of minor characters guards against their melding into an anonymous aggregate, his account of their nature and their past suggests that communal knowledge holds the key to characters' individuality. If the story of Andrew Randle's coprolalia follows him from job to job, how can any character hope to make a fresh start? *The Mayor of Casterbridge* elaborately demonstrates that fundamental dispositions (operating from the inside) and communal knowledge (pressing from the outside) effectively box characters into inescapable outcomes. They certainly prevent Michael Henchard's final evasion of his basic nature as an impulsive alcoholic inclined to alienation.

Infamously, young Michael Henchard takes too much rum in his furmity at the hiring fair and sells his wife, an action witnessed by the inconveniently long-memoried furmity woman. Her testimony represents the communal knowledge that follows characters in Hardy's fiction even when they change locales, jobs, dress, and social status. Known facts about crimes and indiscretions may be temporarily overlooked, but they inevitably come back to identify characters with their past behavior. Hardy depicts in these instances of communal memory the power of social norms that can be invoked when the community has other reasons for bringing down a character. Thus the external pressures on character are represented. The plot of Henchard's rise and fall turns on his pledge not to touch alcohol for a specific period of years. A man wiser about his own tendencies would have made a life-long pledge of abstention, but Henchard's relapse after twenty-one years demonstrates one of Hardy's points about internal dispositions: they do not change, even when a symbolic amount of time has been chosen for maturation to occur.

In Hardy's work, alcoholism is strongly associated with depression and suicidal behavior, though he depicts social groups of cider or ale drinkers without alluding to such dire outcomes. Hardy's personal attitude towards drink and other stimulants may be characterized in his own words, written in response to queries about writers' habitual use of alcohol and tobacco. Alfred Arthur Reade, in *Study and Stimulants* (1883), included Hardy's abstemious statements: "I have never smoked a pipeful in my life, nor a cigar" and "I have never found alcohol helpful to novel-writing in any degree. My experience goes to prove that the effect of wine, taken as a preliminary to imaginative work, is to blind the writer to the quality of what he produces rather than to raise its quality." Hardy acknowledged taking a glass or two of claret or mild ale while rambling on the Continent, but "with these rare exceptions, I have taken no alcoholic liquor for the last two years" (*Public Voice* 16–17). This temperate behavior differentiates Hardy the man from the ordinary folk he represents in his fiction. Alcohol was a part of every day life, and among his convivial social drinkers Hardy also represents those for whom alcohol is an addiction. In *The Mayor of Casterbridge*, Henchard's appetite for drink, expressly labeled as an element of his "perverse character" (*MC* 9), leads to the unorthodox divorce proceeding that will haunt Henchard for the rest of his days.

Hardy charts Henchard's tragedy as a psychological study of impulsive behavior and self-destruction, underscoring the key peripeties with shifts in his techniques for representing Henchard's consciousness. At the outset of the novel, the young family approaches the hiring fair, and their perspectives (moods, thoughts) receive a purely externalized treatment. Their lack of conversation while walking along and their apparent estrangement are inferred from visual cues, reported and interpreted by the narrator. Representation of inner states of mind begins with Henchard's perception that alcohol is available to lace the dish of furmity, a hot cereal of grain, flour, milk, raisins, and currants. Hardy moves inward with his narrator's declaration that "there was more in that tent than met the cursory glance; and the man, with the instinct of a perverse character, scented it quickly" (*MC* 9). Hardy's characteristic thought report gives Henchard's response to the rum-infused furmity: "He found the concoction, thus strongly laced, much more to his satisfaction than it had been in his natural state" (9) and his wife's consciousness that her choice has backfired, as she "Too sadly perceived that in strenuously steering off the rocks of the licensed liquor-tent she had only got into Maelstrom depths here amongst the smugglers" (9). Three pages later her husband has sold her for five guineas in front of a tent-full of witnesses.

The second chapter of the novel opens with a firm situation in Henchard's consciousness. His waking, looking around, discerning the left-behind wedding ring, recalling the events of the night before, verifying them by touching the money in his pocket: these actions tether the subsequent narration to Henchard's center of consciousness, still rendered in thought report: "He went on in silent thought. . . . A difficult problem or two occupied his mind" (*MC* 17), specifically, Did anyone know his name in the tent? and Does his wife take her sale as binding? Hardy renders Henchard's pondering on these subjects in a matrix of thought report, studded with an occasional phrase of narrated or quoted monologue. As is typical in Hardy's representation of mental crisis, private thought yields to speech, and Henchard is roaring his distress aloud before the end of the paragraph of introspection. Then Hardy ups the ante on speech itself, as Henchard enters a church and swears out loud his twenty-one year oath of abstention. That there are no witnesses scarcely matters because Henchard himself informs those who know him in later life that he has taken an oath: to Donald Farfare he actually divulges the entire sordid story.

Page by page, most of *The Mayor of Casterbridge* unfolds in conversations, punctuated by passages of action and description. Hardy's commitment to what Ellis recognized as the psychical element represented through physical correlatives shows forth not only in the formal dominance of dialogue, but in the emphasis on the semiotic import of characters' clothing and the general surveillance of their movements in space. The dramatic conventions of dialogue and blocking of action suit a narrative that hearkens back both to Greek tragedy and Victorian melodrama. Narratorial commentary suggests the pressure exerted on the characters by the observant social world, including respectable opinion and lower-class condemnation.[20] Intermental, communal thought receives representation both through narrator's thought report and through the externalized rendering of the conversation of a chorus of low-lives.

People watch and talk in Casterbridge, arriving close to the truth through observation and gossip:

> Henchard's visits [to Susan's cottage] grew so frequent and so regular that it soon became whispered, and then openly discussed in Casterbridge, that the masterful, coercive mayor of the town was captured and enervated by the genteel widow Mrs. Newson. . . . That such a poor fragile woman should be his choice was inexplicable, except on the ground that the engagement was a family affair in which sentimental passion had no place; for it was known that they were related in some way. (MC 78)

Precisely how they are related comes to public consciousness when the old furmity woman is brought before the magistrates on a charge of urinating in public. She tells her twenty-one year old memory before a packed courtroom, and Hardy shifts Henchard out of the internal perspective he has employed since the second chapter.

The change is abrupt but telling. Before the furmity woman makes her devastating speech, Hardy's narrator still employs thought report to track Henchard's state of mind: "Henchard stared, and quite forgot what was evidence and what was not" (MC 187). After the speech, the communal perspective takes over, regarding Henchard from the outside: "Everybody looked at Henchard. His face seemed strange, and in tint as if it had been powdered over with ashes" (187). At this crisis point in the narrative, Hardy emphasizes intermental, communal opinion about Henchard over his interior states:

> The retort of the furmity-woman before the magistrates had spread; and in four-and-twenty hours there was not a person in Casterbridge who remained unacquainted with the story of Henchard's mad freak at Weydon Priors Fair, long years before. The amends he had made in after life were lost sight of in the dramatic glare of the original act. Had the

---

20. For my reading of Hardy's ambivalent representation of class tension in *The Mayor of Casterbridge*, see Suzanne Keen, *Victorian Renovations of the Novel* (1998) 127–44.

incident been well-known of old and always, it might by this time have grown to be lightly regarded, as the rather tall wild oat, but well-nigh the single one, of a young man with whom the steady and mature (if somewhat headstrong) burgher of today had scarcely a point in common. But the act having lain as dead and buried ever since, the interspace of years was unperceived; and the black spot of his youth wore the aspect of a recent crime. (202)

The texture of the idioms used to disperse and process the scandal comes through in this summary thought report of communal judgment: "mad freak," "wild oat," and "black spot" conjure up the gossips, while "the dramatic glare of the original act" and "the interspace of years" inject the literary voice of the narrator relating that "edge or turn in the incline of Henchard's fortunes" (202).

Henchard has been brought low, but his destruction is not yet complete. Economic crisis swiftly follows, and a vengeful impulse leads him to package up Lucetta's letters and offer them to Donald Farfare, who has replaced him in the town's esteem. The high-minded Farfrae refuses to take the bait, and Henchard foolishly entrusts the revealing correspondence to Jopp, a worker whom he has several times rejected and thwarted. Jopp's prior knowledge of Lucetta from Jersey leads him to open the letters, and before long he is sharing them with the denizens of Peter's Finger, a dive frequented by members of the criminal class. Motivated in part by Jopp's desire for retaliation, the group plans a public humiliation for Henchard and Lucetta, the climactic skimmington ride that indirectly results in the deaths of both characters. For the concluding chapters, in which Hardy relates Lucetta's death, the recognition of the effigy drowned in the pool, and Henchard's dread at Elizabeth-Jane's true father's return, the narrator employs generous passages of psycho-narration trained on Henchard's tormented mind: "There is an outer chamber of the brain in which thoughts unowned, unsolicited, and of noxious kind, are sometimes allowed to wander for a moment prior to being sent off whence they came. One of these thoughts sailed into Henchard's ken now" (*MC* 285). He thinks of disowning Elizabeth-Jane and declaring her illegitimacy. Resisting these impulses by leaving Casterbridge and resuming his youthful occupation as a hay trusser leads Henchard into an embittered solitude that receives expression in passages of quoted monologue:

Very often, as his hay-knife crunched down among the sweet-smelling grassy stems, he would survey mankind and say to himself "Here and everywhere be folk dying before their time like frosted leaves though wanted by their families, the country, and the world; while I, an outcast, an encumberer of the ground, wanted by nobody, and despised by all, live on against my will!" (297)

Though the physical correlatives of this despair receive emphasis in Henchard's clothing, actions, and self-abnegating speeches, it must be acknowledged by any careful reader of the chapter 44 of *The Mayor of Casterbridge* that Hardy shows great interest in the inner thoughts and feelings of his self-alienated character. Hardy seems to be answering Ellis through his close focus on Henchard's suicidal psychology.

Furthermore, Hardy suggests that the survivors of the next generation may benefit from the lessons of their elders' deaths. Not a *bildungsroman* plot of moral education, but a Darwinian narrative of gradual change, *The Mayor of Casterbridge* contains Hardy's earliest published statement of the philosophy he was later to label evolutionary meliorism. Though Elizabeth-Jane is not after all Henchard's natural offspring, she learns through her regrets about his suffering in his last days an attitude of kindly, pedagogical altruism:

> As the lively and sparkling emotions of her early married life cohered into an equable serenity, the finer movements of her nature found scope in discovering to the narrow-lived ones around her the secret (as she had once learnt it) of making limited opportunities endurable; which she deemed to consist in the cunning enlargement by a species of microscopic treatment, of those minute forms of satisfaction that offer themselves to everybody not in positive pain; which thus handled have much of the same inspiriting effect upon life as wider interests cursorily embraced. (*MC* 309)

She cannot teach others this lesson without a "reflex action upon herself" (309). The novel ends with three undiluted paragraphs assessing Elizabeth-Jane's growth in thoughtfulness, thankfulness, and awareness of her good fortune, even as she acknowledges, "happiness was but the occasional episode in a general drama of pain" (310). The choice of thought report for the delivery of these consequential meditations on the mind of a young female character should not distract from the development signaled here: Hardy depicts a female character who can bridge the gap between the social mind (of both high and low society) and her own consciousness. Hardy's conclusion here may represent the apex of his faith in an emotionally driven consciousness of others as an ameliorating force in a sorry world beset by the unforeseen (310).

The End of Intermental Acuity

Of all of Hardy's novels, *Tess of the d'Urbervilles* most generously represents the consciousness and internal states of all its major characters and some of its minor ones. Yet in doing so it inexorably charts the end of intermental accord, where the social mind and the individual consciousness can find ways to accommodate one another's versions of experience. Hardy employs his detailed representation of Angel Clare's thought-stream, in a blend of narrated monologue and thought report, to suggest that readerly access to characters' consciousness does not imply accurate intersubjectivity among persons. Equipped with replete information about individual motives and feeling states of individual characters, the reader observes helplessly as misunderstandings, false moves, and even violent crimes transpire. The two crimes of passion that frame the novel's tragic plot, the rape/seduction of Tess by Alec, and the stabbing of Alec by Tess, take place at a remove from the active agents' perspectives. In the first, the narrator steps in with oblique commentary on the ironies and consequences, using analogies that have led to debate as to whether Tess suffers rape or seduction. The narrator's reference to the prior exercise of *droit de seigneur* on the part of Tess's aristocratic ancestors makes the case for rape strong, in my opinion; certainly, Tess's consent is not recorded (*Tess* 82). Readers must resort to inference because the narrator withdraws from the perspectives of both perpetrator and victim and eschews the task of straight narration of events. Similarly, for the murder scene, Hardy deploys the vantage-point of the landlady Mrs. Brooks in the rooms below Alec and Tess. She hears only an argument, Tess's lament, some rustling, and silence. The bloodstain on the ceiling establishes that something has actually happened upstairs, but the upper-story of the characters' consciousness is completely blocked (403–5). Even when the narrator more generously allows access to the characters' minds, the old culprits, nescience, emotional impulsiveness, and prejudice combine to make *Tess* the most punitive of Hardy's parables of the fates of feeling beings.

The first and last statements about mind-stuff in the novel both refer to absence of thought: John Durbeyfield "was not thinking of anything in particular" (*Tess* 13), when the parson plants the unfortunate knowledge of his distinguished ancestry in his susceptible mind; the ancestors who will do him no good and his daughter a great deal of harm sleep "on in their tombs unknowing" (420) as Tess dangles on the gibbet at the novel's conclusion. At every turn the narrator emphasizes failures of perception, for nescience is the norm and balked expression the signal device of the novel's painful set-up of consequences. Hardy begins to work out in this novel an idea he will express most fully in later poetry, the thought that nescience, or unknowing, is a far more desirable state than that of conscious human beings, afflicted with the disease of feeling.

The surviving Durbeyfield girl who goes off at the end of the novel arm-in-arm with Angel Clare, in Hardy's grim restaging of the expulsion from Milton's Eden, has the advantage of being a complete cipher. Liza-Lu is less voluptuous and more "spiritualized" than Tess (*Tess* 419): Hardy represents this survivor without a single attributed thought. Complete mindlessness and blankness of motive make Liza-Lu's merger into a pairing with Angel Clare possible, though to be sure many critics have objected to the sleight of hand by which this cardboard cut-out of a character comes to take Tess's place. To object to the trajectory that replaces a sensitive if impulsive character with her pale, flat, and inexpressive double misses Hardy's message, however. In Hardy's emergent understanding, lack of feeling and absence of consciousness are positive survival advantages, nescience a state to be desired, perhaps especially for females destined to be treated as chattel. The bitterness of this conclusion should indeed be read as a criticism of things as they are, but the evocation of the conclusion of Milton's *Paradise Lost* also hints that Hardy imagines a different state of affairs, after the likes of Tess have met their extinction. Either the Immortals who sport with human lives will have to evolve compassion, or human beings will have to cultivate numb acceptance until they can achieve true nescience.

The word nescience appears four times in Hardy's work, in *The Dynasts* twice and in two individual lyric poems, "A Sign-Seeker," and "Before Life and After." The latter poem, published in the collection *Time's Laughingstocks* (1909), gives a good sense of Hardy's opinion.

Before Life and After
A time there was—as one may guess
And as, indeed, earth's testimonies tell—
Before the birth of consciousness,
When all went well.

None suffered sickness, love, or loss,
None knew regret, starved hope, or heart-burnings;

None cared whatever crash or cross
Brought wrack to things.

If something ceased, no tongue bewailed,
If something winced and waned, no heart was wrung;
If brightness dimmed, and dark prevailed,
No sense was stung.

But the disease of feeling germed,
And primal rightness took the tinct of wrong;
Ere nescience shall be reaffirmed
How long, how long? (*TL* v. 1, 333, ll. 1-16)

The poem of 1909 posits a lost paradise of unknowingness, with a fall into feeling as a consequence of the birth of consciousness. Yet it also imagines a corrective development of the future, where the reaffirmation of nescience can bring back a way of existence like the deep past of humankind, "when all went well" (l. 4). One way of understanding Hardy's interest in the deep past, read through archaeological remains or geological evidence, is to map it onto the sad evolutionary trajectory that introduces the "tinct of wrong" in the form of "sickness, love . . . loss, . . . regret, starved hope, [and] heart-burnings" of modern human beings.

In the novel *Tess of the d'Urbervilles*, Hardy hints that some traces of that "primal rightness" can still be discerned, especially in the Talbothays Dairy idyll, where an unthinking existence can still be achieved. Or so Hardy has Angel Clare project upon Tess. Clare's back-to-the-land fantasy requires understanding Tess as a creature of pure instinct, while he remains unaware of the power of his own embodied impulses. Watching her milk the cow Old Pretty, Angel muses, "The stillness of her head and features was remarkable: she might have been in a trance, her eyes open, yet unseeing. Nothing in the picture moved but Old Pretty's tail and Tess's pink hands, the latter so gently as to be a rhythmic pulsation only, as if they were obeying a reflex stimulus, like a beating heart" (*Tess* 165). Just pages earlier, the text recalls Angel caught by his father reading some sort of systematic philosophy that cannot be squared with Evangelical Christianity (131), derailing his plains for a university education. Yet Clare is still a reader. It is not too much to imagine that Angel, like Hardy's narrator, knows the contemporary physiology of reflex stimuli, widely diffused by the 1880s, as what Hardy understood as unmotivated, unconscious action (*Life and Work* 152).

Clare's materialism leads him to reject the Resurrection (*Tess* 132), but his skepticism about the supernatural is matched by vulnerability to his own physical responses to external stimuli. Looking at Tess, Clare find that her external qualities of facial beauty, especially her mouth, send "an aura over his flesh, a breeze through his nerves, which well-nigh produced a qualm; and actually produced by some mysterious physiological process, a prosaic sneeze" (166). Marked by this instance of what Freud would later describe as displacement upwards, the ejaculation of the sneeze bowls over the inner bulwarks that have restrained Clare from declaring his passion. Tellingly, Hardy's narrator uses the wise tones of narratorial thought report to establish Clare's tumultuous state of mind: "The influence that had passed into Clare like an excitation from the sky, did not die down. Resolutions, reticences, prudences, fears, fell back like a defeated battalion" and he jumps up to take her in his arms (166). Clare, too, is subject to instinctive action that can change "the pivot of the universe for their two natures" (167). Why then must they go wrong, balked of the fulfillment of the imagery of Adam and Eve that the narrator has dangled before the reader? (145).

Part of the problem lies in Clare's limited understanding of what it means to be instinctive. While he credits Tess with subjectivity and an independent consciousness (*Tess* 172), and worries that she is both "fervid and impressionable" (172), he fails to realize that Tess's instincts include not only the instinct to self-delight (113), but an instinct to self-preservation stronger than candor (207) and an instinct to hide the truth (214). Clare's bitter response to her belated disclosure of the affair with Alec d'Urberville and its outcome takes the form of rejection of the woman he has idealized: "You were one person; now you are another . . . the woman I have been loving is not you," but "another woman in your shape" (248–49). Like Gabriel in Joyce's story "The Dead" (1914), he is taken aback that a separate subjectivity in his beloved entails experiences and memories predating his desire, which apparently endows her with reality. In this case, revelation of the past denudes her of the personality he has projected upon her comely person. Prejudice also plays a role. Idealizing the milk-maid, Clare is distressed by the revelation of Tess's connections with persons of rank and position, even centuries earlier (254). He never understands her, though she apprehends his feelings. In the somnambulism episode, Clare's mind closes to Tess and the reader, but his actions and sleep-talk speak plainly of his love, his murderous grief, and his consignment of his living wife to her stone coffin (266–69). It is no wonder that Sigmund Freud, reading *Tess of the d'Urbervilles* in the 1920s, declared that Hardy "knew psycho-analysis" (Oberndorf 182). As I have argued above, Hardy could have absorbed the notion that sleepwalking revealed the promptings of the unconscious mind from Henry Maudsley's *The Physiology and Pathology of the Mind* (1867) (Maudsley 112).

The central irony of Hardy's handling of Angel Clare's mind lies not in the unconscious impulses that reveal Clare to be subject to conventional prejudices, but in the copiousness of narrated monologue employed for this character, who indirectly destroys Tess through his projective idealism. While for other characters in the novel Hardy still relies largely on thought-report, with occasional brief passages of narrated monologue, the incidence of free indirect discourse in the reports of Clare's thoughts is higher than for any prior character in Hardy's novels. Twenty-six years old at his introduction, well-read, well-travelled, and experienced, Clare possesses the education to match the discourse of the narrator. Thus, while few readers would identify the following language as Tess's own words, "It just crossed her mind, too, that he might have a faint recollection of his tender vagary, and was disinclined to allude to it from the conviction that she would take amatory advantage of the opportunity it gave her of appealing to him anew not to go" (*Tess* 306), most would accept the similarly high-flown mental discourse attributed to Angel Clare as his own, and not the narrator's thought report. "He was incensed against his fate, bitterly disposed towards social ordinances; for they had cooped him up in a corner out of which there was no legitimate pathway. Why not be revenged on society by shaping his future domesticities loosely, instead of kissing the road of convention in this ensnaring manner," thinks Clare as he invites Izz Huett to go along with him to Brazil (288). Though the phrases before the semicolon possess the generalizing qualities of thought report, nothing prevents a reader from taking the words from there as transcription in free indirect discourse of Clare's own musings.

Access to Clare's mind through Hardy's use of narrated monologue reveals a character in an extreme condition of self-unknowing. He scarcely seems capable of recognizing by himself that Tess loves him and that he still loves her. It takes a period of exile and the testimony of several disinterested observers to get him to know his own mind. Thus, even when using narrated monologue more generously than for any prior character, Hardy turns the technique away from its traditional association with transparency and free access to motives and intentions to reveal a habitually allusive and philosophical mind beset by obtuseness, perplexity, and misinterpretation. After an illness that ages him a dozen years (*Tess* 360) and an influential encounter with a worldly stranger, who gets him to see the hypocrisy of his position, Clare finally changes his mind about Tess. As he does so—"Thus from being her critic he grew to be her advocate"— the narrator reverts to a greater measure of thought report (361) and externalized narration until the scene when Clare confronts Tess in the lodging house. She has succumbed to Alec's lies and blandishments, and Clare has come too late.

The narrator ironically merges the dissevered couple in thought report of the crisis: "They stood, fixed, their baffled hearts looking out of their eyes with a joylessness pitiful to see. Both seemed to implore something to shelter them from reality" (*Tess* 401). Fragmentation and dissociation immediately follow, with a vivid psycho-analogy for the death of identity and recognition: "Speech was as inexpressive as silence. But he had a vague consciousness of one thing, though it was not clear to him until later; that his original Tess had spiritually ceased to recognize the body before him as hers—allowing it to drift, like a corpse upon the current, in a direction dissociated from its living will" (401). Hardy renders Clare, in his penultimate actions in the novel, as instinctive and impulsive as Tess, subject to influences he cannot identify: why he does what he does "he could not say, but something seemed to impel him to the act" (407). Hardy does not tell the reader how Clare feels about accepting Tess's suggestion that he take up Liza-Lu as a substitute once she is dead, but he shows the new couple merged in obedience to irresistible forces: "They entered upon the turf, and impelled by a force that seemed to overrule their will suddenly stood still, turned, and waited in paralyzed suspense" (419) for the moment of Tess's execution. Hardy rehearses here the theory of human action that he will elaborate in *The Dynasts*, as planned, a demonstration of "Action mostly automatic, reflex movement, etc. Not the result of what is called motive, though always ostensibly so, even to the actors' own consciousness" (*Life and Work* 152). Thought report, especially accounting of chronic nescience, makes an ideal technique to match Hardy's emergent psychology of the human condition, driven by uncomprehended external forces and condemned to feel.

CHAPTER 3

Emotion and Cognition in Hardy's Verse

Emotive Subjects and Subjectivities

Hardy's poetry—over nine hundred poems written over a period of a half century—resists generalizations and defies expectations, especially those brought to it by readers of his novels. Some of the poems are grimmer than anything in his fiction, some funnier. Their thematic range, extending from the concerns of a striving young man of the Victorian period to those of an intellectual elder confronting modernity, can scarcely be matched by any of his contemporaries.[1] Yet he was also remarkably consistent, writing many variations on his key themes over the years, sometimes to the point of repetitiveness. Change, historical and personal, gave him opportunities: Hardy used his poetry to note chance observations of his environment and to work through the bitterest consequences of the loss of Christian faith that makes his life-story so quintessentially Victorian. The shock of confronting the deep time of evolution and the vast spaces of the cosmos reverberates through Hardy's representations of embodied experience. He used his poetry to teach himself, over and over, what it meant to exist with a creative, feeling mind in a universe resistant to anthropomorphizing analogies. Using inherited forms, he wrote

---

1. In taking this view I concur with Paul Zeitlow's minority view on the diversity of Hardy's verse. See *Moments of Vision: The Poetry of Thomas Hardy* (1974) viii–ix.

himself into modernity. Dennis Taylor has argued that Hardy's preoccupation with time enables him to achieve "an exhilarating intimation of a
true present," dramatizing how points of origin are "at once swallowed
up by the past" ("Riddle" 276). The poet was certainly acutely conscious
of growing older, further away from the links to the Napoleonic era that
always fascinated him, but he was still capable of marshaling past and
present in poems of reverie.[2] Some of his poetry has a universal reach and
cosmic time-scale, while other lyrics are situated precisely in fleeting but
highly particularized moments of vision. Hardy's modernity shows especially in the contents of his poetry, as he ponders the turn of the century,
total war, and even the theory of general relativity.

For better or for worse, Hardy was a philosophical poet, not only a
suffering lover, a tragedian, a self-distancing and ironical chronicler of circumstances, and a bereaved elegist.[3] But his possession of a philosophy
that combined scientific rationalism, Darwinian convictions, and materialist psychology does not result in a consistent view in the poetry. He
documented his monist convictions in some poems, even as he imbued
material reality with haunting animism in others. In addition to the many
masks he wore while speaking for himself in verse,[4] he incorporated the
voices and experiences of characters into his narrative poems and rather
scarcer dramatic monologues, enlivening tales of a generation or two
back with fresh expression. For all his obvious preoccupation with time,
spaces and places also commanded his attention.[5] Beyond his invention
of what would become known as Hardy's Wessex, he marked the literary
map of Dorset, the British Isles, and western Europe with recollections
and reinventions of its loci and landscapes. He was a human geographer
before that discipline existed. He had a wonderful sensitivity to the aura
of inanimate things, and at home on lyric poetry's shuttling path between
here and there, now and then, he projected his imagination into humble

---

2. In addition to Taylor, see Sven Bäckman's chapter on Hardy's intense visionary poems of the past in *The Manners of Ghosts: A Study of the Supernatural in Thomas Hardy's
Short Poems* (2001) 181–231.

3. For works representing the characterizations cataloged here, see the following: on the
philosophical Hardy, Samuel Hynes, *The Pattern of Hardy's Poetry* (1961); on the tragedian,
Katherine Kearney Maynard, *Thomas Hardy's Tragic Poetry: The Lyrics and* The Dynasts
(1991); on the self-distancing ironist, J. Hillis Miller, *Distance and Desire (1970)*; on the
elegist, Jahan Ramazani, *Poetry of Mourning: The Modern Elegy from Hardy to Heaney*
(1994).

4. In this respect Hardy was truly a Victorian poet, as Linda Shires has argued. See
"'And I Was Unaware': the Unknowing Omniscience of Hardy's Narrators" (2002).

5. Hardy's handling of place and space has been detailed in many fine articles, mainly
focusing on the fiction. See, for example, Michael Irwin, *Reading Hardy's Landscapes* (2000).

objects and historic remains.[6] He made a gift of his memories, longings, and qualms, wryly wrought into lines crafted out of an extraordinary vocabulary; he also kept his readers at a distance when he adopted the voice characterized by Bert G. Hornback as "Oz-like," for "awful god-voiced poems of doom" (Hornback 57). A simple record of his reading, the other writers who influenced him, or his philosophy does not emerge readily from this diverse corpus.[7]

Two features of Hardy's art (beyond his experimentation within the constraints of formal verse[8]) that persist throughout this large and various body of work concern me here: his preoccupation with the challenges of knowing, and his commitment to an affective representation of the world. As Dennis Taylor notes, "many of Hardy's archaic terms concern cognition: weet; weeting, unweeting, weetless, wot, fain would wot of (to be ware), ware, unware, warefully, wareful, warely, wareness, unwareness, warefulness, phasm, illuded, forethinking, mindsight, wist, I wis, witlessness, witteth, presciencelessness" (*Hardy's Literary Language* 274). It has often been observed that the various forms of science, as in prescience, conscience, nescience, and impercipient, turn up all over Hardy's work, not only in *The Dynasts*.[9] A related collection might be made of words about the emotions permeating Hardy's language: feeling, emotion, and affective as general terms; the positive words gay, hankering, happy, hearten, love, loving, pleasure, and ratheness (meaning eagerness); neutral terms about the absence of emotion such as impassivity, inexcitability, repressed, and spiritless; and a rich stream of words about negative feeling-states: fearsome, heartlessness, leery, melancholy, painful, tristful, supersensitive, and unhope. Martin Ray's admirable electronic *Variorum Concordance* to the *Complete Poems* (1999) enables users to see how habitually Hardy deployed key emotional words, such as forms of feel, fear, mood, pain, rage, sad, smiles, and tears: he could scarcely write poetry without them.

In a single chapter one cannot hope to do justice to the full range of ways that emotion and cognition appear in and shape Hardy's verse. I address their interaction as contributing to Hardy's demonstration of

---

6. See Seamus Heaney, "Place, Pastness, Poems: A Triptych" (1996).

7. Everyone who writes about Hardy's poetry is indebted to Samuel Hynes, the editor of the *Complete Poetical Works* and an influential critic. I am no exception, and I follow Hynes in seeking correlations between Hardy's ideas and the form of their expression.

8. Dennis Taylor, *Hardy's Metres and Victorian Prosody: With a Metrical Appendix of Hardy's Stanza Forms* (1988).

9. See, for instance, Ernest G. Griffin, "Hardy and the Growing Consciousness of the Immanent Will: A Study in the Relationship of Philosophy to Literary Form" (1961).

a belief in the pitiable but inescapable fact of embodied consciousness. Human beings, through the crass casualty of evolution over time, have been cursed with both thoughts and feelings (and the failings of both, unthinking automatism and heartlessness). Hardy idealizes rationality and lovingkindness and diagnoses nescience and lack of compassion. The criticism of Hardy's poetry has most often seen emotion and cognition in aesthetic opposition to one another: so Hornback regards Hardy as bad when bloviating about big ideas and good only when expressing his feelings in simple diction; and even Taylor, the most understanding critic of Hardy's language, can characterize his poetry's defects as arising from "a sensibility violated by doctrinaire ideas" ("Riddle" 263). I will attempt here to complicate that oppositional structure.

To square the binary opposition of thought and feeling (Hardy's Darwinism encouraged him to see both faculties as evolved characteristics) is to place these tendencies in relation to nescience and emotionlessness.

Cognition, Rationality, Thoughts	Emotion, Sensitivity, Feelings
Not-Thinking, Ignorance, Nescience	Not-Feeling, Impassivity, Heartlessness

Hardy varied in his attitudes towards these: fruitlessly wishing for the human species' restoration to nescience, as we have seen; condemning the empty universe for allowing the evolution of feeling beings; hoping for a growth in rationality; and committed to the practice of altruism. Thus far my procedures only increase the categories at play in a reading of Hardy's poetry, but they have also made it harder to sort many of the individual poems into a single cubby-hole, making the interactions and tensions between thinking, feeling, and their negative doubles more apparent. They are often co-present even in quite brief lyrics, as I will shortly demonstrate. By filtering these interacting terms through the schemas of containers from the small (skull-sized) to the vast (on the scale of the cosmos), on the one hand, and through image patterns of brain and mind, on the other, a start can be made in showing how Hardy's verse documents his emotion-saturated Theory of Mind and its relation to a cosmos without a Creator. While his epistemology might be described as skeptical and materialist (pointing towards Schopenhauer), Hardy's poetic ontology is infused with fervent feeling, not limited to the despair that pessimism regarded as the consequence of the human organism's plight. He was an artist and student of the emotions, ideas, and aspirations that pass from person to person "as a coin," and he suggested, long before Foucauldian genealogies of knowledge, that one might write "the biography" of such transactions (*"Poetical" Notebook* 21).

People were the usual carriers of transient emotion, for Hardy, who thought of this quality as one of the sad consequences of evolution, but considered writing about "A person, or family, [who] may be abnormally developed on the imaginative side. They not only imagine ghosts & personalities in every sound & sight, but converse with them, or about them. Their belief may be that all the world is so many forms of thought & emotion, choosing, or compelled to choose, these infinite varieties of expression. Their attitude imparted by fear of life" (*"Poetical" Notebook* 20). The side-stepping displacements in this passage, from a person, to a family, to those who fear life, should not deter a reader from recognizing something of Hardy himself here, for surely he was one of those persons so abnormally imaginative. Just a few years later he concedes in the same notebook, a place for storing up ideas for poems and drafts, "I cannot help noticing countenances in objects of scenery, e.g. trees, hills, houses, &c" (21). Hardy experienced the effects of prosopopoeia as involuntary perceptions rather than as decorative rhetoric. To see faces is to recognize feelings embodied in expressions, so it was not a reach for Hardy to imagine writing about places as possessing emotional histories. He wrote in his *"Poetical Matter" Notebook,* probably around 1905, "It must be a place which *has* an emotion" (45) and he planned "Place lyrics" that "contemplate any house, village, town, or what not, in respect only of the emotion it recalls. E.g. Sturminster, Wimborne, Bocastle, Enfield, Earl's Court Exh[n]" (44). Places, feelings, and memories layer in Hardy's poetic workshop, to be compressed into verses that re-expand upon close analysis, as Tim Armstrong has demonstrated.[10] The fact that few would spontaneously come up with any of the locations in his catalog of emotion-infused sites indicates how private and personal were the root associations: it must be a place that has an emotion *for Hardy.* An unlikely example recurs in Hardy's emotional representations of the provokingly empty expanse of outer space.

Though he often explored scenarios that would place his characters in emotionally fraught situations, many of Hardy's poems arise directly from his own experiences. Hardy wrote that he had "ever been shy of

---

10. See Tim Armstrong, *Haunted Hardy: Poetry, History, Memory* (2000).

putting his personal characteristics into his novels" (*Life and Work* 76). However, in 1919 he dictated for a letter that was later excerpted in his self-authored biography, "Speaking generally, there is more autobiography in a hundred lines of Mr. Hardy's poetry than in all the novels" (425). Critics alert to Hardy's defensiveness and self-divisions have revealed that he "wrote about 'other' people even when he thought he wrote about himself," in James Richardson's astringent phrase (Richardson 62).[11] This chapter does not attempt to recapture the life from the work, but it does employ motif-tracing, interpretation of image schemas, and close analysis of a necessarily limited number of lyric poems to document Hardy's inward journey into solitariness, moving towards an embrace of nescience (the condition of *not* knowing) and affirming his monist perspective on the universe's organization. This vision was the work of many decades, as his poem "'In the Seventies,'" (published in the poet's late seventies in *Moments of Vision*) establishes. Usually read as a poem about Hardy's blazing ambition ("certain starry thoughts"), it also roots a perception of his philosophical differences from his neighbors in those early decades. While a young man he keeps his knowledge "penned tight," where it is safe from the misunderstanding of conventional arbiters: "In the seventies nought could darken or destroy it. / Locked in me, / Though as delicate as lamp-worm's lucency" (*MV* v. 2, 196, ll. 19–21). Hardy kept his doubts and differences to himself in the early 1870s, but he made up for the early self-silencing in the introspective broadcasts of later years. He insistently signaled to an empty universe his reluctant consciousness's pulse of feeling existence.

The psychological methodology of introspection and the lyric poet's training of attention on his or her own subjective experience have a great deal in common, including their vulnerability to shaping pressures that would present experience according to acceptable social or generic norms ("Heads were shaken," Hardy writes of his neighbors, in "'In the Seventies'" [*MV*, v. 2, 196, l. 9). Strange feelings, odd thoughts, and random impulses do not usually get their due through formal introspection. Even the most confessional poet may elide reports of discomforting sensations if they are not already dignified by a place in a literary history of the emotions. Hardy chased down the expression of these products of embodied consciousness and gave them to his creations. He imagined the pride of the hangman in his handiwork ("The Stranger's Song"), the

---

11. On Hardy's psychological strategy of distancing, see Miller, *Distance and Desire*; on his various critical and fictional personae and narrators, see Linda Shires, "'And I Was Unaware': The Unknowing Omniscience of Hardy's Narrators" (2002).

lethal desire of "The Ivy-Wife," the incredulity of a wife receiving news of her husband's accidental death: she worries about her untidy house, and pines afterward ("The Slow Nature"). Though not an old poet yet in 1890, Hardy documented the pains of aging, as Time chisels at his body: "at night he thinks me sleeping / I feel him boring sly / Within my bones" ("In a Eweleaze near Weatherbury," *WP* v. 1, 92, ll. 13–15). When Hardy was a young poet, his introspective verses (written in sonnet form) emphasized the traditional emotional pairing of love and loss. While these rich Petrarchan tropes never let him down, supplying the pretext for poems throughout his career, Hardy augmented his exploration of emotive subjects by writing poems of place rooted in emotions, brainstorming a list of potential titles organized around feelings: "The Wrath-Fleers: The Etherealists: The Ecstatics: The Erratics: *The Flutter-hearts*. The Emotionalists: The *Life-Fearers*" (*"Poetical" Notebook* 20). He would not exhaust the topic.

Near the end of his life, facing death and the remote possibility that his vision might somehow surprise him by seeing beyond the mortal limits of bodily experience, Hardy "resolves to say no more," asserting "What I have learnt no man shall know" and "I'll let all be, / And show to no man what I see" (*WW* v. 3, 274, ll. 19–20). This resolution reverses a lifetime of practice, as evidenced by the grim little poem that immediately precedes it in *Winter Words* (1928), "'We Are Getting to the End.'" Not yet self-silencing with the concern, "Why load men's minds with more to bear / That bear already ails to spare," ("He Resolves," *WW* v. 3, 274, ll. 6-7), Hardy announces that "We are Getting to the End" of dreams of peace, respect of other nations' heritage, and, most futile of all, dreams of a general turn to rationality. It won't happen: like the imprisoned lark singing in a cage, "We ply spasmodically our pleasuring" (273, l. 8) and succumb to the madness of war. Here the innate emotionality of human beings results in vulnerability to manipulation by violent nationalists and conclusively debunks Hardy's own dream of meliorism: "such as that better whiles may follow worse." The late poetry, particularly the verse written after the Great War, contains a great deal of the evidence for Hardy's pessimism (which Hardy persistently contested). Though the emotional register of his introspection varies, traces of the late pessimism can be seen as early as the poem "Hap," discussed below. He was not above the self-pitying death wish or the peevish complaint that the non-existence of God strips a suicide threat of its force (at least before his friend Horace Moule killed himself). But Hardy was also capable of stern self-judgment, as in "A Confession to a Friend in Trouble," in which Hardy admits that his friend's depression makes him shrink from learning his "griefs." Though he suppresses the impulse, he acknowledges: "such instinct was in me!" (*WP* v. 1, 13, l. 14). He indicts himself for a temporary failure of compassion.

Yet an equally important aspect of Hardy's poetic art sympathetically attends to other minds in the form of fictional characters, recording in ballads, dramatic monologues, and other narrative poems his acute observations of human behavior, of intermental social minds, of individual experience rendered so that his reader may step into someone else's shoes. Though Hardy often explicitly invokes sympathy across class lines, as in "A Trampwoman's Tragedy" (*TL* v. 1, 243–47), he does not always strike the expected notes. The grieving speaker of "A Sunday Morning Tragedy" rebuffs compassionate response: "My punishment I cannot bear, / But pray God *not* to pity me" (*TL* v. 1, 255, ll. 127–28). In other poems Hardy invites the reader to share unexpected emotional responses. For instance, in the comic ballad "The Curate's Kindness," Hardy creates an aged speaker, bitterly disappointed when he is allowed as a boon from the young Parson to remain with his wife when the destitute couple enters the Union workhouse. The speaker had been counting on enforced separation, as per Board rules: "*The men in one wing and their wives in another*" (257, l. 15; italics in original). The promise of freedom from "this forty years' chain" (l. 36) has been the only thing softening the shame and misery of pauperism. The speaker resolves to drown himself instead!

"Perhaps I can do a volume of poems consisting of the *other side* of common emotions" (*Life and Work* 54), Hardy proposed to himself: this other side could be regarded as the stuff either of irony or of empathy, and it could be regarded as genuinely other-directed, or as a bid for the understanding of *himself* that he sought from others, and from himself, through his poems. As Dennis Taylor writes, "The language Hardy uses to characterize his novel characters in turn characterizes his own consciousness; in describing how language controls the consciousness of his characters, he discovers in the poems how it controls his own" (*Hardy's Literary Language* 178). This process became a matter of commitment in Hardy's statements about the purposes of art. In 1918, Hardy reflected, "My opinion is that a poet should express the emotion of all the ages and the thought of his own" (*Life and Work* 417), a task that links an inevitable solipsism with an other-directed vocation. While the conclusion to this study, "Empathetic Hardy," considers what he knew and believed about the altruistic responsibilities of poetic vocation, the present chapter explores the intersections of emotion and thought, mindsight and nescience, in individual lyrics on a human scale and in vatic utterances on the nature of the cosmos. From his early poems of the 1860s, the key elements of emotion, cognition, a cosmic frame and a focus on individual brains appear in close juxtaposition, indicating interests that reach climactic expression in the machinery and imagery of *The Dynasts,* his verse drama with a large cast of characters.

Attention to Hardy's evocation of feeling and the word-work of his unusual phrasing supports his own contention (of 1902) that his poetic art was a matter of both emotion and expression: "Poetry—There is a latent music in the sincere utterance of deep emotion, however expressed, which fills the place of the actual word-music in rhythmic phraseology on thinner emotive subjects, or on subjects with next to none at all. And supposing a total poetic effect to be represented by a unit, its component fractions may be either, say. . . . Emotion three-quarters, plus Expression one quarter, or Emotion one quarter plus Expression three-quarters" (*Life and Work* 334). These quatrain-like fractions suggest a pattern of units arranged around a turn, but they do not predict a smooth integration of emotion and expression. As we will see, the modulation among emotional registers and the integration of thoughts, caviling arguments, and ontological crises trouble the surface of Hardy's sincere utterances from *Wessex Poems* (1898) onwards.

"Locked in That Universe Trackless, Distant, Drear"

Published in 1898, Hardy's first poetry collection, *Wessex Poems,* contains a group of verses written decades earlier. (Hardy continued throughout his poetry-publishing career to mine the products of his early years of writing for verses to fill out volumes, increasing the impression of consistency of theme.) The year 1866 was a particularly prolific one for Hardy the young poet, as he practiced traditional forms and rehearsed some of the ideas that would preoccupy him throughout his life. Of the 1866 sonnets, only "Hap" is usually anthologized or discussed, and I depart here from the usual practice of isolating it as an exhibit by discussing "Hap" in the company of two of its neighboring sonnets, "'In Vision I Roamed,'" and "A Confession to a Friend in Trouble."[12] All three pose imagery of big spaces as rejoinders or revised contexts to dilemmas of the tight time

---

12. Purdy identifies the friend as Horace Moule, according to Samuel Hynes's notes to *Complete Poetical Works* v. 1, 361n.

frame of immediate experience. That Hardy's poetic arguments are constructed as unresolved antimonies or paradoxes, as Hynes has argued, rather than as conclusive answers to questions does not prevent the reader from following the gesture towards a context that stands in for a solution. Long before Hardy worked out the synaptic neural imagery of *The Dynasts,* in which the Will figures as a cosmic brain crackling with the impulsions that drive history and human experience, he positioned the emotional experience of the individual in the largest possible frames: the sky, the "flashing Firmament," the open sea. The alternatives of annihilation, nescience, or the willed fight against natural human instinct show the mind and brain of the individual responding to its condition, "Locked in that Universe trackless, distant, drear" ("'In Vision I Roamed,'" *WP* v. 1, 10–11, l. 14).

The sonnet was not Hardy's most congenial form: its iambic meter constrains his freewheeling rhythm with some resulting awkwardness as he drops words ("From up the sky" in "Hap" [*WP*, v. 1, 10, l. 2)) and counts on unearned Miltonic elisions ("Half-eased in that a Powerfuller than I," also from "Hap" [l. 7]). Hardy scarcely altered the position of the caesura in his sonnet lines, relying instead on rhythmically similar lines in blocky quatrains followed by a heavy sestet, set about with white space. He constructed sonnets like a bricklayer, slab by slab. The sonnet lacks the freedom to vary line length and stanza shape that characterizes Hardy's best lyrics, but he kept some of what he learned from practicing traditional sonnets in his later verse. His rhyme schemes and use of ABAB CDCD quatrains suggest a hybrid of Elizabethan and Italian forms, probably authorized by Shelley's play with blending the two types or inverting their components, rather than by Wordsworth, who mostly cleaved to the Italian model. Hardy's choice of a sestet instead of a third quatrain and concluding couplet suggests his preference for two not-quite balanced perspectives over a reasoned argument that concludes with a punchy rhyme. His was an art of undermining certainties, or qualifying conclusions rather than nailing them down, and he shows a strong attraction to the Italian sonnet's *volte* rather than the Elizabethan sonnet's strong closure in a couplet. A close look at three of his early sonnets reveals not only his characteristic juxtapositions of near and far, small and vast that may owe something to his reading of Petrarchan tropes of unrequitedness, but also his liking for the strong *volte* or turn, a rhetorical device he exploited hundreds of times in lyrics both slighter and more substantial than sonnets. The "But not so" that controverts the wish of the first two quatrains of "Hap" presages dozens and dozens of other abrupt turns in Hardy's poetry. A meta-gloss runs like this: "You might think that [some great force] would do X, so that I might respond accordingly. But not so." The turn acts not just as an argumentative about-face, but also as a suspension of resolution, a fulcrum upon which the contraries of Hardy's poems teeter.

"Hap" complains that the lover's misfortune is just as much an accident as anything else that happens: "How arrives it joy lies slain, / And why unblooms the best hope ever sown? / —Crass Casualty obstructs the sun and rain, / And Dicing Time for gladness casts a moan . . . " (*WP* v. 1, 10, ll. 9-12). The anticipation of the conclave of the Spirits of the Years and the Immanent Will, gaming with human lives without their knowledge, is striking: the Spirit of the Pities, who might be expected to sympathize since it takes the part of humanity, does not appear in this 1866 poem. Random chance seems to produce only disasters, the speaker observes, when it could just have easily as "strown / Blisses . . . as pain" (l. 14). These oversize figures, "purblind Doomsters," take the place of the nonexistent "vengeful god" of the first line and octave, who fails to demand suffering, a demand that would justify the lover's situation by killing him unjustly. The clanking machinery of this sonnet smashes round a vacancy at its core: "But not so." No one "From up the sky" or large enough to get in the way of weather cares one bit about the lovelorn individual looking for someone to blame for his plight. The best word in the poem is "unblooms," from the question "Why unblooms the best hope ever sown?" (l. 10). Not withers, fades, nor fails to flower, but unblooms—the word points to Hardy's self-annihilating emotion, unhope. Like time-lapse photography run backwards, the word takes away as it gives, leaving the ghost image of its positive fulfillment behind. The title word, "Hap," meaning happenstance or chance (the title in the holograph manuscript according to Hynes), also takes a half-step towards happy, but stops short. The worst word in the poem (though "Powerfuller" runs a close second) is "pilgrimage," because nothing in the poem's plaint suggests the traversing of terrain or spiritual journey on the part of the speaker. Something bad has happened to him: "joy lies slain" (l. 9) but all his responses are in the subjunctive mode. He neither steps forward nor back, stuck in the negative space, an agent who cannot act for himself, casting about for universal forces to blame. He is caught in the swerve of the turn; to imagine his condition as a stage of a pilgrimage is self-aggrandizing, if conventional in a Petrarchan sense.

The sonnet "'In Vision I Roamed'" supplies the pilgrimage missing from "Hap" through a strange dissociative journey, an out-of-body experience that brings the speaker the relative peace of emotionlessness and lack of consciousness. In the sonnet Hardy's speaker, apparently a pining lover, travels "the flashing Firmament" (*WP*, v. 1, 10, l. 1) visiting stars in the "last chambers of the Monstrous Dome" (l. 6), so far away from Earth that the bright points of the zodiac cannot be discerned. In the stark "footless traverse," the speaker's spirit roves "through ghast heights of sky" (l. 5), dissociated and unfeeling. This odd sonnet revisits the metaphysical tropes of Donne's "A Valediction: Forbidding Mourning," as it, too, addresses the situation of a distant lover. Rather than solving distance in an alchemical formula for eternity and refined connection, Hardy's sonnet abjures feeling grief in favor of relief that the absent beloved has not been abducted (teleported?) to some other planet! This peculiar consolation uses a fantasy of remoteness to address the more mundane temporal problem of a period of separation. It resolves the speaker's grief by stripping him of yearning, "as day by day / I lived unware, uncaring all that lay / Locked in that Universe trackless, distant, drear" (*WP*, v. 1, 11, ll. 12–14). The insensate body left behind while the spirit roves the universe suggests a coma, an image which may be set in relation to what Hillis Miller has shown about Hardy's use of distance to spur desire. Of course the distance here is an illusion, for the metaphor, a variant of the schema LIFE is a JOURNEY,[13] describes a process in which the speaker's body literally goes nowhere and ends up feeling nothing. Hardy insists at various points of his career, in his fiction, his notes, prefatory apologies, and poems, that it would be better not to feel or know. Yet he cannot flush out all the emotional coloration even of the trackless Universe: it is still "drear," a depressing condition, perhaps worse in the variant reading when it is also "taciturn," not just "trackless." If Hardy dislikes the absence of a path (preferring to fantasize a pilgrimage than to admit he lacks a way forward), he hates the silence of the empty universe, caught in the variant word "taciturn." In both "Hap" and "'In Vision I Roamed'" the absence of a God-like voice, even a cruel and angry one, provokes the speaker to raise his own voice, if to announce his abjuring of thought and feeling.

God, the purblind Doomsters, the Immanent Will: these figures are not good listeners. Hardy's poems show God degrading into empty-headedness (as, for example, in "Nature's Questioning"), and he only hopes in *The Dynasts* that the Will may someday evolve consciousness

---

13. For the schemas mentioned in the following pages of poetic analysis, see George Lakoff and Mark Turner, *More Than Cool Reason: A Field Guide to Poetic Metaphor* (1989).

and compassion, analogously with human beings, who have been selected by evolution to feel in an unfeeling universe. Hardy's sonnet "A Confession to a Friend in Trouble" confides his own impulse to become a bad listener. It draws on Miltonic imagery of the flight of Satan towards Earth, from Books 3 of *Paradise Lost*.[14] Hardy confesses in the poem that he considers tuning out refreshed knowledge of the unnamed Horace Moule's condition: "*I will not show zeal again to learn / Your griefs, and, sharing them, renew my pain . . .* " (*WP* v. 1, 12–13, ll. 7-8 emphasis in original), failing in compassion by enjoying his distance from his depressed friend's troubles. As many commentators have noted, Hardy was more attentive to the dark side of human emotions, more prone to record pain than pleasure. This poem, however, maps the limits of compassion onto a theological ontology of mind, taking as its starting point the recognition that it feels good *not* to be exposed to another's suffering. The poet's brain corresponds to Milton's creation, strange thoughts to Satan (the author of sin), and instinct to human fallenness.

Equating his uncompassionate "thought too strange to house within my brain" with the implied figure of Satan in flight, bent on the ruin of humanity, Hardy figures sin in motion. In Milton's poem Satan flies out of Hell and approaches Earth in winged form (*Paradise Lost* 3, ll. 561–90). In Hardy's sonnet, the "thought too strange" to allow into his brain nonetheless breaches its outer defenses, detected, as Satan is by the archangel Uriel on guard (*PL* 3, l. 694 ff), "Haunting its outer precincts," but released because hypocrisy is invisible (ll. 683–84). As Satan sails down "toward the coast of earth" (l. 739), Hardy's thought similarly "goes, like murky bird or buccaneer / That shapes its lawless figure on the main." In *Paradise Lost* humankind is already foredoomed to fall before Satan even coasts to earth and penetrates Eden, and Hardy sets Adamic "staunchness," which "tends to banish utterly / The unseemly instinct" against the knowledge that already the thought "had lodgment here" as in Eve's dream, presaging her fall. The poem ends echoing the position of Eve's lamenting awareness of her responsibility for sin, asking "can bitterer knowledge be / Than that, though banned, such instinct was in me!"

---

14. Hardy knew Milton's work well. In his library at the time of his death were numerous books by Milton, including *The Poetical Works of John Milton. A New Edition, Carefully Revised,* ed. Theodore Alois Buckley (1864), *Paradise Lost, as Originally Published by John Milton, Being a Facsimile Reproduction of the First Edition,* with an introduction by David Masson (1877), and *Milton's Poetical Works* (1865). According to Millgate, this last volume bears a signature dated 1866 and heavy annotations. See "Thomas Hardy's Library at Max Gate."

Everything in the poem takes place within the container of the speaker's mind, but the cosmology of *Paradise Lost,* evoked by the central comparison of the strange thought to Satan in flight, writes the sinful "instinct" to ignore the compassionate responsibilities of friendship onto the narrative of the Fall of Man. Hardy's penetrable brain contains the banned instinct, the staunch defender, and the guilty fallen creature that errs in feeling happy to be away from a sad friend and in thinking of shutting out further confidences from him. A whole universe of regret is shrunk into this sonnet, which confesses without actually apologizing, and offers chagrin without retraction.

All three of the 1866 sonnets discussed here describe the interaction of emotion and cognition. The feelings come first, as motive impulsions. The fact that in each of the poems thought is balked—unresolved, blessedly alleviated, owned and disowned—dramatizes the painful condition of the speaker, doomed to feel and as incapable of conclusive decision as of permanent nescience. To emphasize the trap sprung on emotional beings, Hardy uses the large-scale frame of the universe itself as the set for the mental movements of the speaker's feelings and thoughts. That the vastness of the universe in two of the three poems explicitly (in "Hap" at least implicitly) turns out to map exactly onto the brain of the speaker asserts that there is no way out. As Hillis Miller writes about another Hardy poem, "The poet's mind comes to coincide with the universal mind," expressed in imagery of astronomical space: "a metaphor for a universal mind capacious enough to contain and keep in existence all the times of human history." ("Wessex Heights" 358).

Mind-Chains and Mind-Stuff

A possible response to the emotional consequences of embodied consciousness doomed to suffer in relationship with others is self-sequestering: for "mind-chains do not clank where one's next neighbour is the sky," as Hardy writes in his famous poem of isolation, "Wessex Heights" (*SC* v. 2, 25–27, l. 8). This poem of 1896 figures the actions of minds as material objects. They are chains, echoing Blake's "Mind-forg'd manacles," they produce visible phantoms and ghosts, and they can penetrate the boundaries of others' bodies: "I am now but a thought of hers, / I enter her mind" (ll. 25–26). These figures may not be entirely a matter of metaphor for Hardy, who read and excerpted the mathematician and philosopher W. K. Clifford, the theorist of "mind-stuff," in his *Literary*

Notebooks (v. 2, 108, 109). Congenial to Hardy because of his monist convictions, Clifford regarded "consciousness as a complex of feelings" and "of ejective facts" (Clifford 64). *Ejects* for Clifford are "inferred existences . . . thrown out by consciousness," as opposed to *objects,* phenomena perceived by consciousness (58). Ejects are bound by the same physical laws that bind matter, and "*Mind-stuff is the reality which we perceive as Matter*" (65, emphasis in original). Clifford explains the phylogeny of human consciousness thus:

> That element of which, as we have seen, even the simplest feeling is a complex, I shall call *Mind-stuff.* A moving molecule of inorganic matter does not possess mind, or consciousness; but it possesses a small piece of mind-stuff. When molecules are so combined together as to form the film on the under side of a jelly-fish, the elements of mind-stuff which go along with them are so combined as to form the faint beginnings of Sentience. When the molecules are so combined as to form the brain and nervous system of a vertebrate, the corresponding elements of mind-stuff are so combined as to form some kind of consciousness; that is to say, changes in the complex which take place at the same time get so linked together that the repetition of one implies the repetition of the other. When matter takes the complex form of a living human brain, the corresponding mind-stuff takes the form of a human consciousness, having intelligence and volition. (65, emphasis in original)

In Clifford's resolutely materialist reading, "the reality external to our minds which is represented in our minds as matter, is in itself mind-stuff. The universe, then, consists entirely of mind-stuff" (66). However, lest we infer a supernatural or idealist consequence of this conclusion, Clifford cautions, "Reason, intelligence, and volition are properties of a complex which is made up of elements themselves not rational, not intelligent, not conscious" (67).

Hardy, like Clifford, also read Spinoza and Kant (Clifford further cites Wundt, whose work Hardy does not mention), and stirred their ideas into the mix. This 1878 formulation, copied out into Hardy's reading notebook,[15] resonates with his poetic presentation of evolved consciousness in a nescient universe. We have already seen how in early poems Hardy conflates the individual mind and the universe, in schemas of

---

15. Hardy excerpted this passage in his *Literary Notebooks* (v. 2, 108), under the heading *Notes in Philosophy,* flanked by notes from Alexander Bain and comments on Spinoza.

containers turned inside out. Later he uses the word "ejection" in *The Dynasts* to refer to the products of the Will's neural network. In his 1887 poem "Rome: The Vatican: Sala Delle Muse," he has the Muse explain that her sisters and she are but "phases of one," adding "And that one is I; and I am projected from thee, / One that out of thy brain and heart thou causest to be" (*PP* v. 1, 136, ll. 20–22). Hardy emphasizes the power of the poet's imagination to create and project the sentient inhabitants of the universe in the form of ejects.

In "Wessex Heights" the wish for liberty from the ejects ("inferred existences . . . thrown out by consciousness") roving the lowland land-scape and towns produces a poem that has often been read as expressing Hardy's flirtation with the supernatural: it is after all, about phantoms, ghosts, and haunting. Reading it as an investigation of the consequences of mind-stuff unleashed in the world and empowered by a distressing inter-subjectivity, we may see it afresh. As a statement of a suffering speaker, seeking relief from his unpleasant memories of rejection and insult, from a disapproving younger self, and from guilty awareness of those he may have injured, "Wessex Heights" reactivates the scheme of distance, this time as a protection from "ghosts" and real men and women who pre-fer not to climb so high. The places named in the poem, Ingpen Beacon, Wylls-Neck, Bulbarrow, and Pilsdon Crest are real hills marking a new Wessex (Gatrell 32–33), but even the self-isolating speaker hardly believes in their power. They are only "shaped *as if* by a kindly hand" (*SC* v. 2, 25, l. 1, emphasis added) and the relief achieved only keeps the revenants at a distance, granting "*some* liberty" (l. 32, emphasis added). The lonely hilltops give the speaker a way of fantasizing an escape from conscious-ness, getting to "where I was before my birth, and after death may be" (l. 4). Hardy follows this often-reiterated wish for nescience with a sequence of stanzas depicting the trail of ejects produced by conscious life,[16] which is inescapably shared with the others who perceive his speaker so malig-nantly. "Wessex Heights" dramatizes one of the immediate consequences of acknowledging one's own subjectivity and its powers: that the others out there possess matching powers of ejection from their own conscious-nesses, and they may not be inclined to construct a forgiving or flatter-ing version of oneself. As Clifford writes, "The complicated processes of your body and the motions of your brain and nervous system, inferred from evidence of anatomical researches, are all inferred as things possibly

---

16. Tom Paulin sees them as "eidetic memories which [Hardy] is projecting outside his own mind" (*Thomas Hardy: The Poetry of Perception* 129).

visible to me" (Clifford 57). Hardy renders them visible and records the discomfort of their gaze upon him, the perceiving subject.

For the speaker of "Wessex Heights," the recognition of what Clifford calls "the kindred consciousness in one's fellow beings" (Clifford 59) produces not gregarious action, but agony and aversion. The second stanza dangles the suggestion that the speaker might under some conditions hope for a comrade in the lowlands, but it complains of the absence of a friend. Fellow-feeling being unavailable, where "nobody thinks as I" (l. 7), the speaker retreats to the solitary hilltop. If only neglect were his only problem: intersubjective experience is worse, or so it seems when imaginatively he returns to the scene of social failures, where "phantoms having weird detective ways" track him (l. 9) and direct harsh remarks, sneers, and disparaging in his direction (ll. 11–12). Clearly these fellow creatures exercise their powers to project images of the speaker from their consciousness, and their ejections seem to overpower his own. The consequence is a dissociative breach, in which the subject sees both "my simple self that was / And is not now" and also the present speaker, "a strange continuator," linked to the chrysalis of the earlier person only through some "crass cause." Having recognized the self as in part the creation of the intersubjective work of others, Hardy's speaker makes the radical leap of questioning the continuous existence of his own individual subjectivity. In effect he turns his current self into a phantom of his own past, the agnostic regarded quizzically by the pious young man, the poet by the earlier novelist.

The fourth stanza relates the sinister barring of the way to "the great grey Plain" (l. 17) and the "tall-spired town" (l. 19), locales that invite the reader to imagine the novelist's own word-wrought landscapes of 1891 and 1895 (possibly Salisbury Plain and Christminster) as already inaccessible to the poet of 1896. This stanza animates figures and forms that no one else can see in quite the same way: fictional characters, conjured up by Hardy the novelist, as Frank Giordano suggests (63). This suggestion meshes well with J. O. Bailey's idea that the men and women of the prior stanza include hostile critics of Hardy's *Tess* and *Jude* (Bailey 278). The speaker seeks to avoid the harsh disparaging of the critics by retreating to the heights, but he cannot forget his creations: they, too, are subjected to scathing criticism, and his imaginative sympathy extends to their sense of grievance. Hardy declared in a note of 1886 that novelistic worldmaking ought to go forward by "rendering as visible essences, specters, &c. the abstract thoughts of the analytic school" (*Life and Work* 183). What if those forms and figures—Tess, Jude, even the unsympathetic masters of the colleges of Christminster—having been conjured up by Hardy as visible essences, also look back at their maker and bar his way back into the fictional world he created? The "forms" are kept alive by readers, "in whose long vision they stand there fast" (l. 20).

The fifth stanza follows out the logical consequences of this common illusion of authors, that characters and fictional beings possess independent agency[17] to chide, haunt, follow the author around, and even advocate for an alternative version of the story than the one Hardy the poet has chosen to tell: "There is one in the railway-train whenever I do not want it near, / I see its profile against the pane saying what I would not hear" (ll. 23–24). This interpretation makes sense of the estranging pronouns Hardy employs in these two stanzas alone: "one," and "it" rather than "he" and "she," indicating the liminal status of his own fictional characters, embodied and figured forth by his imagination and then abandoned. Also in 1886, Hardy had imagined turning the material world inside out through imaginative reversal of the position of ejects and objects: "The Realities to be the true realities of life, hitherto called abstractions. The old material realities to be placed behind the former, as shadowy accessories" (*Life and Work* 183). To embrace this strategy is one thing when you are the active agent arranging new and old realities, but what if it happens to you, and you become a "shadowy accessory" replaced by an abstraction (for instance, by a rival you do not know)?

To give Hardy credit, he also imagined that the minds of others could carry out the same procedure, and he cites an example in "Wessex Heights" of his own denaturing by another's mind. Characteristically the injury has occurred as a consequence of unrequited, possibly even unnoticed, love. The speaker claims injury by "one rare fair woman," in whose mind he exists only as a displaced thought. She prefers another, or perhaps only another thought (l. 26). This could explain a lot about the injured self who climbs to the heights to avoid the company of men and women. She fails to apprehend the speaker's warm ejection, which almost takes on a body: "my love for her in its fullness she herself even did not know." In the one positive or at least therapeutic line in the poem, the speaker allows that the passage of time "cures hearts of tenderness, and now I can let her go" (l. 28). It is hard to hold the "rare fair woman" responsible, for the poem invites the reader to wonder whether the speaker has been haunting her himself all this time. It suggests the self-injury of the super-

---

17. On psychologist Marjorie Taylor's work on the Illusion of Independent Agency (IIA) and its implications for an author's empathetic imagining of characters, see Keen, *Empathy and the Novel* 125–27.

sensitive: in clinging to this old rejection, has the speaker dealt his "simple self" the first dissociative wound? She hardly seems as implacable as the fictional ejects of stanzas 5 and 6, nor as aggressive as the "shadows of beings who fellowed with myself of earlier days" from stanza 3 (l. 10).

If "Wessex Heights" offers to quarantine the speaker in the safety of isolation, it still only promises "some liberty" (l. 32) from men, women and ghosts. Hillis Miller suggests that the spatial trope of the heights actually defines "distance as an escape into the atemporal realm which exists before birth and after death, the realm from which Tess and her fellow sufferers came and the realm to which they have now returned" (*Distance and Desire* 264). But as Miller observes, the speaker has not obtained a release from time. He is "still open toward a future which will be the re-enactment of episodes from the past, in an always unsuccessful attempt to free himself from them completely" (264–65). The mind-chains may not clank, but they still bind as long as life persists, because they are a consequence of existing in time.

Time-Wraiths

Two of Hardy's later poems, "The Unborn" of 1905 and "The Pedigree" of 1916 consider the degree to which human life is bound by mind-chains from the very outset, driven by the "all-imminent Will" into birth and doomed to repeat the actions and decisions of its begetters. In these poems Hardy employs imagery of brains, thoughts, and feelings to debunk both freedom and responsibility. Evoking pagan ideas, in the Platonic scene of the Cave of the Unborn and the ancestors entered in the recorder's book, the poems present tacit rejoinders to Christian theology. It is not surprising to find Hardy engaging in theological argument in his verse. Hardy thought poetry was a better vehicle for the expression of his views than prose, writing in his journal in 1896 (the year of "Wessex Heights"):

> Poetry. Perhaps I can express more fully in verse ideas and emotions which run counter to the inert crystallized opinion—hard as a rock— which the vast body of men have vested interests in supporting. To cry out in a passionate poem that (for instance) the Supreme Mover or Movers, the Prime Force or Forces, must be either limited in power, unknowing, or cruel—which is obvious enough, and has been for centuries—will cause them merely a shake of the head; but to put it in argumentative prose will make them sneer, or foam, and set all the literary contortion-

ists jumping upon me, a harmless agnostic, as if I were a clamorous atheist, which in their crass illiteracy they seem to think is the same thing. . . .
If Galileo had said in verse that the world moved, the Inquisition might
have let him alone. (*Life and Work* 302)

This passage explicitly names "ideas and emotions" as the proper subject of verse, and although he eschews argumentative prose, Hardy does
not reject the goals of argumentation. Indeed, his reference to Galileo's
ideas (and tacitly his martyrdom) clarifies that some theses are better off
presented in a "passionate poem" than in a tract or treatise. Though he
disingenuously suggests that verse is preferable because dismissible with
a "mere shake of the head," Hardy also shows some pride in linking his
"obvious" view that "the Supreme Mover or Movers, the Prime Force or
Forces, must be either limited in power, unknowing, or cruel" with Galileo's heliocentrism. By naming Galileo (rather than Darwin, a more likely
suspect!), Hardy indicates his interest in opposing the views of the insti-
tutional church, that rock of crystallized opinion. If Hardy was a "harmless agnostic," as he calls himself here, not an atheist, he certainly felt
empowered to clamor and cavil in his poetry. Like Galileo, he had differences with the theologically acceptable vision of the universe's organization, but Hardy's critique attacked the temporal, not spatial, dimensions
of the world.

Both "The Unborn" and "The Pedigree" confute the Christian idea of
eternity: for Hardy there is no timelessness outside of time and no access
to the mysteries at the beginning of time. "The Unborn" relates the trick
of the Will, fulfilling the desire of the "crowding shapes" in the Cave of
the Unborn to enter a life about which they entertain false hopes:

A scene the loveliest, is it not? A pure delight, a beauty-spot
Where all is gentle, true and just,
And darkness is unknown?
(*TL* v. 1, 344, ll. 9-12)

These hapless refugees from a Blakean or Wordsworthian vision of the
soul's preexistence question the poem's speaker with "artless trust," but
he cannot "frame a word" to break the news that his anguished expression conveys to the unborn. These beings will not enter life trailing clouds
of glory. Out of pity he says nothing as they are "Driven forward like a
rabble rout" into life (l. 22), hounded by the "silent Head" (l. 5), the "all
imminent Will" (l. 24) to whom they have prayed. Their desire to be born

into time is to be cruelly gratified, but if they knew what they were getting into, Hardy suggests, they would not crowd round "for tidings of the
life to be" (l. 4). Indeed, Hardy notoriously regarded the death of a child
as a lucky break, a fortunate escape from life that, as Sally Shuttleworth
has recently demonstrated, extended to his views of child suicide (Shuttleworth 346–47).

The cancelled last stanza of the earlier 1904 version of the poem,
published under the alternate title "Life's Opportunity"[18] in the collection *Wayfarer's Love,* twice mentions the consolatory "Lovingkindness"
that the unborn will find scope for in life. The context helps to explain
the more positive vision of the first version. This was a volume intended
to benefit the Potteries and Newcastle Cripples' Guild, filled with poems
solicited by Millicent, the Duchess of Sutherland, from living poets. AE
(Alfred Douglas), Binyon, Bridges, Chesterton, Housman, Masefield, and
Yeats also contributed. The brief of the volume demanded an upbeat tone
and Hardy delivered. By 1909, however, when Hardy published *Time's
Laughingstocks,* he had replaced the celebration of compassionate life
with pity for those doomed to birth. Far from getting credit for choosing
mortal life, where "Life's gladdening star" can be followed, these guileless shapes come out "helter-skelter" (l. 21), driven into a world that can
only crush their hopes.

A later poem, "Copying Architecture in an Old Minster," revisits this
idea, imagining that the dead memorialized in the nearby tombs speak
with the "yet unborn"

> And caution them not to come
> To a world so ancient and trouble-torn,
> Of foiled intents, vain lovingkindness,
> And ardours chilled and numb.
> (*MV* v. 2, 172–73, ll. 26–30)

Hardy is not terribly far removed from Philip Larkin's sentiment of "This
Be the Verse": "Man hands on misery to man. / It deepens like a coastal
shelf. / Get out as early as you can / And don't have any kids yourself"
(*Collected Poems* 180). Hardy rendered childlessness as a form of social
responsibility. Possibly the childless poet consoled himself by envisioning
this wise counsel to the unborn, though he was also to focus on the especially vulnerable, the offspring of the poor. In the 1901 poem, "To An

---

18. See Thomas Hardy, "Life's Opportunity" (1904) 16.

Unborn Pauper Child," Hardy counsels the "wombed souls" to "Breathe not" and "cease silently," in preference to entering the world where "The Doomsters heap / Travails and teens around us here, / and Time-wraiths turn our songsingings to fear" (*PP* v. 1, 163, ll. 4-6).

The Doomsters we have already met, in "Hap" and other poems, but what does Hardy mean by the threatening "Time-wraiths" who convert joyful singing into fear? A consequence of being born into time is evidently to be victimized by them. Are they like the phantom-ejects of "Wessex Heights," the inevitable product of intersubjectivity, or do they haunt the newly born from the past, the legacy of human ancestry? "The Pedigree" gives a glimpse of time-wraiths—figured as ancestors who in the end evade the visualizing of a living being seeking an understanding of his existence. In this 1916 poem, Hardy describes a scene in which the speaker scrutinizes his family tree by moonlight. The branches of the genealogical table interact with the window through which moonlight streams, becoming a "mirror" into the past. The speaker discovers

> And in it a long perspective I could trace
> Of my begetters, dwindling backward each past each
> All with the kindred look,
> Whose names had since been inked down in their place
> On the recorder's book,
> Generation and generation of my mien, and build, and brow.
> (*MV* v. 2, 197, ll. 16–21)

So far, so good: the family tree shifts from the two-dimensional chart to a vertiginous regress of mirroring ancestors, recognizable to their descendent, and possibly based on a reflection of him cast down the *mise en abyme*. However, the speaker realizes two paralyzing thoughts at once: first, that his own actions are not original to him, but "in the glass portrayed / As long forestalled by" the ancestors (ll. 25-26); and second, that he cannot discern his forefather, "the first of them, the primest fuglemen of my line" and therefore cannot see the sources of "every heave and coil and move" made within his brain (ll. 23). The speaker comes to understand that even though his thoughts and actions are predicted by his "primest" ancestor, he cannot know them by looking for that first source. He cannot claim free will honestly: "'I am merest mimicker and counterfeit!— / Though thinking, *I am I, / And what I do I do myself alone*'" (ll. 30–32).

This view of the generations as time-wraiths who bind humans unlucky enough to be born into repetition of acts and impulses that they cannot even claim to have chosen freely arises from Hardy's understanding of and the imagination. As Stephen Kern observes, a generation of European intellectuals including Ibsen, Strindberg, and Hardy settled in the 1880s into "a fatalistic pessimism based on biological, historical, and psychological theories to the effect that we are fated to inherit our parents' diseases and repeat their vices" (Kern 327n45). Hardy goes deeper, seeing "every heave and coil and move I made / Within my brain, and in my mood and speech" as a belated repetition of ancient ancestors' originary impulses, which, in a Maudsleyan echo, "forestall" the present generation. It would be one thing to know this if you could see into those precursors' brains, but at most the vision reveals their familiar "mien, and build, and brow." As the prior chapter suggests, Hardy was comfortable implying thoughts though externalized cues of physiognomy and behavior, but this technique does not work if you can't see the person. Thus the vision fails him by fogging "in far antiqueness" the readable traits of his "primest" ancestor.

Even if you can know a family and recognize its inherited face, as he described in another poem, "Heredity," Hardy knew the limits of surmise and reason when it came to predicting human behavior. Environment puts its own pressure on the inherited personality, as Hardy emphasized by focusing on character and circumstance. In his *Literary Notebooks* he excerpted a passage from an 1885 essay by Vernon Lee that has bearing on this view of human character:

> By the fatality of heredity, on one hand, a human being contains within himself a number of different tendencies, all moulded, it is true, into one character, but existing none the less each in its special nature, ready to respond to its special stimulus from without; on the other hand, by the fatality of environment every human being is modified in many different ways; he is rammed into a place until he fits it, & absorbs all fragments of all the other personalities with whom he is crushed together. So that there must be, in all of us, even in the most homogeneous, tendencies which, from not having met their appropriate stimulus, may be lying unsuspected at the very bottom of our nature, far below the level of consciousness; but which, on the approach of the specific stimulus, or merely on the occasion of any violent shaking of the whole nature, will suddenly come to the surface. (*Literary Notebooks* v. 1, 165)

Lee's theorizing, a part of "A Dialogue on Novels," published in 1885 in *The Contemporary Review*, represents a novelist's effort to come to terms with Darwin (and possibly also Fourier), and it would be a relatively simple matter to apply her ideas to fictional characterization. The circumstances of plot shifts or peripeties could provide the stimuli that violently shake a hitherto hidden trait into sudden expression. However, the character here is that of general human nature, looking inward at the diverse tendencies inherited from ancestors. This character, like the forms that evanesce in Hardy's poem "The Pedigree," is plural and composite, a product of diverse fragments crushed together, as much a product of the social circumstances that surround him and pressure him into the available space. Far from giving the inward looking person a glimpse into the causal chains that stretch back into deep time, an understanding of heredity makes externalized behavior the only observable data. In "The Pedigree," the vision seems to promise a way towards explanation of motives and causes, but it ends up in an obscuring blur, as Hardy's paper, reflective surfaces, windows, and mirrors block access. He arrives at something like the behaviorist's black box: research into the deep past does not afford insight. Going back to "where I was before my birth," in the escapist wish of "Wessex Heights" (*SC*, v. 2, 25, l. 4) does not solve the problem of living in time, a condition that the speaker must endure under "the stained moon" (*MV*, v. 2, 198, l. 36) and "the green-rheumed clouds" (l. 6) of temporality. What starts out looking like an eternizing conceit, demonstrating the living person's long pedigree through the generations, ends up "having wrought its purport wry," depriving the speaker of a sense of meaningful continuity. The poem leaves the speaker staring out the window at the moon and clouds, none the wiser for his vision.

Nescient Witnesses and Victims of Consciousness

When Vernon Lee wrote about Hardy's craft (in another context), she was a perceptive if unforgiving critic. Describing his style in a 500-word passage excerpted from *Tess of the d'Urbervilles*, Lee writes: "The woolly outlines, even the uncertain drawing, merely add to the impression of primeval passiveness and blind, unreasoning emotion; of inscrutable doom and blind, unfeeling Fate which belong to his whole outlook on life. And the very faults of Hardy are probably an expression of his solitary and matchless grandeur of attitude" (Lee, *Handling* 240–41). These faults are perhaps most noticeable in Hardy's many staged confrontations with Nature, God, the Earth, and the Prime Mover in its many guises. A bombastic tone, exaggerated—sometimes incoherent— imagery, and strained vocabulary show the difficulty of rendering materialist philosophy, evolutionary theory, a monist world view, and human experience in poetic form. The fact that Hardy kept at it, reiterating the facts that were so obvious to him in poems that gave voice to a variety of ejects, projections of his imagination, in pageants of plaint and argumentation, has made his ideas relatively accessible and thus easy targets of criticism. These poems have probably done more to damage Hardy's reputation as a lyric poet than anything else he wrote, but they, too, record the experience of being Thomas Hardy, "No answerer," but a tireless questioner. He risked flagrant exhibition of his most portentous tone in order to work out the various angles of his convictions, at length and in visionary high dudgeon.

"The Mother Mourns," a poem in the 1901[2] volume *Poems of Past and Present,* is a case in point. Its "dirgelike refrain" of lamentation from Mother Nature features an incredible twenty-two rhyme-words to end the stanzas with the same sound: lane, unchain, pain, refrain, disdain, brain, strain, reign, grain, domain, inane, rain, gain, sane, train, unrein, vain, preordain, strain, wane, appertain, and (could Hardy hear his own joke?) *not again* (*PP* v. 1, 144–47). One can only express gratitude that in pushing the limits of experimentation in formally echoing a droning complaint through rhyme, Hardy did not persevere and finish the job with bane, cane, deign, feign, Jane, seine, and thane. The twenty-two quatrains afford Hardy ample space to rehearse many of the points that recur in his philosophical poems and to try out representational strategies that he will reuse over the next two decades.

Like "The Pedigree," "The Mother Mourns" begins with a natural scene, transformed by a trick of the imagination into a vision: "dimly / Came wheeling around me / Those phantoms obscure and insistent / That shadows unchain" (*PP* v. 1, 144, ll. 5–8). Like "The Unborn," the scene of the vision quest evokes classical tropes, in this case a scene of Ovidian transformation: "as though from a tree-god disheartened, / Perplexed or in pain" (ll. 11–12). But the visual yields to the auditory, arresting the speaker to listen to Nature's grievances with mankind, spoken by a voice that blows through "the needle thicks" (l. 9). Once she gets going in her soughing voice, Nature ticks down a laundry list of complaints. First she objects to the intellectual powers that humans have developed, "such brightness of brain / As to read my defects . . . / Uncover each vestige / Of old inadvertence, annunciate / each flaw and each stain!" (ll. 24–28).

Human beings affront Nature by their insight, their scientific exploration of the heavens, and their "mountings of mind-sight" (l. 37), all of
which exceed Nature's original plans. Human cognition (not coinciden-
tally comprised of natural science, materialist philosophy, skepticism, and
introspection that Hardy values) affronts Nature and "tops [her] intent"
(l. 39). Loss of faith makes an appearance—"He holds as inept his own
soul-shell" (l. 41)—though Nature seems more concerned that humans
neither worship the sun and moon, nor read the stars. These debunked
perceptions refer to a lost natural religion that Nature doesn't defend, but
"the Mother" seems especially irritated at pessimism's critique of sexual
desire (the drive that leads to reproduction): Mankind "Reckons gross
and ignoble my teaching, / Immoral my story, / My love-lights a lure,
that my species / May gather and gain" (ll. 49–52). Man goes so far as
to claim that he could do better, given the powers and materials: "My
brain could evolve a creation / More seemly, more sane" (ll. 55–56). The
Mother feels unappreciated, and regrets the moment when she let imagination and the visionary capacity evolve (l. 64).

This poem incorporates Hardy's conviction that the consciousness
and critical faculties of modern humans evolved over time, and shows
Nature regretting that she permitted the development. "His guileless
forerunners, / Whose brains I could blandish, / To measure the deeps of
my mysteries / Applied them in vain" (ll. 65–68). These dupes believe
that everything Nature made and did was for the best and fore-ordained.
Motivated by a desire to receive praise from the "sage," not just from
the "simple," Nature is herself responsible for "unreining" Man's brain-
power. Hardy renders pagan the theology of free will, adopting a version
of Milton's argument about the Father in *Paradise Lost*: the omnipotent
parent prefers "adulation / from creatures more keen than those crude
ones / That first formed my train" (ll. 58–61). Notably, Hardy substitutes
"Vision unruly" for free will, since he can imagine the evolution of reason and emotion, but not a human species endowed with real power over
their decisions.

That rational human beings, endowed with intellectual powers sufficiently potent to outstrip the Mother, would actually go about ruining the
natural world, Hardy observes in a proto-environmentalist protest:

> . . . My species are dwindling,
>   My forests grow barren,
>   My popinjays fail from their tappings,
>   My larks from their strain.

'My leopardine beauties are rarer,
My tusky ones vanish,
    My children have aped mine own slaughters
    To quicken my wane.
(ll. 73–80)

In an anticipation of Rachel Carson a half century later, combined with an appropriately Victorian protest about cruelty to animals through big-game hunting, Hardy's Mother Nature commits herself to growing only the "slimy distortions" of a contaminated creation. Though she resents the pessimistic critique of the sex-drive that perpetuates life, Mother Nature petulantly vows to grow only a distorted, unlovely environment of "mildews and mandrakes" (l. 81). That will show her brainy human children, who will not be permitted to resume nature worship, because they have irreversibly despoiled the temple.

In another poem from the same volume, "By the Earth's Corpse," Hardy imagines the Lord and Creator taking the blame for extinguishing life on earth as well as for creating it in the first place. Heat death of the universe has put out that "late earthly scene" (*PP* v. 1, 161, l. 12), but still the old dialogue of abstractions maunders on! Time itself poses the opening question, asking why the Lord cares: " . . . why grievest Thou?— / Since Life has ceased to be / Upon this globe, now cold / As lunar land and sea" (ll. 1–4). The Lord defends his right to feel bad about the whole endeavor:

"So at this last, when flesh
    And herb but fossils be,
And all extinct, their piteous dust
    Revolves obliviously,
That I made Earth, and life, and man,
    It still repenteth me!"
(ll. 27–32)

But at the same time he shifts the blame: "Written indelibly / on my eternal mind / Are all the wrongs . . . / Which my too oft unconscious hand / Let enter undesigned" (ll. 17–22). This startling disavowal of knowledge and intention suggests that the Lord inhabits a similar position to the speaker of "The Pedigree," searching his memory for the traces of the past, but unable to get at their sources. Who was in control when the Lord's hand unconsciously permitted wrongs to enter his creation? Since he is apparently awake and regretful at the moment of the earth's extinction, the Lord tacitly confesses lapses in his omniscience, and the poem flirts with a Manichaean explanation for evil's perpetration of wrongs. Having disempowered the Lord, however, Hardy's speaker is unlikely to conjure up an equally strong evil power embodying malign intentions. The closest he comes to that occurs in the closing lines of *Tess of the d'Urbervilles,* where he refers to the President of the Immortals' cruel sport with the victim Tess (*Tess* 420). There the resonance with the capricious inhabitants of Mount Olympus differentiates the malign agent from a Manichaean Satan. In "By the Earth's Corpse" the Lord does not name an opponent; he simply confesses to having let wrongs occur unnoticed. Possibly his own unconscious hand does the deeds.

Hardy explored several ways of figuring the cognitive failures of God in his lyric poems, and he often mapped these explanations using brain imagery. These are the possibilities broached in the early work "Nature's Questioning," published in *Wessex Poems.* Here God is a powerful imbecile, who can create but could never manage his creation. He made us as a joke and left us to chance (*WP,* v. 1, 86, ll. 13–16). God was always "an Automaton / unconscious of our pains" (ll. 17–18). God once had a good brain, but now has senile dementia (ll. 19–20). Or possibly a final battle between principles of good and evil will eventually demonstrate the existence of "some high Plan . . . / As yet not understood" (ll. 21–22). The chorus of natural questioners, "pool, / Field, flock, and lonely tree" (ll. 1–2), receive no answer from Hardy's speaker in this poem. A decade later in *Satires of Circumstance,* Hardy was still thinking about what had gone wrong with God, but this time he lays the blame on humankind, who can "no longer keep alive" the "man-projected Figure" of "God's Funeral." The collective power of human minds have created a vast eject, "Framing him jealous, fierce, at first" (*SC,* v. 2, 35, l. 25), then adding properties of justice and mercifulness (ll. 26–28), and fantasizing his role as Creator (ll. 29–32). Human beings create the myth in the first place, and then "Uncompromising rude reality / Mangled the Monarch of our fashioning" (ll. 34–35). Here God never has a mind of any kind, for it is only ever an amorphous shape, man-like, phantasmal, and a symbol of human wishes for potency and lovingkindness (ll. 9–16). If God is only an eject, as "God's Funeral" asserts, then human beings themselves are responsible for his lapses of attention.

This shared culpability, diagnosed by Hardy's lyric speaker, does not prevent him from recording the emotional impact of God's death on his mourners and himself. Indeed, the speaker of "God's Funeral" empathizes with the members of the funeral procession:

And by contagious throbs of thought
Or latent knowledge that within me lay
And had already stirred me, I was wrought
To consciousness of sorrow even as they.
(ll. 5–8)

Though humankind is "tricked by our own early dream / and need of solace" (ll. 29–30) into self-deception, the grief is genuine as scales fall from
the eyes of the mourners. Sympathizing "with all" (l. 54), even with those
obstinately insisting that the real God is not dead, Hardy's speaker does
not exempt himself from the general bewilderment, "dazed and puzzled
'twixt the gleam and the gloom" (l. 67). In a way this is a more appealing stance than the belligerent interrogation that some of Hardy's other
speakers employ when they question God, and a silent corpse makes a
more dignified figure than the defensive God of a poem like "New Year's
Eve," in which God responds to Hardy's heckling:

. . . "My labours—logicless—
    You may explain; not I:
Sense-sealed I have wrought, without a guess
That I evolved a Consciousness
    To ask for reasons why.

"Strange that ephemeral creatures who
    By my own ordering are,
Should see the shortness of my view,
Use ethics tests I never knew,
    Or made provision for!"
(*TL,* v. 1, 334, ll. 16–25)

It is one thing to assert a nescient, "unweeting" God (l. 30), and another
thing entirely to present one so nonsensical as this bombastic juve-
nile delinquent. Hardy does better when he focuses on the conundrum
of human consciousness, for there he need not explain the oxymoronic
model of God's unaware mind and booming voice.

"The Aërolite" of *Human Shows* is one of the most fanciful of Hardy's poems on this topic, describing the accidental infection of planet
earth by an alien life form from "some far globe" (*HS* v. 3, 86–87, l. 4).
The "germ of consciousness" arrives on earth via a falling meteorite, or
aërolite of the title, and becomes an invasive disease, wiping out "Earth's
old-established ignorance" (l. 17) with an epidemic of conscious aware-

ness. Back on its original planet, Hardy's dreaming speaker explains, the perfect beings who experienced consciousness felt "a gift uncloyed / Of gladsome glow, / And life unendingly displayed / Emotions loved, desired, enjoyed" (ll. 7–10). On Earth quickening awareness reveals a nasty truth, and "show[s] to us the worm / That gnaws vitalities native here" (ll. 14–15). The consciousness-bearing aërolite does not cause the misery and grief of the human condition; it simply "unblinds" humans, so that they can know their plight, waking "on earth / The mortal moan / Begot of sentience" (ll. 32–34). This late poem of Hardy's rehearses and reverses the imagistic schemas normally associated with consciousness. MIND is a BODY moving in SPACE; LIFE is a BURDEN; SEEING is KNOWING: these schemas all pertain, but negatively. Consciousness becomes an unwelcome and destructive visitor from outer space, crash landing on Earth and infecting life with an alien disease that makes its inherent condition unbearable. The Seers of the poem seek not to recognize all that consciousness reveals, wishing for blinders that would "hide from it all anguishment" (l. 30). In a variant of DEATH is DELIVERANCE, Hardy concludes with the vain hope, "Maybe now / Normal unawareness waits rebirth" (ll. 34–35).

Occasionally Hardy wrote a restrained and effective lyric complaint about the pains of "thought-endowment." The trochaic trimeter ditty "'Freed the Fret of Thinking'" (*HS* v. 3, 67–68) imagines the restoration of humankind to an innocent state of nescience:

> Loosed from wrings of reason
>   We might blow like flowers,
> Sense of Time-wrought treason
>   Would not then be ours
> In and out of season;
> Loosed from wrings of reason
>   We should laud the Powers!
> (ll. 15–21, 68)

Whereas most poets handling the image schema PEOPLE are PLANTS echo the Psalmist's identification of stages of growth and decline (*More Than Cool Reason* 5), Hardy uses the metaphor to imagine how blissful it would be to "blow like flowers," entirely lacking cognitive capacities. Humans in this natural state would be "light of lot" (*HS* v. 3, 67, l. 2), performing their functions of labor and reproduction without worrying about the future, the past, mortality, the meaning of life. This 1925 vision abjures time-wraiths, laments human awareness of "Creation's groan" (l. 14) and promises praise songs in exchange for nescience. This poem does not express a death wish. Hardy wants to live without knowing that he does, in a natural body, "like to bird or bee" (l. 4). To retain embodied experience without emotion and feeling would lead to desirable states of not-thinking and not-feeling. Hardy knows that the trick would be to achieve this state of nescience while shedding the heartlessness and ignorance that impede altruism.

Linda Shires observes that although Hardy's narrators and personae often assert unknowingness, "It was not until his last three novels that his doctrines [became] more insistent" ("Unknowing Omniscience" 35). Certainly the emphasis given to representation of states of nescience increases in *The Woodlanders* (1887), *Tess of the d'Urbervilles* (1891), and *Jude the Obscure* (1895) and receives elaborate dramatization in *The Dynasts*. The research that Hardy conducted in the 1880s, in preparation for the composition *The Dynasts,* went well beyond the oft-noted culling of historical sources on the Napoleonic wars. Hardy also undertook a serious course of reading in the current psychological literature, making notes on ideas about minds and brains that would show up in the later novels, as well as in the poems discussed here. Both were needed for *The Dynasts,* but their impact can be observed in works of the 1880s and later. Nescience of individual humans and the lack of compassion of the Immanent Will combine in Hardy's late fatalism. He hardly knew what to hope for: restoration of a fully unconscious universe, or evolution of a feeling cosmos. He knew enough about brain science to understand that much of what brains and nerves perform occurs behind the curtain: we only know the actions that appear on stage. Yet even if his characters cannot know their own minds, and if the impulses of the Will are neither intentional nor feeling, Hardy insists on showing that consequential events in the lives of people, communities, and nations still happen and bring on palpable emotional responses. He schematizes this in his epic abstractions, the Spirits of the Years and Pities, and figures it in his neural imagery of a cosmic mind. How his particular studies supported this neurological turn in Hardy's representations is the subject of the next chapter.

CHAPTER 4

The Neurological Turn

Hardy's Victorian Psychology

It is perfectly understandable that earlier psychological approaches to Thomas Hardy have often adopted twentieth-century, largely psycho-analytic, frames of reference. He is after all considered a modern poet, and the modernists engaged with Freud's ideas, sometimes directly, as in the case of H. D.[1] The dates come so close to working. Hardy lived until 1928; in 1938 Freud moved to London. Had that happened two decades earlier they would almost certainly have met, given Hardy's club member-ships and his connections to the elders of the Bloomsbury Group mem-bers, such as Leslie Stephen. Tantalizing chains of connection exist: Hardy knew Siegfried Sassoon and Henry Head (Gibson 87–88); Sassoon was treated for shell shock by W. H. R. Rivers (1864–1922), a neurologist and psychologist, close friend and collaborator of Head's. Though Riv-ers was not a Freudian *per se,* he commented on and criticized Freud's analysis of dreamwork in his posthumously published book, *Conflict and Dream* (1923). The language of the interpretation of dreams was certainly in circulation in English after 1913, when A. A. Brill's authorized English translation of *Die Traumdeutung* (1900) was published by Macmillan. In

---

1. On H. D.'s 1933–34 treatment by Freud in Vienna, see her own accounts in Susan Stanford Friedman, ed., *Analyzing Freud: Letters of H. D., Bryher, and Their Circle* (2002).

the same year Macmillan also brought out the three parts of *The Dynasts* in a single volume, so Hardy and Freud crossed paths in the virtual space of the publisher's list.[2] Yet they did not meet in Hardy's lifetime, and as I have argued in chapter 1, Hardy makes no mention of Freud or his ideas.

It may be objected this is too austere a standard for attributing influence. Further, a temporal match has not always been regarded as essential when theorists or critics discuss the ideas they can discern in works of an earlier period. Indeed, the interpretive tools of literary Freudianism, Jungianism, and Lacanianism have often enough been put to work on texts authored long before the language of psychoanalysis became well known. A special critical pleasure arises from the revelation of an unwitting writer's unconscious demonstration of what will become a commonplace of psychoanalytic criticism: the interrelation of Eros and Thanatos, the mirror stage, the return of the repressed. But analogues are not necessarily sources, and we should ask why we more readily value Hardy's prescient anticipation of ideas he did not know than those he belabored in poems, notes, and prefaces. Certainly the terms of psychoanalytic criticism[3] resonate with twenty-first-century readers in a way that Hardy's ejects, impulsions, nescient beings, automatons, and pulsing cosmic brains cannot rival. Nonetheless, Hardy's terms belonged to the late Victorian interdisciplinary flowering of materialist science and monist philosophy, and it is there that we should turn to seek the sources of Hardy's psychology.

Making a strong case for the significance of the 1860s in Thomas Hardy's intellectual development, Dennis Taylor writes:

> Many of the traditions which Hardy carried on or reacted against underwent important developments in the 1860s. Indeed the decade was a decisive stage in the evolution of architecture, in the growth of public art collections, in discussions of the grotesque, in the collecting of ballads, in the Victorian novel, in philosophy and epistemology, in philology and prosody, in archaeology and history, even in photography. These developments profoundly impressed Hardy's mind at a formative stage. (*Hardy's Poetry* xvii)

---

2. Sigmund Freud, *The Interpretation of Dreams* (1913); Thomas Hardy, *The Dynasts: An Epic-Drama of the War with Napoleon, in Three Parts, Nineteen Acts, and One Hundred and Thirty Scenes* (1913).

3. Fine readings of Hardy's poetry and fiction employing psychoanalytic terms include Marjorie Levinson, "Object-Loss and Object-Bondage: Economies of Representation in Hardy's Poetry" (2006); Judith Bryant Wittenberg, "Early Hardy Novels and the Fictional Eye" (1983); Linda M. Austin, "Reading Depression in Hardy's 'Poems of 1912–13'" (1998).

This is certainly true: Hardy was shaped by his consciousness not just of the official Darwinian theory of evolution but by his knowledge of discoveries, innovations, new practices, technological advances, and other forms of Victorian progress.[4] The sources of what he would call his evolutionary meliorism lay deep in the Whiggish meta-narratives of High Victorianism. Yet he was also perceived by his contemporaries as a gloomy pessimist,[5] and despite his insistent rejection of the label, Hardy did entertain ideas about human automatism and an indifferent universe that resist recuperation to narratives of progress. As we have seen in the prior chapter, he fantasized about regress and regarded nescience as a desirable condition for human beings, given their painful circumstances. Hardy was simultaneously a pessimist and a meliorist, and he set this apparent conflict imaginatively to work in his representation of a cosmic will not yet evolved to feel, not yet as sensitive as the humans it impels into action. His vision is cosmological, evolutionary, and neurological, and it would not have fused into the first literary representation of the monist universe as a vast neural net had Hardy relied only on intellectual influences from mid-century.

A chronological reading of selected sources of the 1880s and after shows that while aspects of Hardy's psychology were in place by the beginning of his writing career (as his early verse shows), a period of reading in the 1880s was to provoke a noticeable change in his figuration of minds, their actions, and their physiological components. Abstract though it may seem in retrospect, for Hardy the imaging of a neurally linked creation was also a matter of intense feeling. Comparative soundings from *Two on a Tower* (1882) and *The Woodlanders* (1887) suggest the emotional valence Hardy woefully attached to his more elaborated understanding of human psychology. *Two on the Tower* employs the plot devices of sensation fiction to evoke readers' sympathies for insignificant characters set against the vast backdrop of interstellar space. In *The Woodlanders* Hardy represents medical neurological work directly in Dr. Fitzpiers's researches, but the brain anatomy is only the most obvious impact of his developing psychological interests in his fiction, as his

---

4. In his Max Gate library at the time of Hardy's death was a copy of *Arcana of Science and Art: Or, An Annual Register of Useful Inventions and Improvements, Discoveries and New Facts in Mechanics, Chemistry, Natural History, and Social Economy* (1830–33), and John Beckmann's eclectic *A History of Inventions, Discoveries and Origins* (1846). See Michael Millgate, "Thomas Hardy's Library at Max Gate."

5. See the frequent remarks on pessimism scattered throughout reviews collected in R. G. Cox, *Thomas Hardy: The Critical Heritage* (1979).

image schemas and allusions reveal. Hardy's reading of W. K. Clifford, Henry Maudsley, Eduard von Hartmann, and George Romanes contributed elements to his neurological turn, altering schemas that had been in place since his earlier absorption of Fourier and Comte. Then, as he reflected in the late 1880s and early 1890s on the novelist's craft, Hardy's augmented knowledge of psychology shows in the way he writes about the conditions for authorship and the impact of fiction on readers in "The Profitable Reading of Fiction" (1888), "Candour in English Fiction" (1890), and "The Science of Fiction" (1891).[6] This chapter culminates with a tracing of brain imagery in *The Dynasts,* through close readings of the Fore Scene and After Scene of the Overworld, in which Hardy's most explicit neurological representation and his most ambitious brief for altruistic development of the universe appear. A seeming outlier in my otherwise chronological survey of Hardy's reading and writing between 1881 and 1891, *The Dynasts* belongs to the decade of Hardy's neurological turn. Despite the fact that *The Dynasts* is by date and acclamation a thoroughly modern poem, often seen as anticipating filmic techniques,[7] its neurological imagery marks it as a product of Hardy's engagement with late Victorian scientific speculation.

"Drooping Periods"

In the early 1880s Hardy was already an accomplished professional writer, author of the acclaimed novels *Far from the Madding Crowd* (1874) and *The Return of the Native* (1878). Hardy had every reason to feel ambitious as well as successful; he was making a living by the products of his pen and moving in intellectual circles in London. His election to the Savile Club in 1878, the year *Return of the Native* was published, had indicated the esteem of fellow professionals. His marriage had not yet soured. Yet the early 1880s were also to prove personally challenging, as he suffered periods of depression and at least one serious illness. In terrible pain,

---

6. "The Profitable Reading of Fiction" first appeared in *Forum* (New York) in March, 1888. The version cited here is from Harold Orel, ed. *Thomas Hardy's Personal Writings* (1966). "Candour in English Fiction" was a contribution to a symposium in *The New Review* (January 1890). References cite Orel, ed., *Personal Writings* 125–33. "The Science of Fiction" was first published in *The New Review* (April 1891). Citations come from Orel, ed., *Personal Writings* 134–38.

7. For a recent example of this observation, see Herbert F. Tucker, *Epic: Britain's Heroic Muse, 1790–1910* (2008) 585–86. See also Chester A. Garrison, *The Vast Venture: Hardy's Epic Drama* The Dynasts (1973) 187–203.

Hardy had to dictate part of his novel *The Laodicean* (1881) to Emma from his sickbed, with his feet raised higher than his head, and his sense of obligation to his publishers goading him on (*Life and Work* 150). He persevered, but he also meditated on what it meant to depend upon the work of a mind tethered to a frail human body. He extrapolated from his experience a grim little model of society, suggesting that Positivist dreams of social improvement had been long since abandoned:

> Discover for how many years, and on how many occasions, the organism Society, has been standing, lying, etc, in varied positions, as if it were a tree or a man hit by vicissitudes.
>
> There would be found these periods:—
>   1. Upright, normal, or healthy periods.
>   2. Oblique or cramped periods.
>   3. Prostrate periods (intellect counterpoised by ignorance or narrowness, producing stagnation.)
>   4. Drooping periods.
>   5. Inverted periods.
>   (150)

Though in transcribing this scrap into his biography decades later, Hardy characterized it as an "irrelative note of rather vague import" (150), it documents a radical change in one of Hardy's major image schemas. Provoked by his own recent experience of losing uprightness, suffering cramped, prostrate, drooping and even inverted postures during his illness, Hardy supplants the gothic architectural imagery of organic forms arching, thrusting, reaching, and supporting with imagery of lost vigor: the swamp takes over the forest as the sap drains out.

In a striking contrast to the tree-diagram Hardy transcribed from Fourier (discussed above, chapter 1), the life stages of man are no longer characterized by upright trunks and twining vines, issuing in blooms of amalgamated moral harmony (*Literary Notebooks* v. 1, 4), but by imagery of decline and even inversion (roots metaphorically in the air). Hardy would take this declinist version of the man/tree/society schema even further in *The Woodlanders* to excellent psychological effect. The vehicles of organic metaphors could carry freights of disease, decay, and death: by appearing to promise growth and fruitfulness, Hardy decided, "Nature is an arch-dissembler" (*Life and Work* 182). Laid low by illness, Hardy saw new truths about human nature. He learned how to use his suffering like a professional, never wasting material. While he convalesced, Carlyle and George Eliot both died, "vanished into nescience while I have been lying here" (152), but Hardy was thinking hard. He conceived the "philosophic scheme or framework as the larger feature of *The Dynasts,* enclosing the historic scenes" (152), writing this preliminary plan: "Mode for a historical Drama. Action mostly automatic, reflex movement, etc. Not the result of what is called *motive,* though always ostensibly so, even to the actors' own consciousness. Apply an enlargement of these theories to, say, 'The Hundred Days'!" (152, emphasis in original). The enlargement of his theory from the elementary neurology of reflex action to a full-blown universal brain would take several years to develop, in tandem with his vision of the human race as a unified species linked through shared sensations (183); in the meantime, Hardy read steadily and conceived lyric poems such as "The Mother Mourns" that explored how humans "have reached a degree of intelligence which nature never contemplated when framing her laws, and for which she consequently has provided no adequate satisfactions" (169). Illness and injury often inspire sufferers to return to their neglected God as supplicants: not Hardy. Having turned away from religious faith, Hardy sought but did not find consolation in philosophy. Hardy's 1882 character Swithin St. Cleve finds after a severe disappointment as a research astronomer, "the Goddess Philosophy, to whom he had vowed to dedicate his whole life, would not in return support him through a single hour of despair" (*TT* 69). About Hegel's dicta, Hardy wrote "having been thinking over . . . that real pain is compatible with a formal pleasure—that the idea is all, etc. But it doesn't help much" (*Life and Work* 185).

This sense of grievance would follow Hardy even through years when he was enjoying professional success, socializing with the interesting, influential, and high born, designing his house, Max Gate, and moving back in triumph to the county of his origins, a well-known author.[8] In 1881, the year in which Hardy suffered the debilitating health crisis (probably a malady of his bladder or kidneys—certainly a very painful experience)[9] that drove him out of London, he wrote "the emotions have no place in a world of defect, and it is a cruel injustice that they should have developed in it" (*Life and Work* 153). The physical pain appears to have brought on mental anguish. While we cannot know precisely what Hardy was feeling,

---

8. Fame had its downside. In 1882 Hardy was troubled by an imitator publishing "wretched ungrammatical verse" under his name (*Letters,* v. 1, 108).

9. Millgate suggests, variously, that Hardy had a bladder inflammation, possibly a kidney stone, with complications from typhoid fever (*Biography Revisited* 201).

he left a very good record of what he was thinking about, reading for the first time, and studying in depth. Hardy's biography records the periods in the mid 1880s when he sought lodgings in Bloomsbury "to have the Reading Room of the Museum at hand" (184) or accounts for his activities thus: "The remainder of his spare time in London this year appears to have been spent in the British Museum Library and elsewhere considering the questions of *The Dynasts*" (190). Though the work was dedicated to his future project, it had an immediate impact. It combined with his personal experience to encourage a dissociative habit that we have seen Hardy indulging since early childhood.

This course of reading, resulting in the cosmic vision of *The Dynasts,* was to induce a neurological turn in his representations of brain, mind, consciousness, and nescience, but first it made Hardy giddy with the fusion of time and space, and vertiginous perceptions about material forms of immortality. Cognition takes on physicality as human bodies and knowledge stored in books intermingle materially when people gather to read. In 1888 he wrote a note, nearly a poem in itself, about his experiences in the British Museum Reading Room. Not for Hardy the commonplace about famous predecessors in particular seats of the library; instead, he combines the eternizing conceit that ideas live forever in books with the corporeal, soul-screening and cough-producing bodies of the readers:

> Souls are gliding about here in a sort of dream—screened somewhat by their bodies, but imaginable behind them. Dissolution is gnawing at them all, slightly hampered by renovations. In the great circle of the library Time is looking into Space. Coughs are floating in the same great vault, mixing with the rustle of book-leaves risen from the dead, and the touches of footsteps on the floor. (*Life and Work* 215)

Like his "irrelative" model of society in decline, this comment emphasizes the embodied nature of cognition. Dissolution gnaws at souls and the building itself (despite efforts at renovation). Borne up by the coughs of readers, the sound of page turning resuscitates books that have been hauled out of the stacks to live in human minds, where before they were unread and dead. This could happen to anyone's books! To have one's own immortality tethered to the behavior of these flighty readers, "gliding about here in a sort of dream," is to confront the liabilities of corporeality, the short attention span of human beings, under the daunting dome where Time looks into Space.

Hardy resolves upon a strategy of dissociation that helps him protect himself from the disappointing conduct of his fellow humans, who obey impulsions that they do not understand, arising from cognitively impenetrable areas of the mind. Ill again, this time with a rheumatic attack, Hardy reflects on the "value of life" after a conversation with Mrs. Ritchie (the former Miss Thackeray):

> For my part, if there is any way of getting a melancholy satisfaction out of life it lies in dying, so to speak, before one is out of the flesh; by which I mean putting on the manners of ghost, wandering in their haunts, and taking on their views of surrounding things. To think of life passing away is a sadness; to think of it as past is at least tolerable. Hence when I enter into a room to pay a simple morning call I have unconsciously the habit of regarding the scene as if I were a spectre not solid enough to influence my environment, only fit to behold as say, as another spectre said: "Peace be unto you." (*Life and Work* 218)

The grandiosity of Hardy's justification for his self-protective demeanor, issuing in his imitation of the resurrected Christ's greeting to his traumatized disciples, incompletely conceals the cry of pain this passage contains. To cope with social interactions by pretending to be dead already, to tolerate fear of mortality by making one's own death into history, to claim that these strategies give a melancholy satisfaction: is this grandstanding or an authentic transcript of depression? In London in 1889, oppressed by the four million individuals surrounding him there, Hardy writes

> A woeful fact—that the human race is too extremely developed for its corporeal conditions, the nerves being evolved to an activity abnormal in such an environment. Even the higher animals are in excess in this respect. It may be questioned if Nature, or what we call Nature, so far back as when she crossed the line from invertebrates to vertebrates, did not exceed her mission. The planet does not supply the materials for happiness to higher existences. Other planets may, though one can hardly see how. (227)

Here self-pity disappears, replaced by an abstracted compassion for the entire human species.

The conundrums of Hardy's understanding of psychology can be traced in a chain. If one human suffers, they all may. Yet humans often fail in compassion to one another. That human emotional life is inextricably bound to bodily experience shows everywhere in Hardy's work, even down to his complaint in 1892, when he had hurt his tooth—"Why should a man's mind be thrown into such close, sad, sensational, inexplicable relations with such a precarious object as his own body" (*Life and Work* 265). Lamentably, but inexorably, the body mediates all experience, and its corporeal conditions do not favor happiness. Nor does the shared condition of human life guarantee shared sympathy, an observation that prompts Hardy's abstracting dissociations, which fall short of outright stoicism.

Hardy's productivity, however, tells a different story about this time. For if Hardy's reflections and notes from this time record drooping periods of depression, illness, and revel in his strategies of dissociation and self-alienation, something was still right in his work-life. In the decade after his severe illness, he published *A Laodicean* (1881), wrote and published *Two on a Tower* (1882), *The Mayor of Casterbridge* (1886), with its great study of suicidal depression, *The Woodlanders* (1887), *Wessex Tales* (1888), *A Group of Noble Dames* (1891) and *Tess of the d'Urbervilles* (1891). This magnificent period of work would secure Hardy's literary reputation for the future. For many novel readers, the works that keep Hardy alive today in that reanimating miracle of reading had all been written by the conclusion of these ten years. Even the mixed reception of the controversial *Tess* contributed to Hardy's accelerating financial success (his wealth at his death would be £95,428).[10] All the while he was studying the sources that he would bring together in his epic-drama, his Vergilian bid for literary immortality.[11] In the meantime he did not stop thinking about how to square the facts of individual experience with his developing sense of human psychology too evolved in affective sensitivity for its environment. Humans feel their own pain, but can they extend themselves to others? Does general nescience vitiate the countervailing possibility of lovingkindness? His insight that societies, too, go through phases under no one individual's control, puts pressure on those, like the sensitive Hardy, who can recognize the symptoms of prostration: "intellect counterpoised by ignorance or narrowness, producing stagnation" (*Life and Work* 150). Could a public diagnosis of social ills, especially those inflicted on individuals by society's narrow-mindedness, hold off "drooping periods"? Possibly the most an individual could do would be to stay

---

10. See Michael Millgate, "Hardy, Thomas (1840–1928), Novelist and Poet."

11. On Hardy's fascination with the Virgilian model of a poetic career, see Charles Lock, "Hardy Promises: *The Dynasts* and the Epic of Imperialism" (1998).

wide-awake, documenting the decline. Hardy committed himself officially to few causes,[12] but he was determined not to be a somnambulist.

Infinitesimal Lives in the Stellar Universe: *Two on a Tower*

Hardy's *Two on a Tower* (1882) shows the novelist trying to reach his growing readership with an exemplary study of the consequences of social narrowness, in this case enforced by a suspicious brother who represents contemporary social mores. As Pamela Gossin has expertly revealed, Hardy draws on contemporary astronomy, particularly the work of John Herschel and the popularizer Richard A. Proctor, in creating his scientist character and in employing stellar thematics and allusions.[13] Swithin St. Cleve and Viviette, Lady Constantine come together because he has an interest in astronomy and she has a tower on her property. Though she is older and from a higher social class, they secretly marry, thus accidentally committing bigamy. Viviette's husband, long disappeared to South Africa, has been reported dead of malarial fever. Months into the concealed and apparently unconsummated marriage to St. Cleve, Viviette learns that her first husband has in fact only recently died, a suicide. That he himself had contracted a liaison with a native woman only heightens the sense that Viviette is justified in planning on remarrying Swithin at the earliest possible moment. Before she can do so, she discovers that an interfering uncle has left St. Cleve a generous bequest, designed to support his scientific career, with the provision that he remain unmarried until age twenty-five. She resolves, altruistically, to send Swithin away to pursue his career—at least until he turns twenty-five. Viviette's rigidly conventional brother Louis encourages Swithin to go, but not before the lovers at last consummate their union—technically out of wedlock—in a farewell meeting. Nature intervenes to thwart Viviette's benevolence when she discovers her pregnancy. She tries and fails to contact Swithin before he sails; meanwhile her pandering brother encourages the Bishop who has earlier made Lady Constantine an offer of marriage. Viviette's instinct of self-preservation combines with her resolve to leave Swithin

---

12. During the decade under scrutiny in this chapter, Hardy officially supported those who advocated for international copyright and art appreciation in the National Schools, as well as the Society for the Protection of Ancient Buildings. He did not support the extension of the franchise to agricultural laborers, as can be seen in *Letters* v. 1, 121, 123.

13. See Pamela Gossin, *Thomas Hardy's Novel Universe: Astronomy, Cosmology, and Gender in the Post-Darwinian World* (2007) 155–95.

free; she marries the Bishop and gives birth to a seven-months, apparently premature son. Years pass, Swithin eventually finds out about the marriage and its issue, but providentially the Bishop dies, only a middle-aged man. Swithin is now old enough to claim his prize without forfeiting his uncle's bequest, and he returns to England. His son, about whom he has obtusely remained unaware, is a lovely little boy, but Viviette has aged. Reading his dismay in his face, she tries to send Swithin away; he bites the bullet and insists that he intends to marry her; she dies in his arms of joy or shock. Hardy concludes with striking insincerity, "The Bishop was avenged" (*TT* 281). *Two on a Tower* is a sensational story in which a contorted plot employs long distances and temporal gaps to churn up ingredients of abandonment, bigamous liaisons, class boundary crossing, an older woman's desire, and out-of-wedlock sex. Yet Hardy meant to achieve something more ambitious than this bald synopsis can convey.

About his intentions for *Two on a Tower,* Hardy wrote in an 1895 preface to a reissue, "This slightly built romance was the outcome of a wish to set the emotional history of two infinitesimal lives against the stupendous backdrop of the stellar universe, and to impart to readers the sentiment that of these contrasting magnitudes the smaller might be the greater to them as men" (*TT* 3). The awkwardness of the plan shows early on, when Hardy introduces his "stupendous" theme as the material of a flirtatious conversation between the young scientist and his aristocratic patron. Lady Constantine perceptively observes that the study of astronomy "makes you feel human insignificance too plainly" (32). Swithin takes this cue to launch into a lecture on the scope of his ambitions, to chart the reaches beyond the solar system. Swithin's annihilating preoccupation with the "horror" of the actual sky, rather than the conventional imagery of domes and constellations, makes a large theme for his proud elucidation:

> Until a person has thought out the stars and their interspaces he has hardly learnt that there are things much more terrible than monsters of shape; namely, monsters of magnitude without known shape. Such monsters are the voids and waste places of the sky. . . . In these our sight plunges quite beyond any twinkler we have yet visited. Those are deep wells for the human mind to let itself down into, leave alone the human body! (33–34)

Swithin's vision of interstellar mental travel employs bilocation imaginatively to engage the real woman next to him in the makeshift observatory. As in the 1866 sonnet "In Vision I Roamed," mental travel into the trackless universe threatens the mind that voyages there: "am I not right in saying that those minds who exert their imaginative powers to bury themselves in the depths of the universe merely strain their faculties to gain a new horror?" asks Swithin rhetorically (34). Yet the increasing scale of the "grandeur," "solemnity," and "ghastliness" of space is nothing to the record of deep time that the decay of stars implies; "they are not everlasting, they are not eternal; they burn out like candles. . . . The senses may become terrified by plunging among them as they are, but there is a pitifulness even in their glory! Imagine them all extinguished, and your mind feeling its way through a heaven of total darkness, occasionally striking against the black invisible cinders of those stars" (34–35). Unlikely though it may seem, this melancholy harangue charms Lady Constantine, "crushes" her personal troubles into their proper insignificance, and perhaps more to the point, achieves a class-leveling effect: "In the presence of the immensities that his young mind had, as it were, brought down from above to hers, they became unconsciously equal. There was, moreover, an inborn liking in Lady Constantine to dwell less on her permanent position as a county lady than on her passing emotions as a woman" (35). It is almost touching to imagine Hardy's hope that readers' interest in Lady Constantine's dilemma, abandoned and in love with a younger man, would awaken "social sympathies" with the "pathos, long-suffering, and divine-tenderness which in real life frequently accompany the passion of such a woman" (3). Over a century later, she would still risk mockery for desiring a younger man.

An earlier chapter explores Hardy's frequent use of narrator's thought report to detail a character's unawareness of the mental contents of another, a condition that may be inferred to impair potential sympathy between characters. As Anna Henchman has observed, "Hardy uses images of looking at stars, planets, comets, or the moon to reflect on the difficulty of taking in information about other people and understanding their mental lives" (Henchman 37). Yet in *Two on a Tower* Hardy explicitly labels a character's mental inaccessibility as a positive attraction to the gazing lover:

Looking again at him her eyes became so sentimentally fixed on his face that it seemed as if she could not withdraw them. There lay . . . a guileless philosopher. His parted lips were lips which spoke, not of love, but of millions of miles; those were eyes that looked, not into the depths of other eyes, but into other worlds. Within his temples dwelt thoughts, not

of woman's looks, but of stellar aspects, and the configuration of constellations. . . . Thus to his physical attractiveness was added the attractiveness of mental inaccessibility. (*TT* 44)

Sighing without knowing why even as she clips a lock of the sleeping
Swithin's hair, Lady Constantine at least registers that she is already forgiving him "childlike faults of manner which arose from his obtuseness
to their difference of sex" (44); paradoxically, his inattention to her as
a woman ennobles him in her eyes (as Bathsheba Everdene has earlier
experienced, going unnoticed can be an aphrodisiac). The beginning
of such a story, in Hardy's logic, can scarcely avoid ending in disaster,
since Swithin is equally unaware. Only late in the novel does he startle
into consciousness, recognizing his responsibility: "He felt like an awakened somnambulist who should find that he had been an accessory to a
tragedy during his unconsciousness" (266). The narrator knows about
Swithin St. Cleve what neither Swithin nor Viviette can grasp, that "He
was a scientist, and took words literally" (279). Hardy's narrator opines,
"There is something in the inexorably simple logic of such men which
partakes of the cruelty of the natural laws that are their study" (279).

Intermental cognizance thus balked, Hardy performs one of his oddest
operations of thought report, in which the two lovers share undifferentiated extremes of dissociation provoked by star gazing. Their perspectives
are formally fused without a gain in mutual understanding:

> Thus, the interest of their sidereal observations led them on, till the
> knowledge that scarce any other human vision was travelling within a
> hundred million miles of their own gave them such a sense of the iso-
> lation of that faculty as almost to be a sense of isolation in respect of
> their whole personality, causing a shudder at its absoluteness. At night,
> when human discords and harmonies are hushed, in a general sense, for
> the greater part of twelve hours, there is nothing to moderate the blow
> with which the infinitely great, the stellar universe, strikes down upon
> the infinitely little, the mind of the beholder; and this was their case now.
> Having got closer to immensity than their fellow-creatures they saw at
> once its beauty and its frightfulness. They more and more felt the con-
> trast between their own tiny magnitudes and those among which they
> had recklessly plunged, till they were oppressed with the presence of a
> vastness they could not cope with even as an idea, and which hung about
> them like a nightmare. (*TT* 63–65)

To some degree Hardy simply rehearses the tropes of gothic night thoughts and the underpinning qualities of the sublime in this passage: in the dark they see a beauty that is accompanied by frightfulness, yielding nightmare.[14] Without knowing one another's thoughts, they share a fused mind and the feelings it produces as a result of the universe's assault on their insignificance. Hardy suggests some consequences of the experience, beginning with a sense of isolation that will lead both lovers to imagine, falsely, that they are so obscure as to remain unnoticed by others in their neighborhood. There is a risk that abandoned behavior could be provoked by such a conviction of one's minuteness. Holding out disinterestedness as a potential effect of insignificance, Hardy then unfolds a plot that awkwardly grafts altruistic self-sacrifice onto a narrative of headlong desire.

Lady Constantine's altruism, though brief in duration, points in the direction that Hardy wishes to posit the future evolution of the cold and terrifying universe that afflicts him and his characters so grievously. Later, in *The Dynasts*, Hardy will reuse the same imagery that he gives to Swithin in *Two on a Tower* to characterize the mechanical action of the "Great Foresightless" Will, which can only be traced a strand at a time by the limited narration of The Spirit of the Years:

> *Yet but one flimsy riband of its web*
> *Have we here watched in weaving—web Enorm,*
> *Whose furthest hem and selvage may extend*
> *To where the roars and plashings of the flames*
> *Of earth-invisible suns swell noisily,*
> *And onwards into ghastly gulfs of sky,*
> *Where hideous presences churn through the dark—*
> *Monsters of magnitude without a shape,*
> *Hanging amid deep wells of nothingness.* (*Dynasts* v. 5, 251, ll. 10–13,
>   italics in original)

Hardy sets a compassionate principle against this vision of the universe, in the aerial music of the Semichorus of the Pities, where "*a food for final Hope*" takes the form of "*The Wellwiller, the kindly Might / That Balances the Vast for weal, / That purges as by wounds to heal*" (253,

---

14. In Hardy's library at the time of his death was a 1776 copy of Edward Young's *The Complaint: Or, Night-Thoughts on Life, Death, and Immortality* (1776). See Michael Millgate, "Thomas Hardy's Library at Max Gate."

ll. 45-47 original italics). According to the Pities, who take the part of humanity, the birth of universal altruism should awaken the heart of the All-mover, "*Promptly tending / To its mending / In a genial germing purpose, and for loving-kindness' sake*" (255, ll. 97–99, original italics). To get to this point, the catastrophe of Napoleon's ambition must lay all Europe low in a "prone and emaciated figure" stripped of its skin. That is, agony precedes the hope of lovingkindness.

In *Two on a Tower*, Hardy emphasizes the painful parturition of altruism. Lady Constantine realizes that she has an opportunity to free Swithin from a marriage that holds back his scientific pursuits and deprives him of the financial assistance of his uncle's bequest. In sketching Viviette's response to this "unique accident," Hardy describes the protracted labor necessary for the birth of benevolence:

> Thus she laboured, with a generosity more worthy even than its object, to sink her love for her own decorum in devotion to the world in general and to Swithin in particular. To counsel her activities by her understanding, rather than by her emotions as usual, was hard work for a tender woman; but she strove hard, and made advance. The self-centered attitude natural to one in her situation was becoming displaced by the sympathetic attitude, which, though it had to be artificially fostered at first, gave her, by degrees, a certain sweet sense that she was rising above self-love. (*TT* 231)

The psychological process sketched here closely resembles that theorized in Herbert Spencer's 1855 *Principles of Psychology*, including the ultimate triumph of the ego over the sympathetic impulse that Hardy orchestrates by arranging for Lady Constantine's pregnancy. As soon as she knows it, "the instinct of self-preservation flamed up in her like a fire. Her altruism in subjecting her self-love to benevolence, and letting Swithin go away from her, was demolished by the new necessity, as if it had been a gossamer web" (244). Like Spencer, Hardy sees the impulses of the ego as considerably more robust than other-directed moral emotions, and it is hard not to see his account of sexual desire here as both selfish and annihilating to the human agents caught in the consequences of acting upon instinct. The gossamer web of altruism is brushed aside to reveal a stickier web, from which neither of Hardy's tragic agents can escape. When in the conclusion of the novel Swithin acts compassionately in promising to remarry Viviette, who is showing her age, Nature steps in to strike the woman down with a heart attack.

If it is true, as Pamela Gossin suggests, that Hardy writes *Two on a Tower* to explore the "chance that humanity might successfully adapt a compassionate value system to a scientific world view" (*Novel Universe* 159), he surely broaches the question to answer it firmly in the negative. In a note that reflects both his reading of Comte and his Darwinian convictions, Hardy remarks "These venerable philosophers seem to start wrong; they cannot get away from a prepossession that the world must somehow have been made to be a comfortable place for man" (*Life and Work* 185) and he would not fall victim to that anthropocentric error. It is certainly possible to discern what Gossin calls a "new cosmological myth" (*Novel Universe* 156) in *Two on a Tower,* so long as it is not a cheery origins story: how humanity got compassion. Not yet. Thinking back on his novels in an 1889 letter to John Addington Symonds, Hardy writes, "I often begin a story with the intention of making it brighter & gayer than usual; but the question of conscience soon comes in; & it does not seem right, even in novels, to belie one's own views. All comedy, is tragedy, if you only look deep enough into it" (*Letters* v. 1, 190). Hardy's commitment to this tragic perspective would not waver, but his reading in the psychological and the materialist philosophy would provide him with the ingredients of a slightly more hopeful vision of the interaction of individual minds and an indifferent universe, leading to guarded optimism, in the short term, about the potential impact of a writer's work on readers and, in the long term, about the possibility that the cosmos could develop the consciousness required for imaginative sympathy with its creatures.

Brain and Nerves in the Vast Interplanetary Spaces: Sources and Influences

As the first chapter of this study details, Hardy read authors contributing to Victorian psychology from the 1860s through 1928, his entire working career as a writer. His reading notes from the 1880s reveal an assiduous interest in key ingredients: the possibility of a cosmic brain, the link between individual minds and this neural network, and the power of minds to create ejects. But this was by no means all he learned from his stints in the Reading Room of the British Museum. Hardy's notes reveal that he consulted Leslie Stephen's redaction of Mill (*Literary Notebooks* v. 1, 132) in 1880 or thereabouts. In 1881 he read essays on materialism and referred in a note to W. K. Clifford's mind-stuff (148) a concept he had earlier encountered in an article by W. H. Mallock (135). In 1883 he took in G. H. Lewes, more Mill, and Herbert Spencer. An 1885 note refers to F. W. H. Myers on the supernatural (167). In 1886 he was reading Spencer's *Principles of Psychology* (172), the monists George Romanes and W. K. Clifford on ejects (174), and in counterbalance, he also took notes on the utility of sympathy (176–77). He wrote in 1887, "*Find utterance for the deepest emotions of your contemporaries,*" a thought inspired by reading Leslie Stephen (180). Between 1886 and 1888 Hardy read G. T. Bettany's *Life of Charles Darwin* (1887), which included a précis of Darwin's *Expression of the Emotions* (1872) (Bettany 126–35). He also read Henry Maudsley (*Literary Notebooks* v. 1, 184), Eduard von Hartmann's *Principles of the Unconscious* (185), more W. K. Clifford (187), Herbert Spencer on sympathy (191–92), and publications of the Society for Psychical Research on dreams and automatic writing (192–93). In 1888 Hardy took copious notes on Henry Maudsley's *Natural Causes and Supernatural Seemings* (195–201) and consulted surveys of contemporary psychology in French (208–10).

Hardy's philosophical interests extended to Schopenhauer, supporting his imagery of the Immanent Will (*Literary Notebooks* v. 2, 28–29), whose lack of awareness of its own impulsions would be a central element of Hardy's figuration. He learned, by 1891, about the right and left brain, excerpting "It wd. seem that to the left brain we must assign the chief control over speech, writing, & gesture—the methods, that is, of expressing ideas . . . also . . . reasoning . . . & control of motions & organs of right side of body . . . Right side of brain . . . emotional manifestations, including those called hysterical . . . also nutrition . . . also left side of bodily organs" (27).[15] The book from which Hardy made this extract also contains an essay on "The Growth and Decay of Mind," with this remark, "Men often die as trees die, slowly, and at the top first" (Proctor 299), an image Hardy would use in his poem "Nature's Questioning" (*WP* v. 1, 86–87). The idea that a divided brain might not be aware of the commands issued by its other side provided a good foundation for Hardy's vision of the unconscious volition of the Immanent Will. This source may also have suggested to Hardy a therapeutic way forward for the Will. For while the discovery of our two brains does not promise doubling of brain power, Proctor does suggest that "it may, for instance, be an especially desirable change . . . to have [the] emotions called into play, because the

---

15. Hardy indicates this note as coming from his reading of *Our Two Brains,* attributed to Proctor. Björk does not identify a source. I identify here Hardy's likely source, Richard A. Proctor's book *Science Byways* (1875), especially page 324. Hardy's extract comes from the essay, "Have We Two Brains?" 302–37.

over-worked reasoning part of the brain obtains in that way a more complete rest" (Proctor 336). Though Hardy would persistently represent the emotions as contributing to human beings' unhappy victimization by little-understood impulses, he also saw affect as the key to a compassionate relationship with other beings in the web of life. "The human race to be shown as one great network or tissue, which quivers in every part when one point is shaken" (*Life and Work* 183), he jotted in his notebook.

Intellectual networks such as the one he joined through his friendship with his editor Leslie Stephen provided a model for the transmission of ideas, of which Hardy entertained transformative expectations. Reading had changed his own life, after all, and he was sometimes impatient in his expectation that his contemporaries ought to catch up with his doubts and convictions through reading. Responding in 1888 to the Reverend Alexander Balloch Grosart, for instance, Hardy tartly recommends a course of reading that will answer Grosart's search for reassurance of "the absolute goodness and non-limitation of God acting in the universe" (*Life and Work* 214). Hardy demurs to supply that evidence, writing "Perhaps Dr Grosart might be helped to a provisional view of the universe by the recently published Life of Darwin, and the works of Herbert Spencer and other agnostics" (*Letters* v. 1, 174). Hardy received support in his response to this clerical harassment from his intellectual mentor Leslie Stephen, who had also exchanged words with Grosart. This was to be in good agnostic company from Hardy's point of view. Stephen's example, advice, and writings were to prove a life-long influence on Hardy's reading, as he himself testified. That extended to the thinkers Stephen wrote about, recommended, and edited.

One such thinker was the mathematician and philosopher W. K. Clifford, whose posthumous essays and lectures were edited by Stephen and brought out just in time (in 1879) for Hardy's study of psychological literature.[16] Writing in a source excerpted by Hardy in his *Literary Notebooks*, Clifford considers the notion that the universe might be "a vast brain," the stars "atoms in some vast organism."[17] Clifford asks, "Can we regard the universe . . . as a vast brain, and therefore the reality that

---

16. A copy of the 1904 edition of Clifford's *Lectures and Essays* (1904) was in Hardy's library at the time of his death. The date of the edition suggests that Hardy was revisiting Clifford's work as he wrote the first volume of *The Dynasts*. See Michael Millgate, "Thomas Hardy's Library at Max Gate."

17. W. K. Clifford, "Body and Mind" (1874) 67. Clifford is most celebrated for anticipating aspects of Einstein's Theory of General Relativity. On Clifford's influence on subsequent psychology, see G. E. Berrios, "Body and Mind: W. K. Clifford" (2000).

underlies it as a conscious mind?" Hardy was to answer this question in the negative in *The Dynasts,* depicting the Immanent Will as not yet conscious, but he held out the hope that evolution of the cosmos itself could still occur. It is instructive for Hardy's vision of a nescient cosmic brain to see how Clifford (and his source before him) had reasoned through the faulty analogy:

> This question has been considered by the great naturalist Du Bois Reymond, and has received from him that negative answer which I think we must also give. For we have found that the particular organisation of the brain which enables its actions to run parallel with consciousness amounts to this—that disturbances run along definite channels, and that two disturbances which occur together establish links between the channels along which they run, so that they naturally occur together again. It will, I think, be clear to every one that these are not characteristics of the great interplanetary spaces. Is it not possible, however, that the stars we can see are just atoms in some vast organism, bearing some such relation to it as the atoms which make up our brains bear to us? (Clifford, *Lectures and Essays,* v. 2, 46–47)

The lack of a material correlate for neural pathways, the "definite channels" along which "disturbances" run weakens the analogy for Clifford, but his mathematician's sense of comparative scale pushes the speculation into an alignment where stars equate not to objects so crude as nerve cells, but to the very atoms that comprise cellular structures. Even if this undetectable but potentially functional cosmic brain could exist, Clifford still rejects a materialist explanation for a God-like power with particular interests in human beings: "it seems clear that the knowledge of such an organism could not extend to events taking place on the earth, and that its volition could not be concerned in them. And if some vast brain existed far away in space, being invisible because not self-luminous, then according to the laws of matter at present known to us, it could affect the solar system only by its weight" (270). Hardy will tweak this model just slightly in *The Dynasts,* connecting the volition of the Will and the actions of unwitting human agents, but preserving the nescience of the vast brain as to the consequences of its impulses. Following Clifford's logic, it would be as if our own minds could attend to the unconscious commands of our brains over motor functions or the spinning of electrons in our atoms.[18]

---

18. That atoms possessed an indivisible electric charge was theorized in 1838 by Richard Laming, in his *On the Primary Forces of Electricity* (1838). G. J. Stoney named this charge

Monist philosopher Eduard von Hartmann also proved a stimulating source for Hardy, who transcribed pages of extracts from his 1869 *The Philosophy of the Unconscious* (published in English translation in 1884),[19] including the following passage. Hartmann's ideas support the nescience of a cosmic brain as Hardy would later represent it:

> Only if the existence of the world was decided by the act of a *blind will* . . . only then is this existence comprehensible: only then is God as such not to be made responsible for the same. . . . But why did not God when he became *seeing,* i.e., his all-wise intelligence entered into being, repair the error? . . . Here we are again aided by the inseparability of the idea from the will in the Unconscious . . . the dependence of the idea on the will; [and] the whole world-process [i.e., throughout time] only serves the one purpose of emancipating the Idea from the will by means of consciousness. (*Literary Notebooks* v. 2, 111)

While Clifford's speculations reached out into the great interplanetary spaces, monist philosophers extrapolated from introspection about the function of microscopically small vibrations. In *The Philosophy of the Unconscious,* Eduard von Hartmann considered how individual brains perceive Time (through sensations) and Space (unconsciously):

> Space and Time are forms both of Being and of (conscious) Thought. Time is immediately translated into sensation from being, from the vibrations in the brain, because it is contained in the form of the *single* cerebral molecular vibration in the same way as in the external impulse. Space, as a form of perception, must be created by an act of the Unconscious, because neither the space-relations of the *single* cerebral molecular vibration, nor the space-relations of the different vibrating parts of the brain, have an similarity or direct relation to the spatial figures and the spatial relations of positions either of the real things or of the objects presents; but the spatial determinations of perceptions are probably governed by the system of local signs in the senses of Sight and Touch. (*Unconscious* 348)

---

electron in 1894, and in 1897, the electron was identified as an elementary particle by J. J. Thomson. See Theodore Arabatzis, *Representing Electrons: A Biographical Approach to Theoretical Entities* (2006) 70–74. These latter discoveries came too late for W. K. Clifford, who died at age 33 of tuberculosis, but not too late for Hardy.

19. The edition cited here is Eduard von Hartmann, *The Philosophy of the Unconscious* (1893), v. 1.

Here Hartmann rejects the world/brain analogy that would explain perception by miniaturized correspondences. From another source Hardy had harvested a doubt about the morphological resemblance of the human brain and the universe. His notes on George Romanes's "The World as an Eject," published in *The Contemporary Review,* record an early impact of imagery that Hardy will reconfigure in *The Dynasts:* "unless we can show in the disposition of the heavenly bodies some morphological resemblance to the structure of the human brain, we are precluded from rationally entertaining any probability that self-conscious volition belongs to the universe" (*Literary Notebooks* v. 1, 174). If the astronomy of the day yielded too little evidence definitively to show that the universe was in fact a vast neural net, as Hardy's sources agreed, these passages still attracted Hardy's attention, for the notion was evocative enough to develop and subject to critical questioning. Some of those questions stimulated Hardy's scrutiny of the function of human brains, as the near-at-hand elements in the tempting analogy: how did they process stimuli (apparently without knowing how they did it)?

Hardy found an answer to this question in the anti-supernaturalist and materialist writings of medical psychologist Henry Maudsley, who wrote in 1870,

> [W]hen a shock imparted to the mind through the senses causes a violent emotion, it produces a real commotion in the molecules of the brain. It is not that an intangible something flashes inward and mysteriously affects an intangible metaphysical entity; but that an impression made on the sense is conveyed along nervous paths of communication, and produces a definite physical effect in physically-constituted mind-centres; and that the mental effect, which is the exponent of the physical change, may be then transferred by molecular motion to the muscles, thus getting muscular expression, or to the processes of nutrition and secretion, getting expression in modifications of them. (*Body and Mind* 94)

Maudsley thinks in terms of nerve cells, chemistry, and electricity, as he theorizes the physical path of conveyance of affective and cognitive impulses, from perception to mental effect, all the way to muscular reaction. For more than a century, brain scientists had known about the electricity emitted by the brain, as Alan Richardson has demonstrated, and Maudsley's language captures the relation between the shock of trauma and the electrically charged chain of reactions that course through the brain. Hardy later transposes this description onto a universe in which

all is one, with no "intangible somethings" stimulating metaphysical entities, but only an impercipient cosmic unity that neither notices nor cares
for the human creatures caught up in the commotion of its impulses. Just
as our own bodies have no awareness of how our brain directs the processes of digestion or secretion, the cosmic brain can stimulate physical
changes in the real world without consciousness of its actions. Hardy
wondered about how much minds were under conscious control: as early
as 1882 he inscribed in his notebook, "Write a history of human automatism, or impulsion—viz., an account of human actions in spite of human
knowledge, showing how very far conduct lags behind the knowledge
that should really guide it" (*Life and Work* 158). He did not fail to apply
the same questions to the Immanent Will. Like this passage from Maudsley, Hardy's neural imagery in *The Dynasts* will be electrical as well as
organic, impulsive both in the sense of the electrical pulse and the affective swerve. But these figurative overlays did not solve the problem of the
connection between the vast cosmic brain and tiny human beings. If the
analogy breaks down for lack of evidence of interstellar pathways, how
does the relationship work?

Hardy incorporated another idea from W. K. Clifford and monist
George Romanes to bridge the gap between individual mind and a cosmic
mind: the concept of ejects. As I have already suggested and documented
in chapter 3, Hardy knew Clifford's idea of ejects and mind-stuff. His
poetry of 1898 and later shows the action of ejects as ghost-like projections haunting the mental landscape of *Wessex Poems*. How early did
Hardy know about ejects? He came across these ideas during his 1880s
studies of the psychological literature. In 1886 George Romanes's essay,
"The World as an Eject," Hardy found a monist argument about the
Problem of other Minds: in Romanes's terms, "ejects" refers to those
other subjectivities. Hardy did not accept without question the theory
of ejects, by which means a mind effectively creates the world that sur-
rounds it through projection of its perceptions. He questioned the idealism of Clifford's vision of ejects, because he could not square his own
experience with the idea that the boundary between individual minds
could be erased. Hardy wrote to Roden Noel, who had suggested that
Hardy join the Psychical Research Society (*Letters* v. 1, 260n) of his "mis-
trust of metaphysic." In this 1892 letter, Hardy explains the experiential
barrier to belief:

> [I]f the body be only sensations *plus* perceptions & concepts, then to
> hold that the ego may be related to many more forms of corporeity than

the one our senses inform us of at present is a gratuitous assumption without ground. You may call the whole human race a single *ego* if you like; & in that view a man's consciousness may be said to pervade the world; but nothing is gained. Each is, to all knowledge, limited to his own frame. Or with Spinoza, & the late W. K. Clifford, you may call all matter mind-stuff (a very attractive idea this, to me) but you cannot find the link (at least I can't) of one form of consciousness with another. (*Letters* v. 1, 262)

Though Hardy will supplement the monist vision of a cosmic brain with neural imagery to create imaginatively the missing connections, in his fiction of the 1880s and early 1890s he took pains to figure the absence of the link. One form of consciousness does not connect with another, and each butts up against the delimiting barrier of his or her own frame. Even to comprehend the workings of human impulsions requires cracking open the skull or stripping off the skin in the style of an anatomical illustration. Even then the body does not readily yield its mysteries.

The Condition of Organic Life in *The Woodlanders*

No novel of Hardy's explores the limitations of individual understanding in the context of social relations more thoroughly than his 1887 work *The Woodlanders*. Here the known world of his pastoral characters is in fact a misunderstood world, because it is not really separate from the rest of the universe: "To hear these two Arcadian innocents talk of imperial law would have made a humane person weep who should have known what a dangerous structure they were building up on their supposed knowledge. They remained in thought, like children, in the presence of the incomprehensible" (W 253). To imagine, as Giles and Grace do, that there might be a way out of the trajectory of inexorable causation, which moves from little accidents towards decay and disorder, is invariably a mistake in a world where heat does not flow spontaneously from cold to hot bodies,[20]

20. Rudolf Clausius's formulation of the second law of thermodynamics, an extension of Sadi Carnot's work, was published in 1850 and appeared the next year in English translation. See "On the Moving Force of Heat, and the Laws Regarding the Nature of Heat Itself Which Are Deducible Therefrom" (1851) 1–21, 102–19. By 1900 Hardy certainly knew of the heat-death of the universe, as indicated by his excerpting a review mentioning Haeckel's description of a world grown cold in his *Literary Notebooks* v. 2, 98–101. Swithin St. Cleve's speeches about the decay of stars (see above, 206) suggest that Hardy was aware in the 1870s of the prior decade's advances in theoretical physics, including the concept of entropy.

consciousness is trapped in its embodied containers, and communications fail. Though the reader of this novel's familiar love triangle may wish for the connection of the right pair of lovers, Giles Winterbourne's death in the cold just outside the little building sheltering the warm-blooded Grace Melbury, Grace's restoration to a loveless union with Fitzpiers, and Marty's vigil at Giles's grave assert Hardy's conclusion: the only separation that can be reversed is one with no heat, and the dead can give no warmth to the living. A rich pattern of image-schemas shows verticals falling into horizontals, structures collapsing, and marriages failing, all aspects of the "Unfulfilled Intention, which makes life what it is, was as obvious [in the woods] as it could be among the depraved crowds of a city slum. The leaf was deformed, the curve was crippled, the taper was interrupted; the lichen ate the vigour of the stalk, and the ivy slowly strangled to death the promising sapling" (48). Though this passage has been read as reflecting the ideas of Schopenhauer (345n48), it also resonates with the mid-century account of the universe ruled by physical laws inimical to progress. The woodlands are not exempt from entropy, not even with Giles's husbandry and Marty South's cultivation of saplings set against its destructive force. Giles's last name, Winterbourne, predicts his downhill flow (a bourne is both a creek and a goal) to a cold end.

The Woodlanders provides a useful glimpse of Hardy's darkening views about human psychology in a chilling universe for several reasons, not least its two phases of composition. As Peter J. Casagrande shows, the novel's conception in the mid-1870s shows in its pastoral imagery and setting, which situates it near *Under the Greenwood Tree* and *Far from the Madding Crowd*. The psychological imagery associated with the native inhabitants of the woodlands links their connection to the earth, their rooted existences through the generations, their planting and tending of trees, and their old-fashioned minds. They have container brains that can only hold so many thoughts: Grace's lady's education has driven out her childhood knowledge of the different types of apples (W 38). They adhere to a traditional morality of wrongs righted, even if there must still be winners and losers in competitive life. This psychological backwardness might appear to afford some protection against the crushing insights of modern thought, but Hardy does not spare his characters. The idyllic scene is also penetrated by the science, philosophy, social changes, and sexual mores of the 1880s, with destructive impact on Giles Winterbourne, the novel's most rooted inhabitant and representative forester. This is not entirely the fault of Mephistophelean intruders, for the woodlanders have broken their own quarantine. Melbury, the timber merchant, has a tradesman's link to the outside world, as well as the prosperity to educate his daughter in town. His waffling about Grace's marriage prospects shows the appeal of a rise in social position by marriage with an outsider when he abandons his original plan to match her with Giles. Characters from the outside bear the blight of modernity, including the deceptive rumor of a liberalized divorce law that will fail to permit the potentially restorative dissolution of Grace and Fitzpiers's broken marriage. The blend of traditional and modern affects in the local but educated Grace causes suffering from the combination of "modern nerves with primitive emotions" (267).[21]

Though he sticks to his technique of narratorial thought-report to render it, Hardy shows the outsiders of the novel, Felice Charmond, Dr. Edred Fitzpiers, and the returned native Grace Melbury as possessing modern interiority: these characters have weird dreams, dwell on metaphysics, and fall into reveries of unruly desire. Not surprisingly for Hardy, those with modern consciousness still obey the commands of affective impulses, which may even be heightened by the isolation of the woodlands, and intersect with the narrower understandings of the natives disastrously. As Hardy's narrator announces,

> [T]his self-contained place . . . was one of those sequestered spots outside the gates of the world where may usually be found more meditation than action, and more listlessness than meditation: where reasoning proceeds on narrow premises, and results in inferences wildly imaginative; yet where, from time to time, dramas of a grandeur and unity truly Sophoclean are enacted in the real, by virtue of the concentrated passions and closely knit interdependence of the lives therein. (W 7–8)

Hardy dramatizes the consequences of narrow premises and unjustified inferences in the tragic results of a clash in psychologies. The traditional, closely knit interdependence that many readers have idealized as Hardy's depiction of the country turns into liability.[22] The novel is full of failures to imagine the facts, extrapolations from misinformation, and abrupt realizations of the truth, each imparting a mental shock. In the educated

---

21. Many critics have noticed the clash of attitudes embedded in Hardy's contrast of rural and cosmopolitan life, but the one who comes closest to the concerns of my treatment of *The Woodlanders* is Robert C. Schweik, "The Ethical Structure of Hardy's 'The Woodlanders'" (1996).

22. For a survey of attitudes towards Hardy's representation of the country, see Jonathan Bate, "Culture and Environment: From Austen to Hardy" (1999).

country girl Grace Melbury's attraction to representatives of both the older and the newer way of thinking, Hardy illustrates the disruptive force of sexual desire, a condition of organic life but not a guarantor of moral harmony. Indeed, the neutral force of the universe, the "Unfulfilled Intention," uses sexuality to propagate its victims even as it subjects them to degeneracy and decay.

Hardy works through the inevitable consequences of Grace's choice (the newer is not inevitably the better, the more learned not necessarily the good) using an entwined set of image schemas related to the tree/man/society complex. Earlier in this chapter I have suggested Hardy's association of horizontality with illness and decline, to felled trees and decay. *The Woodlanders* enforces this association with its depiction of prostrate sick and injured people. Maintaining verticality, or uprightness, pertains not only to trees but also to human characters, who struggle to keep their heads and what's inside them or growing out of them. Hardy suggests that the orchard region cultivates not just apples but other products for harvest: hair, brains, people. All have their uses, even if they must be cut or crushed first. This treatment, too, is natural, for nothing in organic or human nature guarantees kindness, fairness, or justice. At best, cruelty and lovingkindness cancel each other out, given the commonality of all living and dying things. As Peter Casagrande observes, "Tree-like men coexist with and contend with man-like trees" in *The Woodlanders* (Casagrande 117). Hardy shows this through what happens to heads, both on the inside and the outside, persistently linking states of mind to the condition of trees and branches.

For his setting, woods that stand both for an Edenic garden of orchards and the wilds of people's minds, Hardy explicitly overwrites the form of the individual brain with a stage for his characters' desire-driven behavior. The very land takes the shape of a skull, encouraging mythic readings of the inhabitants of the woodlands, as a comparison of British and American early editions shows. In 1886, Hardy produced two different versions of his opening paragraph for the British and American serialization (in *Macmillan's Magazine* and *Harper's Bazaar*, respectively). In the American serial, the first paragraph makes an analogy between the woods and a lonely human head, using a favorite image, road as hair-parting: "the largest of the woods shows itself bisected by the highway, as the head of thick hair is bisected by the white line of its parting. The spot is lonely."[23] This image, familiar to Hardy readers from his poem "The

---

23. Thomas Hardy, "The Woodlanders, Chapter 1" (1886) 318.

Roman Road" (*TL* v. 1, 320), points directly to Marty South's chestnut hair, coveted and finally acquired by Felice Charmond. It suggests that loneliness is a prerequisite of luxuriant growth. In the British version of the text, the head-like quality of the setting appears as the "bold brow" (*W* 5) of the highest hill. There, the hair-parting vanishes, in favor of the thickly strewn leaves scattered over the path, in an image that echoes an ancient simile for the innumerable souls of men:[24] Both versions contribute salient resonances to the setting of *The Woodlanders:* A lonely place where lives come and go like the fallen leaves, a naturalistic view, consistent with Darwin; a place where isolation converts the merely solitary person into "an incubus of the forlorn" (5), an affective transformation. This strange phrase, suggesting a demon who takes advantage of sad women while they sleep, applies to the barber whose journey into the woodlands opens the action, only in the sense that he hopes to play on Marty South's poverty to acquire her hair. It more appropriately describes the serial seducer Dr. Edred Fitzpiers, rumored to live so remotely "because they say he is in league with the devil" (8). Whether the worse incubus is the one who seduces, or the one who gets into one's head, or even into one's brain, Hardy does not resolve: Fitzpiers will do all these things, without supernatural aid. He is a psychology-reading and philosophy-spouting bounder, transported into the natural world of the *Woodlanders* like a bad idea.

Hardy's drafts from the early stages of the composition of *The Woodlanders* (after 1874) do not survive, but we may posit that it could already be the Darwinian world that has attracted much of the critical commentary on the novel.[25] The contribution of the 1880s can be seen in its effort to eschew any consoling dualism (no enduring spirit to survive the process of decay) and to tarnish idealism by association with Dr. Edred Fitzpiers's aims. In planning stages he was Fitzpaine;[26] by publication time he has

---

24. Hardy knew *Paradise Lost* well, so it is possible that he echoes Milton (Book 1, ll. 299–313), as James Gibson suggests (Penguin Classics edition, 451n3), although the strewn leaves are likened to angel forms, and only indirectly the souls of men. A more likely echo, considering the sense, points all the way back to Homer: "Very like leaves / upon this earth are the generations of men— / old leaves, cast on the ground by wind, young leaves / the green forest bears when the spring comes in. / So mortals pass" (*The Iliad* Book 6, ll. 148–52, translated by Robert Fitzgerald, 146). Hardy might also have noticed the simile in Vergil's *Aeneid* (Book 6, ll. 305 ff) or in Dante's *Inferno* (Book 3, ll. 112–17).

25. See for example, George Levine, "*The Woodlanders* and the Darwinian Grotesque" (2006); David Lodge, ed. "Introduction," *The Woodlanders,* by Thomas Hardy (1975) 13–22; Phillip Mallett, "Noticing Things: Hardy and the Nature of Nature" (2000); Ronald D. Morrison, "Love and Evolution in Thomas Hardy's *The Woodlanders*" (1991).

26. The name was suggested by the locality Okeford Fitzpaine, associated in *The Wood-*

become "dread," ("Dr. Ed"). Hardy's explicit reference to recent neurological research comes in through Fitzpiers's collection and opening up of brains, with the implication that he is driving his specimens crazy before their decease. Hardy's interest in medical neurology shows in his representation of an anatomist intent on carrying out studies of brain tissue. Weighing the brain, then extracting and examining tissue samples under a microscope mark the limits of Dr. Fitzpiers's scientific investigations: he does not get far in his quest to identify the point of contact between the material world and the ideal (W 119) because his own carnal impulses involve him in the everyday coils of marriage and adultery. A collector of women, Fitzpiers attempts to secure old Grammer Oliver's brain, seduces Suke Damson, marries Grace Melbury, only to betray her in his adulterous liaison with Felice Charmond. Sexual contacts, not the idealist's quest to connect physiology and transcendental philosophy, rule the plot of the promiscuous male, an outsider who invades the hamlets of *The Woodlanders* with his disquieting modern philosophy.[27]

We are never very far from skulls and their contents in this novel, for the motif of brain as container runs through the book. Literal references to brains support an old-fashioned view of physiology, while the predicaments of the sympathetic characters run ahead of their physical capacities as they deal with unwelcome intrusions of modernity. Headaches, miseries, intoxication, and fires of indignation are located by Hardy specifically in the brains of his woods-bound characters. A repressed thought is relegated to "the obscurest cellarage" of Melbury's brain. Plans, thoughts, business appointments, obsessions ("maggots"), stimulants, and fears go in and out of characters' heads, which are most often mentioned turning this way or that in an externalized report of distracted attention. Only Marty South carries out her work without turning her head, and although it garners unwanted comment when she chops off her hair, she never wavers in her concentration on her work and her unrequited love, Giles Winterbourne. Giles himself is often depicted ruefully shaking his head, especially when out-of-control events dislocate him from his home: "The sense that the paths he was pacing, the cabbage-plots, the apple-trees, his dwelling, cider-cellar, wring-house, stables and weathercock, were all slipping away over his head and beneath his feet, as if they were painted on a magic lantern slide, was curious" (W 83).

landers as Buckbury Fitzpiers where the doctor's ancestors were supposed to have dwelt. See F. Outwin Saxelby, *Thomas Hardy Dictionary* (1911) 155.

27. This behavior is consistent with Fitzpiers's Shelleyan traits, capably traced by George Fayen in "Hardy's Woodlanders: Inwardness and Memory" (1961).

He is indeed in jeopardy: John South's lifehold on his property will lapse at his death, and later Giles will lose his home because he has annoyed Felice Charmond by refusing to back up his wagon. His bewilderment and anxiety temporarily dislocate his perceptions from material reality as the ground beneath his feet dissolves in the Victorian special-effects style of the magic lantern.[28] When his own perception of the solidity of the world and its arrangements fails, Giles can scarcely keep his balance. His plot trajectory that will lead to the horizontal of prostration begins in the destabilizing imagery of mental confusion.

Hardy ties Giles's fate to John South. The ill man enjoins Giles to tackle the elm tree that haunts his imagination: "Whenever the wind blew, as it did now, the tree rocked, naturally enough; and the sight of its motion, and the sound of its sighs, had gradually bred the terrifying illusion in the woodman's mind," a fear that the tree is about to fall down and crush his house (W 83). Giles "shrouds off" the limbs of the tree, climbing far above his ladder and "leaving nothing but a bare stem below him" (84). From the ground, Giles ascends into a "skyey field" (84), "cutting himself off more and more from all intercourse with the sublunary world" until he is only "a dark grey spot on the light grey zenith" of the tree (85). At this precipitous peak of his vertical ascent, Giles receives the news from Grace Melbury that her father has called off their presumed engagement. He has nowhere to go but down, all the way to the earth ("This severance was in truth more like a burial of her than a rupture with her" [87]), but in fact Hardy will bury Giles before the novel's conclusion, leaving Grace alive to learn something close to altruism from the ironic buffetings of her experience. For the operation on the tree only worsens John South's mania, and soon he is dead with his brain sectioned under Dr. Fitzpiers's microscope. Though Grace goes to Fitzpiers's house to enjoin him to release Grammer Oliver from her promise to surrender her brain for his studies, once she gazes at the "usual circle of light patterned all over with a cellular tissue of some indescribably sort," in fact "a fragment of old John South's brain" (119), she is lost in her wondering admiration of Dr. Fitzpiers.

---

28. Hardy will recycle the imagery of magic-lantern slide show in *The Dynasts* in order to suggest that the Will, a showman and deft-manipulator "Might smile at his own art" as he projects the phantasmagoria of Austria's surrender at Ulm (*The Dynasts* v. 4, 109), a scene that also emphasizes a move to horizontals in the symbolic laying down of arms. On the popularity of magic-lantern shows from the 1860s through the 1890s and the technology of moving images, see Joss Marsh, "Dickensian 'Dissolving Views': The Magic Lantern, Visual Story-Telling, and the Victorian Technological Imagination" (2009).

That this is a mistake, Hardy makes obvious even before he brings the two together. Fitzpiers describes his own responses to an earlier sight of Grace, as "charged with emotive fluid like a Leyden jar with electric," which is to say, fleetingly (W 106). The doctor's reference to Spinoza's ideas about love, "a subjective thing . . . we project against any suitable object in our line of vision" does not reassure Giles that it would truly have made little difference which woman appeared at the particular moment for Fitzpiers's interest to light on. Intellectually, Fitzpiers is inconstant, moving through disciplinary areas of reading like houses of the zodiac, studying anatomy, metaphysics, poesy, literatures "of emotion and passion," and science (111). Though he carries out empirical investigations, "being in a distinct degree scientific," Fitzpiers is an "idealist" (120). Hardy damns this flaw in a man of science by remarking that Fitzpiers believes "that results in a new and untried case might be different from those in other cases where the material conditions had been precisely similar" (120) and especially faults him for thinking himself exempt from the determining conditions that have already produced sorry results "for thousands" (120). Apparently his reading of Spinoza has not sunk in, for Fitzpiers clearly does not believe in a universe run by unavoidable mechanical laws, nor in the unity of body and mind that can be investigated by scientific methods without recourse to the transcendental (119). This intellectual sleight-of-hand is as damning as Fitzpiers's habit of opportunistic sexual conquest.

Curiously, Hardy gives the libertine, mischief-making Fitzpiers much of his own reading, including the variety of disciplines into which the medical man dips in his course of study. Hardy, too, read German metaphysics, poetry, prosody, and "psychological literature" (W 181), but he came to rather more ethically upright conclusions than he gives his character. The impact of Hardy's recently acquired knowledge of psychology and related philosophy shows clearly in the allusions Fitzpiers makes, as well as in his activities as a brain anatomist. Yet Hardy also shows Fitzpiers as intellectually flighty and lacking in compassion. He depicts the doctor using an exhibition of brain science to shock and titillate. Fitzpiers combines the acquisitive habits of an amoral user and the hollow rhetoric of an idealist clinging to dualism in spite of the evidence. Looking into the bright circle of the microscope to see the cellular pattern of a brain section should not lead to imaginative leaps of metaphysics; it should be subjected, Hardy thought, to rigorously materialist logic. Hardy judged harshly such evasions of what he took to be the obvious conclusions from a serious reading of Darwin, Spencer, and the

monists. Some years later, writing about his attraction to but final dis-
agreements with Henri Bergson, Hardy writes, "I fear his theory is, in the
bulk, only our old friend Dualism in a new suit of clothes,—an ingenious
fancy without real foundation, and more complicated than the fancies he
endeavors to overthrow" (*Life and Work* 400, 489).

Yet Hardy was still open, in the late 1880s and 1890s, to hopes that
physical laws could leave room for progress from liberty to love, from
competition to combination. In a conversation with the medical neurologist James Crichton Browne in 1893, Hardy wondered whether, as
Browne had suggested, "the doctrines of Darwin require readjusting
largely" (*Life and Work* 275) especially as concerned survival of the fittest. Hardy records, "There is an altruism and coalescence between cells
as well as an antagonism. Certain cells destroy cells; but others assist and
combine.—Well, I can't say" (275). From a journal of the same year, an
extract from F. W. H. Myers's essay "Modern Poets and the Meaning of
Life" wonders

> Does the law of the conservation of energy condemn man's consciousness
> to extinction when the measurable energies which build up his chemi-
> cal texture pass back into the inorganic world, or may his conscious life
> be a form of activity which, just because it is not included in our cycle
> of mutually transformable energies, is itself in its own proper form as
> imperishable as they? What does evolution mean. . . . Does it apply to
> the moral, or only to the material world? (*Literary Notebooks* v. 2, 55)

That modern writers should be tackling such questions, while the scientists stuck to their inexorably simple extension of logic from literal fact
to cruel conclusions, meant that poets and novelists had a special duty to
discharge. How Hardy saw that working emerges clearly in his three published essays about the art of fiction, essays that also show the impress of
his 1880s reading in psychology and neurology.

Schooling Readers: Hardy's Essays on Fiction

In 1889, between the publication of *The Woodlanders* and *Tess of the
d'Urbervilles*, Hardy wrote to John Addington Symonds about his ambitions for his fiction, which were directly linked to his gravitation toward
tragedy and a natural scientist's desire for empirical verification:

A question which used to trouble me was whether we ought to write sad stories, considering how much sadness there is in the world already. But of late I have come to the conclusion that, the first step towards cure of, or even relief from, any disease being to understand it, the study of tragedy in fiction may possibly here & there be the means of showing how to escape the worst forms of it, at least, in real life. (*Letters* v. 1, 190)

This comment echoes one of the main points of Hardy's 1888 essay, "The Profitable Reading of Fiction," that novel-reading can be therapeutic and even elevating, so long as readers approach the task in the right spirit, not in the "mentally and morally warped" way that seeks to be offended by "an honest picture of human nature" ("Profitable" 125). The dependent relationship between an unfettered representation of life, including the physical condition of the characters, and the promise of readers' "humanizing education" through "fictitious narrative" (120) shows Hardy working his way towards his strongest statements in favor of an "illuminant" method.

This essay, too, reflects the neurological turn in Hardy's imagination, in his contrast between novelists' techniques, more or less revealing of the "waves of human impulse on which deeds and words depend" ("Profitable" 124). In a great deal of fiction, Hardy complained, a sense of refinement interferes with "vigorous portraiture, by making the exteriors of men their screen rather than their index" (124) and in some "the author's word has to be taken as to the nerves and muscles of his figures" while "in the other they can be seen as in an *écorché*" (124–25). The image of the *écorché* recurs in *The Dynasts* to figure forth the embodied recumbent Continent, contorted by war. There it stands both for what an observer sees from a visionary distant view of actions and reactions, and for the implicit pain of the evisceration that reveals what goes on under the skin. In "Barbara, of the House of Grebe" in *A Group of Noble Dames* (1891), the masked Edmond Willowes appears a living *écorché* to his recoiling wife Barbara, displacing the pain of surgery and disfiguration onto the beholder, who cannot stand the horror of his mutilation. Good novelists, Hardy asserts in his analogy in "The Profitable Reading of Fiction," are like good visual artists and anatomists, who do not allow conventional decorum or body boundaries to interfere with their representations of characters. Good readers are those who can master their distaste and look clearly at what they are shown without horror or offense. They exercise "generous imaginativeness" (112) and gain a "true

exhibition of man" from the renderer who throws "a stronger irradia-
tion" over his human-like subjects (115). Hardy favors novelistic figuration that shows the connection between the impulses and the muscular
actions that a skinless model or illuminated specimen reveals, bound as
good novelists are to the facts of human nature (124–25).

That novelists are fettered by the context in which they publish Hardy
knew from long experience. He had willingly negotiated with the editors
of his serialized novels, often removing or replacing risqué passages, consoling himself by reinserting the self-censored words, phrases, and episodes into the later editions of his novels. He wanted to deal honestly
with life as "a physiological fact" including "the relations of the sexes,"
as he wrote in his 1890 essay "Candour in English Fiction" ("Candour"
127). That Grundyism afflicted all English novelists, Hardy averred,
writing "If the true artist ever weeps it probably is . . . when he first discovers the fearful price that he has to pay for the privilege of writing in
the English language—no less a price than the complete extinction, in the
mind of every mature and penetrating reading, of sympathetic belief in his
personages" (130). In 1891 Hardy wrote appreciatively to H. W. Mass-
ingham, who had favorably reviewed Tess in the *Daily Chronicle,* "Ever
since I began to write—certainly ever since I wrote "Two on a Tower"
in 1881—I have felt that the doll of English fiction must be demolished,
if England is to have a school of fiction at all: & I think great honour is
due to the D. Chronicle for frankly recognizing that the development of a
more virile type of novel is not incompatible with sound morality" (*Letters* v. 1, 250). Because of the domination of magazine publication of fiction, Hardy wrote, prudery interferes with representation of both natural
actions and thoughts. He imagined a future in which a mature fiction
could contain "the position of man and woman in nature, and the position of belief in the minds of man and woman—things which everybody
is thinking but nobody is saying." If only these interdicted materials
"might be taken up and treated frankly" ("Candour" 133), then a more
virile English novel could grow up. Oversensitivity on the part of cultural
watchdogs and deference to dominant modes of publication constrain
the development of a sophisticated novel tradition in English. Change
would require different conditions for publication, an open-minded readership, but also penetrating insight on the part of authors who would see
under the skin to reveal true human nature.

Hardy's third and last essay about his novel-theory, "The Science of
Fiction," throws down the gauntlet in its title and opening premises: "The
materials of Fiction being human nature and circumstances, the science

thereof may be dignified by calling it the codified law of things as they really are. . . . The Science of Fiction is contained in that large work, the cyclopaedia of life" ("Science" 134). However, Hardy does not unfold the expected defense of the novelist as required by art to record everything accurately as a photographer. He instead advances *sympathy* as the necessary quality for successful fiction writing. For Hardy the Science of Fiction precedes composition: it is a burden that must be taken up the aspirant realist, who must achieve "comprehensive and accurate knowledge" (134) before he can begin to create an "illusion of truth" (135) through selection. Hardy draws on the psychology of perception when he doubts the theory of scientific processes of realism, pointing out "the impossibility of reproducing in its entirety the phantasmagoria of experience with infinite and atomic truth, without shadow, relevancy, or subordination" (135). The novelist must always highlight and downplay, note "adventitious externals" without "neglect of vital qualities" (137). Furthermore, Hardy's successful novelist has "a power of observation informed by a living heart" (138) and possesses the "mental tactility that comes from a sympathetic appreciativeness of life in all of its manifestations" (137). Hardy explains that the machine-like recording of data, or even a reliance on empirical facts, yields not the materials necessary for truly realistic fiction writing: "why such a keen eye to the superficial does not imply a sensitiveness to the intrinsic is a psychological matter beyond the scope of these notes; but that a blindness to material particulars often accompanies a quick perception of the more ethereal characteristics of humanity, experience continually shows" (137). Blindness, lack of sympathy, and stunted emotional intelligence are all fatal deficiencies in a novelist, and no amount of scientific recording can make up for the absence of an attentive, feeling observer. Hardy's description of the scientific realists closely resembles his depiction of the Inadvertent Mind, authoring all human action but comprehending nothing of human nature.

"Fibrils, Veins, / Will-tissues, Nerves, and Pulses of the Cause" in *The Dynasts*

On the relationship of the Fore Scene and the After Scene of the Overworld to the historical action in *The Dynasts*, Walter F. Wright comments approvingly, "It is to his credit that, though [Hardy] did make use of a supernatural network of nerves, he did not preach his theory obtrusively in the action of his poem" (Wright 113). Indeed, his theory precluded such preaching, for the Immanent Will that Hardy figures as a giant brain and network of neurons acts on human agents without their knowledge. Since the Will is itself unconscious, the reader relies on the remarks of the Spirit of the Years and the Spirit of the Pities, as well as the anonymous narrator of the phantasmagoric stage directions, for descriptive passages. The Will cannot and does not describe itself, and the most the human actors of the historical scenes can do is to accidentally echo the unheard speeches of the phantasmal Intelligences (*Dynasts* v. 4, 7). Herbert Tucker, the most recent of many commentators who have noticed Hardy's neural imagery in *The Dynasts*,[29] describes the special effects of the Overworld well: "For these uncanny transparencies the poet contrives an imagery combining the organic pulse of neurochemical science with the winking circuitry of an electronic system . . . somewhere between a lobed brain and an automated switchboard" (Tucker 588). Further, Tucker observes, "If the Will is to be imagined as a vast network of fibers interconnected in patterns of mutual response, the spirits constitute a higher-level function that the network has somehow, curiously, generated in response to itself" (589). Hardy explained in his 1903 Preface to *The Dynasts* that these "impersonated abstractions" were "intended to be taken by the reader for what they may be worth as contrivances of the fancy" (*Dynasts* v. 4, 6). That is, they resemble the imagination-formed ejects of Clifford's psychology of mind, a point Hardy underscores by using the word "ejections" to describe the action of the Will at the battle of Austerlitz: "The controlling Immanent Will appears therein, as a brain-like network of currents and ejections, twitching, interpenetrating, entangling, and thrusting hither and thither the human forms" (v. 4, 160). The Will makes and moves the universe: nothing exists outside the "*ordered potencies, / nerves, sinews, trajects, eddies, ducts of It / The Eternal Urger*" (ll. 59–61, original italics). As discussed in chapter 3, the process of eject-formation explains how a mind makes spirits apparently external to and separate from itself, so the Years, who has the instrumental role of showing "with preternatural

---

29. For some of the most prominent of the earlier commentators to discuss the imagery of brain and nerves in *The Dynasts*, see G. Glen Wickens, *Thomas Hardy, Monism and the Carnival Tradition* 51–73; Miller, *Distance and Desire* 267; Susan Dean, *Hardy's Poetic Vision in The Dynasts* 257–58; and Samuel Hynes, *The Pattern of Hardy's Poetry* 161. Of these, Wickens is most interested in the monist thinkers who influenced Hardy's imagery and he provides the best account of Hardy's synthesis of these sources. Wickens joins a discussion whose emphasis has been philosophical, led by Dean and F. R. Southerington, *Hardy's Vision of Man* (1971), as well as earlier critics debating the impact of Schopenhauer (Garwood, Wright, Orel). Paradoxically, the critics most interested in Hardy's psychology (Björk, Sumner, Dale, Thurley) do not comment on the brain imagery in *The Dynasts*.

clearness" the anatomized battle scene (v. 4, 160), is itself a product of the Will, and knows it: "*Our scope is but to register and watch / By means of this great gift accorded us— / The free trajection of our entities*" (v. 4, 16, ll. 44–46, original italics). We may translate trajection as transmission. The Spirits, spectators and commentators upon the terrestrial action, have different roles and attitudes. The Years "approximates to the passionless Insight of the Ages," while the Pities corresponds to the "Universal Sympathy of human nature" (v. 4, 7), and their knowledge and hopes for the Will differ accordingly.

The action of *The Dynasts* takes place not on a real stage (though excerpted versions of it were in fact performed[30]) but in a series of views and scenes nearer and farther from the action. Hardy wrote that it was "intended simply for mental performance" (*Dynasts* v. 4, 8), making stages of the brains of his readers. Though early critics were struck by the filmic qualities of *The Dynasts,* formally its descriptions, dialogues, scenes, and narrated dumb-shows come closer to the polyglossia of the radio play.[31] The Overworld, however, is a blank stage for oratorical recitation by the Spirits and their choruses, into whose utterances we must move to discern the outline of Hardy's "Immanent Will and its designs," in the words of the opening line of the poem (v. 4, 14). That in the first speeches of the Spirits the Will is disclosed as working unconsciously, mechanically, automatically, making "flesh-hinged mannikins . . . click-clack off Its preadjusted laws" (v. 4, 17, ll. 86–87) suggests a mechanistic vision of a clock-work universe. It does not prepare the reader for the sudden visualizing of an organic "Will-web," revealed by the special power of the Years for the interpretation of the Pities (v. 4, 21). Using a device that combines microscopy with telescopy, the stage directions show "A new and penetrating light descends on the spectacle, enduing men and things with a seeming transparency, and exhibiting as one organism the anatomy of life and movement in all humanity and vitalized matter included in the display" (v. 4, 21). While this imagery, with its emphasis on illumination and transparency, clearly derives from the examination of animalcules and cellular tissues under the microscope, it somehow also anticipates the summation of visual data presented by satellite imagery. Hardy would have loved Google Earth.

---

30. See Keith Wilson, "'We Thank You . . . Most of All, Perhaps, for *The Dynasts*': Hardy's Epic Drama Re-evaluated" (2006) 237.

31. For an excellent Bakhtinian reading of *The Dynasts,* see Glen Wickens, *Thomas Hardy, Monism and the Carnival Tradition: The One and the Many in* The Dynasts (2002).

The Spirit of the Pities must pause to ponder the strange image. It seems to show not only *"bodies substantive"* but also *"Strange waves . . . like winds grown visible, / which bear mens' forms on their innumerous coils, / Twining and serpentining round and through"* (*Dynasts* v. 4, 21, ll. 161–64, italics in original). These mysterious "retracting threads like gossamers" apparently exert irresistible influence on everything they touch. The Years explains in the manner of a scientific lecturer:

> *These are the Prime Volitions,—fibrils, veins,*
> *Will-tissues, nerves, and pulses of the Cause,*
> *That heave throughout the Earth's compositure.*
> *Their sum is like the lobule of a Brain*
> *Evolving always that it wots not of;*
> *A Brain whose whole connotes the Everywhere,*
> *And whose procedure may but be discerned*
> *By phantom eyes like ours; the while unguessed*
> *Of those it stirs, who (even as ye do) dream*
> *Their motions free . . .*
>
> . . .
>
> *Though they subsist but atoms of the One*
> (v. 4, 21–22, ll. 168–77, l. 180, italics in original)

As we have earlier seen, Hardy's monist sources consider the possibility of a cosmic brain, but question the analogy because the neural channels that would comprise it cannot be detected by astronomy. Hardy supplies what no one but "phantom eyes" can see, the *"Prime Volitions,—fibrils, veins, / Will-tissues, nerves, and pulses of the Cause"* (ll. 168–69), and he imagines the instruments that can reveal the composition of the universe as a *"lobule of a Brain"* (l. 171), of which human beings are an unperceiving portion. Clifford had imagined that stars might be the atoms of a cosmic brain; Hardy makes *"atoms of the One"* (l. 180) out of human agents who *"dream / Their motions free"* (ll. 176–77).

In *The Dynasts*, Hardy takes on the task of historical narration, featuring great men, but denying them true motive influence on events. Unlike his classical models, Hardy's epic does not substitute supernatural agency for human decisions: for the *"Will has woven with an absent heed / Since life first was; and ever will so weave"* (v. 4, 16, ll. 39–40, original italics). A short while into the historical action of the poem, when Napoleon almost hears the warning that the Spirit of the Pities whispers in his ear, Years rebukes his younger colleague: there can be no helping or interfering in the action below. All that can be done is witness *"the very streams / And currents of this all-inhering Power"* (v. 4, 58, ll. 99–100), by observing the scene, which "assumes the preternatural transparency" and is "beheld as it were the interior of a brain which seems to manifest the volitions of a Universal Will, of whose tissues the personages of the action form portion" (v. 4, 58–59, original italics). Clearly microscopic investigations lend the qualities of transparency and brain anatomy suggests that looking at tissues from the interior of a brain could allow an observer to trace motive causes or volitions. Hardy's 1887 notes from the French psychologist Pierre Janet included these evocative scraps: "mouvemens cérébruax . . . vibrations des cellules cérébrales . . . contagion des imaginations . . . vibrations nerveuses" (*Literary Notebooks* v. 1, 209). Something like these movements and vibrations is revealed by the Years, in an historical account that displaces motivation from individuals and nations to the universe itself. Late in the action of the poem, the Spirit of the Years hauls out his instruments one last time:

> A transparency as in earlier scenes again pervades the spectacle, and the ubiquitous urging of the Immanent Will becomes visualized. The web connecting all the apparently separate shapes includes WELLINGTON in its tissue with the rest, and shows him, like them, as acting while discovering his intention to act. By the lurid light the faces of every row, square, group, and column of men, French and English, wear the expression of people in a dream. (v. 5, 230)

Two possibilities open out from this image. One, human beings themselves could wake up and stop sleepwalking. They, at least, have consciousness and feelings, even if they are deceived about their free will. Two, the unconscious Immanent Will itself could wake up, and at the very least recognize what its own transmission the Spirit of the Pities can see about the effects of its ubiquitous urging. Hardy chooses the second option because it fits with the evolutionary long view of change in the universe.

Before the third part of *The Dynasts* was published, Hardy asserted moral rights to this idea. He wrote in 1907 to Edward Wright,

> That the Unconscious Will of the Universe is growing aware of Itself I believe I may claim as my own idea solely—at which I arrived by reflecting that what has already taken place in fractions of the Whole (i.e., so much of the world has become conscious) is likely to take place in the Mass; & there being no Will outside the Mass—that is, the Universe—the

whole Will becomes conscious thereby; & ultimately, it is to be hoped, sympathetic. (*Letters* v. 3, 255)

His Spirit of the Pities would put the possibility this way:

> *Men gained cognition with the flux of time,*
> *And wherefore not the Force informing them,*
> *When far-ranged aions past all fathoming*
> *Shall have swung by, and stand as backward years?*
> (*Dynasts* v. 5, 252, ll. 19–22, original italics)

If an awakening from nescience to consciousness could occur, with a role even for a motherly "*mild-eyed Prescience*" (v. 5, 253, l. 41 original italics), then the next desirable step is the development of "*tendermercy*" (v. 5, 252, l. 33) and "*kindly Might*" in the Will (v. 5, 253, l 45, original italics). Back in 1886, Hardy took notes from an article on "Callousness" in the *Spectator* that anticipated his hope that sympathy could break out even in a self-interested world: "The human world as a whole, with its predominant strain of selfishness, so curiously blended with the most tender affection, the large surface of supreme callousness . . . is not half so surprising as the large & increasing surface of sensitiveness to those sufferings [of other persons]" (*Literary Notebooks* v. 1, 177). The conclusion of *The Dynasts* establishes the high watermark of Hardy's hopes for an affectively responsible and sentient Will: "*must not Its heart awake, / Promptly tending / To its mending / In a genial germing purpose, and for loving-kindness' sake?*" (v. 5, 255, ll. 96–99 original italics). Still he posed it as a question of the Semichorus I of the Pities, not a foregone conclusion.

Hardy's conception of the universal brain as yet unconscious, but potentially evolving to feel, takes the seeker of sources back to an early note from Comte. Hardy's extracts from Comte included this jotting: "*The Brain*—The Active region: the Contemplative region: the Affective region: the last accessible only through the other two, which act upon it; that, conversely, upon them" (*Literary Notebooks* v. 1, 74). The role of the feelings in thinking and acting could not be omitted from Hardy's vision of an Immanent Will awoken to justice through empathy. This brings us to the last problem of Hardy's psychology: he could not help understanding through his feelings even though he could see that feelings motivated most peoples' thoughtless actions. He never gave ground on the centrality of lovingkindness even as he documented human cruelty and indifferent circumstances. Matthew Campbell's nice phrase about Hardy's central, productive contradictions, notes how his "dualist empathy creat[es] monist necessity" (Campbell 220). This raises a question seldom squarely faced by the psychologists and materialist philosophers that Hardy read: is there room for a truly other-directed empathy in a universe in which all things are one? The conclusion to this study shows how Hardy built strategic empathizing for human and inanimate others into his poetic and fictional worlds.

CHAPTER 5

Empathetic Hardy

Hardy's work demonstrates engagement with a variety of empathetic narrative strategies outlined in my book on the subject, *Empathy and the Novel* (2007),[1] from the fellow-feeling of eighteenth-century moral sentimentalism, to the role-taking imagining of Romanticism, to the projection of feeling onto inanimate objects theorized by late-nineteenth-century German aesthetics as *Einfühlung*. His work reveals *bounded strategic empathy* for his fictional creations, Wessex countrymen and women; his *ambassadorial strategic empathy* for animals and select members of despised outgroups; and his *broadcast strategic empathy* for feeling humanity in an indifferent, Godless universe. As Eve Sorum has described, Hardy forges a geo-empathy, which brings a geographical viewpoint into near fusion with an empathic perspective (Sorum 180). His targets of strategic narrative empathy[2] provide a case study of a single author employing all three modes, bounded, ambassadorial, and broadcast empathy, over the course of a career of writing. I extend here my earlier theorizing about strategic empathy with a sampling from a writer whose articulation of altruistic representational goals parallels the elaboration of empathy and *Einfühlung* by psychologists and aestheticians in the same years. The

1. See Keen, *Empathy and the Novel* 142–43; see also Keen, "A Theory of Narrative Empathy" (2006).
2. See Keen, "Strategic Empathizing: Techniques of Bounded, Ambassadorial, and Broadcast Narrative Empathy" (2008).

chronology of the examples I employ suggests, moreover, a development in Hardy's work, with bounded empathy obvious in Hardy's earliest fiction (especially his pastoral novels such as *Under the Greenwood Tree* and *Far from the Madding Crowd*), ambassadorial empathy for animals and outgroups showing forth in his mature fiction, and broadcast empathy in the strange form of *Einfühlung* for inanimate objects and impersonal forces in his narrative poetry (mainly a product of his later years). Yet close analysis of passages from Hardy's narratives, as in *A Pair of Blue Eyes,* show a characteristic blend of situational empathy, personal distress, and broadcast *Einfühlung* within a novel that provides an early example of Hardy's ambassadorial errand on the part of auto-didactic young men who would attempt to transcend artisan-class origins.

Hardy's diction and notes show his knowledge of the related concepts, sympathy and altruism. During Hardy's writing career, the term sympathy (feeling *for* someone) was differentiated from empathy (feeling *with* someone). The "evolutionary significance of sympathy" had been established by Darwin in 1871 in *The Descent of Man*.[3] For Hardy altruism (now seen as a consequence of empathy and sympathy) included what his contemporaries were already parsing as empathy. Focusing on Hardy's strategic empathizing in selections from his novels, in his epic poem *The Dynasts,* and in several of his shorter verses links Hardy's representational strategies to his evolutionary meliorism and his belief that individual altruism might yet diminish the painful drama of human existence. This chapter details Hardy's employment of aesthetic *Einfühlung* to represent inanimate objects, to feel with the dead, and paradoxically to imagine the evolution of consciousness on the part of the unfeeling Immanent Will.

Einfühlung and Empathy

A contextualist reading of a late-nineteenth-century and early-twentieth-century English author's empathetic imagination might seem perfectly suited to match such a writer's disposition, preoccupations, and developing knowledge of contemporary psychology with developments in the history of science. The articulation of *Einfühlung* and empathy as concepts separate from sympathy in psychology and aesthetics[4] occurs during

---

3. For an excellent treatment of the evolutional debate about sympathy and Hardy's moral agency, see Caroline Sumpter, "Of Suffering and Sympathy: Jude the Obscure, Evolution, and Ethics" (2011).

4. I rely here, for the early history of empathy and *Einfühlung,* on Lauren Wispé, "His-

Thomas Hardy's reading, research, and publishing career (1871–1928). It might be predicted that Hardy, a writer whose works reveal serious study of the psychology and neurology of his day,[5] would be aware of developments in psychological aesthetics that so closely matched his own convictions about human emotions.

The timing is perfect. In 1873 the first important philosophical discussion of *Einfühlung* appeared in a work of visual aesthetics, *Über das optische Formgefühl: Ein Beitrag zur Ästhetik* (*On the Optical Sense of Form: A Contribution to Aesthetics*) by Robert Vischer,[6] just two years after Thomas Hardy published his first novel, *Desperate Remedies* (1871). There Vischer describes a process of human engagement with inanimate forms, one that transports and transplants the viewer into the object, imagining the dead form as living (Vischer 104). Mysteriously, magically, the spectator relates to the object in a way that *reminds* Vischer of the way a human being puts his trust in another human (104), but at this early date in the development of the concept (1873), *Einfühlung* had not yet acquired its central meaning as a description of emotional attachment to other human beings. For Vischer as for other German aestheticians and psychologists of perception in the late nineteenth century, *Einfühlung*, or "feeling into," described an embodied (emotional and physical) response to an image, a space, an object, or a built environment. Vischer described a psychological phenomenon that had already been demonstrated by nineteenth-century poets. As early theorists of literary empathy argued, the Romantic poets not only articulated oneness with the inanimate world but also projected feelings into insensate objects.[7] Hardy was steeped in the poetry of Wordsworth, Keats, and Shelley, whose works demonstrate the action of *Einfühlung* through motor and kinesthetic imagery that evokes a physiological and emotional response in a reader (Fogle 149). Outside of poetry and psychology, the term empathy gained currency among art historians over the next two decades, as it accrued key elements of inward imitation of movement (later known as motor mimicry) and perspective taking. For Hardy, who was trained as an

tory of the Concept of Empathy" (1987).

5. See Lennart A. Björk, *Psychological Vision and Social Criticism in the Novels of Thomas Hardy* (1987); see also Keen, "Psychological Approaches to Thomas Hardy" (2010).

6. Robert Vischer, *Über das optische Formgefühl: Ein Beitrag zur Ästhetik* (*On the Optical Sense of Form: A Contribution to Aesthetics*) (1873). Page number citations refer to the English translation, in Robert Vischer, *Empathy, Form, and Space: Problems in German Aesthetics, 1873–1893* (1993).

7. See Richard Harter Fogle, "Empathetic Imagery," *The Imagery of Keats and Shelley: A Comparative Study* (1949).

architect, serious study of art theory and history was an early project. His "Schools of Painting" notebook, dated 12 May 1863, records the start of an autodidactic project that was to continue, in more desultory fashion, through reading, museum visiting, and European travels.[8] He certainly could have become aware of *Einfühlung* as early as the 1870s, though he does not refer in his notes, self-scripted biography, or letters to Bernard Berenson, the most likely art-historical source in English after 1895.[9]

Though Hardy was proud of his ability to read ancient languages and could get around in French, among the modern European languages, he gained most of his knowledge from works written or translated into English. His German was weak, so transmission of *Einfühlung* to an English language context in the 1890s thus makes Hardy's awareness of the concept and term more likely. In 1895, just as *Jude the Obscure* came out, the English novelist Vernon Lee (Violet Paget) introduced the concept of *Einfühlung* to a London audience (Colby 155–58), later publishing the lecture[10] as articles in *The Contemporary Review,* a journal from which Hardy frequently made extracts. By 1913 Vernon Lee had adopted Lipps's "empathy" for *Einfühlung,* following Titchener's coinage of empathy as a translation of *Einfühlung* that chimed with but distinguished the concept from sympathy (Titchener 21). Lee's aesthetic theory thus shifted from *Einfühlung's* motor mimicry (bodily sensations and muscular adjustments) to empathy's inclusion of memories and awakened emotional states as key elements of an audience's collaborative responsiveness to art, indeed to perception broadly construed. In her most elaborated version of the concept, Lee argues that empathy is a constitutive element of "imagination, sympathy." Lee, like Hardy, was reading the French Darwinian psychologist Ribot, but, as Carolyn Burdett has suggested, she set her theorizing against Spencer's evolutionary psychology.[11] Her emphasis shifted from the largely physiological response of *Einfühlung* to a mental conception of empathy (Burdett). Lee described empathy as "that inference from our own inner experience which has shaped all our conceptions of an outer world, and given to

8. Thomas Hardy, "Schools of Painting" notebook, in Richard H. Taylor, ed., *The Personal Notebooks of Thomas Hardy, with an Appendix Including the Unpublished Passages in the Original Typescripts of* The Life of Thomas Hardy (1979).

9. For the relationship of Berenson's tactile imagination to *Einfühlung,* see Wellek, *Discriminations* (1970) 173–74, 178.

10. For the article version of this lecture, see Vernon Lee and C. Anstruther-Thomson, "Beauty and Ugliness" (1897).

11. See Carolyn Burdett, "'The Subjective Inside Us Can Turn into the Objective Outside': Vernon Lee's Psychological Aesthetics" (2011).

the intermittent and heterogenous sensations received from without the framework of our constant and highly unified inner experience" (Lee, *Beautiful* 68). This view certainly resonates with Hardy's depiction of the limited, partial, and affectively charged perspective of human agents in a complex universe that he was to develop most fully in his long Napoleonic dramatic epic, *The Dynasts* (1904, 1906, 1908).

The Dynasts relates history through dramatic scenes of famous individuals and ordinary citizens, who do not realize that they are not in control of their own actions. Scenes of an Overworld populated by Phantom Intelligences (the Spirits and Choruses of the Years, Rumour, Sinister, Ironic, and the Pities; the Shade of the Earth, Recording Angels, and Spirit-Messengers) provide the explanations that human agents cannot perceive. One of these, the Spirit of the Pities alone has the job of articulating the emotional responses to events, through its universal sympathy with human nature (*Dynasts* v. 4, 7). Like Lee's empathy, Hardy's brief for the function of the Spirit of the Pities in *The Dynasts* mediates between inward emotionality and the events of the outer world, registering the impact of blows dealt by the uncaring Will. The Spirit of the Pities, though impressionable and inconsistent in its responses to human events (7), provides an emotional version of their meanings that make better sense to humans, with all their limitations, than the dispassionate historicizing of the Spirit of the Years or the grim commentary of the Spirits Ironic and Sinister. Empathizing with the participants in and victims of the events of *The Dynasts* is a fruitless task for the Spirit of the Pities, because it cannot act compassionately or altruistically to intervene and avert the disasters into which human agents blunder. Yet for Hardy, the Spirit of the Pities' strenuous insistence on responding feelingly to those actions assists readers' comprehension of the workings of a vast, indifferent universe. To paraphrase Lee on empathy, the Spirit of the Pities speaks inferences about humans' inner experience in the face of confusing and various stimuli from the Immanent Will driving the universe (*Beautiful* 68). Hardy's empathetic Spirit of the Pities testifies to the way inner experience feels even if the human agents cannot understand the reason for their actions, and points with some hope to a future in which the Will, who impels those actions without knowing it, might evolve into consciousness.

Hardy often pointed out the cruel irony that evolution had resulted in an unfeeling universe populated by emotional creatures (*Life and Work* 153, 227). That affective impulses drive human and animal behavior was an article of faith in Hardy's "evolutionary meliorism" (*LL* v. 2,

319), and he knew that literature "must like all other things keep moving, becoming" (324) to keep up with natural, if gradual change. As a poet of juxtaposed tones and moods, alternatively satirical, poignant, and humorous, he depended upon an empathetic reader, whose role he described thusly: "I must trust for right note-catching to those finely-touched spirit who can divine without half a whisper, whose intuitiveness is proof against all the accidents of inconsequence" (322). That an intuitive and bodily responsiveness to art verified the alert consciousness of an onlooker Hardy was convinced. Not everyone was equipped to respond feelingly, and even fewer to craft the works that called out to an audience of finely touched spirits. Artists enjoyed a Shelleyan status in Hardy's understanding, and he described poetry and literature as "the visible signs of mental and emotional life" among humans (324). Where that life was evident, hope for further evolution of an intuitive audience for art, and effective techniques for striking the right notes for them to receive, could be sustained.

In the same period as Hardy's installments of *The Dynasts*, early-twentieth-century psychologists and aestheticians considered the relationships between empathy and the literary techniques that called upon readers' feeling responses. Informed by the experimental psychology of Titchener and the aesthetic psychology of Theodor Lipps,[12] Vernon Lee's book *The Beautiful: An Introduction to Psychological Aesthetics* (1913) solidified the place of empathy (*Einfühlung*) in English-language theories of aesthetic response (*Beautiful* 66–67). Empathy, asserts Lee, "explains why we use figures of speech" even when we know a figurative phrase expresses the "exact reverse of the objective truth" (62). Lee was especially concerned to explain human responses to the inanimate world (putting this habit of mind ahead of responses to art and to other humans). According to Lee, we understand better when we project bodily sensations, memories and emotions onto the inanimate objects we behold and describe in figures of speech. The facts may confute figures of speech, but we authenticate figures of speech through our feelings. The mountain persists in rising above us even though we know it is actually stationary or shrinking, through erosion (65–66). Paradoxically, Lee argues: "Without [empathy's] constantly checked but constantly renewed action, human thought would be without logical cogency, as it certainly would be without poetical charm" (69). For Lee, vertiginous waves of empathetic feeling

---

12. See Theodor Lipps, *Äesthetik: Psycholgie des Schönen und der Kunst* (1903, 1906); "Das Wissen von Fremden Ichen" (1906); and *Zur Einfühlung* (1913).

for the size of the mountain are checked by cognition (awareness that the mountain doesn't really "rise") but come right back as we gaze up at its height. Again it seems to rise as we perceive it, trumping knowledge with the experience of embodied cognition, in this case of geological features, mass, and scale in relation to a small human body. For Lee the vacillation between a felt perception and a known object of perception brings about both logic and aesthetic pleasure.

Like the early-twentieth-century aesthetic theorists who speculated about the operation of human emotions on understanding and responsiveness to artistic representations, Hardy explored different roles of the emotions in reaching or balking understanding. Hardy not only theorized the emotional transaction between artist and audience, but also depicted emotional responsiveness to things, events, and other people on the part of his fictional characters. Emotions were a strong force but they did not invariably lead to improved perception, as in his aesthetic theory, where only a few finely touched spirits could catch the right notes, a musician's metaphor for attuned perception. Hardy was a committed monist and materialist writer who read the evidence of his senses. He thought that the action of the emotions on and through human behavior led to tangles of unintended consequence and misunderstanding. He saw these as the basis for tragic narratives; responding to sexual desires, for example, inevitably revealed characters' "monstrous dysfunctions of natural instinct and passion," as John Kucich puts it (Kucich 131).

For Hardy human feelings and impulses typically failed to lead to understanding and right decisions—as I have earlier shown, nescience was one of his keywords—but his authorial empathy still provided a way into the thicket of memory and experience in his work. Hardy recorded intense emotional fusion with others (alive and dead), with objects redolent of past lives, and with earlier versions of himself, in what he called "moments of vision."[13] He narrated his characters' and speakers' feeling connections with absent others and the objects that provoked memories of them, as in "The Workbox" (SC v. 2, 117–18). He dramatized the physiological responses of his characters to things and to one another. In *Poems of the Past and the Present,* he humanized material surfaces: "Here is the ancient floor, / footworn and hollowed and thin" ("The Self-Unseeing," PPP v. 1, 206, ll. 1–2). He generalized from his own experience to those of others:

---

13. *Moments of Vision and Miscellaneous Verses* (1917).

Childlike, I danced in a dream;
Blessings emblazoned that day;
Everything glowed with a gleam;
Yet we were looking away!
(ll. 9–12)

To fail to perceive a moment in the moment and to grant it all its emotional force in retrospect describes an operation of empathy on the poet's own memories, in which the dead past is reanimated through emotional fusion.

Einfühlung and empathy resonate in Hardy's poetry of bereavement. The year Lee published *The Beautiful,* Thomas Hardy wrote most of the poems that would appear in his elegiac sequence *Poems of 1912–13,* later published in *Satires of Circumstance* (1914). In the Emma poems, Hardy's materialist, anti-supernatural philosophy seems to relent into a wistful credulousness, even a belief in ghosts, but Hardy the poet never stops the introspective investigation of the operations of his own (and his speaker's) mind in mourning. His figures of speech and descriptions invest a landscape with a whole emotional history (in "The Going," "I Found Her Out There," and "Beeny Cliff," among others), an effect stronger than memory. Empathetic feeling for his grieving self, for his younger persona and his beloved, and for the very places of their courtship in years past makes palpable to readers the emotional memories evoked by places and sensations. The empathetic imagining initiates a process of transferring private memories and sensations to a verbal form that makes them public. The specific representations of cliff top rides or ordinary days are not in themselves empathetic, but the process by which Hardy revisits and revivifies memories thematizes aspects of empathy. For instance, in "Under the Waterfall" (*SC* v. 2, 45-46) where the poet gives voice to the beloved's perspective with a female speaker,[14] Hardy describes how strong emotion marks the woman's body forever, so an arm plunged into cold spring water inevitably recalls a particular day of courtship, when a drinking glass fell, irretrievable, into a "little abyss" (1. 37) in a spring-

---

14. "Under the Waterfall" is the last poem in *Satires of Circumstance* before the elegiac sequence "Poems of 1912–13" begins (*SC* v. 2, 45–46). It can be regarded as a prefatory memory, spoken in the voice of the once-beloved wife before she dies, but set outside the poems that mourn her passing. Evidence that the episode belongs to Hardy's and Emma's courtship survives in Hardy's sketch of Emma reaching for the glass, reproduced in Claire Tomalin, *Thomas Hardy: The Time-Torn Man* (2006), illustration 14.

water stream. The poem represents the physical evocation of memory twice, balancing on a fulcrum in which an interlocutor questions it:

> "Whenever I plunge my arm, like this
> In a basin of water, I never miss
> The sweet sharp sense of a fugitive day
> Fetched back from its thickening shroud of gray" (ll. 1–4)

> . . .

> "And why gives this the only prime
> Idea to you of a real love-rhyme?
> And why does plunging your arm in a bowl
> Full of spring water, bring throbs to your soul?" (ll. 17–20)

> . . .

> "And, as said, if I thrust my arm below
> Cold water in basin or bowl, a throe
> From the past awakens a sense of that time,
> And the glass we used, and the cascade's rhyme" (ll.. 39–42)

The bodily memory of the past, linking temperature, motion (the sudden plunge or thrust), sound, and the specific August picnic-day, regularly recurs ("*whenever* I plunge my arm"): the speaker can count on it happening every time. This emotion-generating recurrence of the fleshly sensation connects in the verse to the metaphor of an unbroken loving-cup, "that chalice of ours" (l. 48) from which the couple long ago "In turns therefrom sipped lovers' wine" (l. 52). As long as the bodily rush of feeling calls back the remembered day, as long as the dropped glass remains under the waterfall contributing to its sound, the love-communion reactivates its eternizing promises. In direct contradiction of experience, for Hardy and Emma's marriage was strained and other love memories evidently leave a painful "smart" (l. 8), the poem's insistent reenactment of emotional fusion (of the physical response to cold water and passionate recollections), in "constantly renewed action" testifies to the power of *Einfühlung* to animate a figure of speech, as Lee theorized (Lee, *Beautiful* 69). Through its repetitions the poem calls on readers' empathy to feel what the speaker has felt, overwriting their own neutral experiences of arms reaching into cold water with her charged narrative reenactments. It also implicitly raises the question of whether the love embedded in the glass survives when the speaker's particular arm can feel no more.

Hardy does not shy away from the question of whether an empathetic projection into an inanimate object persists when the living and feeling body is gone. It is one thing to imply that a dropped goblet preserves a love-memory after the loving person dies: indeed, "Under the Waterfall" enacts the indefinite prolongation of just such a joined memory and sensation. What about a sensation attributed to a formerly live, but now inanimate body? Can the imagination feel what the corpse cannot sense? According to the projective aesthetic theory of empathy, it can. In "Rain on a Grave" (*SC* v. 2, 50–51), Hardy projects himself into the burial place of his dead wife Emma, flinching for her as the rain falls on her insensate body:

> Clouds spout upon her
> Their waters amain
> In ruthless disdain,—
> Her who but lately
> Had shivered with pain
> As at touch of dishonour
> If there had lit on her
> So coldly, so straightly
> Such arrows of rain (ll. 1–9)

As *Einfühlung* does not require an animate target for emotional projection to work, Hardy's grieving imagination does not just feel for, but feels *with* the unfeeling corpse. This retroactive empathy for a dead woman's body paradoxically emphasizes both its lifelessness and its corporeality. Later in the poem he wishes to swap places with Emma's buried body, or better yet, to join her in the ultimate corporeal fusion, "Would that . . . . together / Were folded away there / Exposed to one weather / we both" (ll. 19–24). The conventional expressions of elegy, which Hardy knew well from his studies of the classical and English tradition,[15] could provide models for both his extreme death wish and his more moderated pleasure in the daisies that grow from her decaying corpse. He combines this with affective stages of projection, shared sensation and withdrawal. We may venture this much: In Hardy's Emma poems, a living body haunts itself using the projections of *Einfühlung*. This helps to solve the conundrum of these elegies, which show so much feeling for a woman with whom the writer was so manifestly out of sympathy. Guilt may have been the driver, but empathy was the device.

---

15. On the relation of Hardy's elegies to the tradition, see Jahan Ramazani, *Poetry of Mourning: The Modern Elegy from Hardy to Heaney* (1994) 33–68.

The coincidences of theme and form, the felicitously overlapping dates that document the migration of an emergent understanding of empathy in psychology and aesthetics into an English-language context through the popular media of the day, may verify Hardy's awareness of the concepts, empathy and *Einfühlung*. The debut of empathy, so named, occurs during the very years when Thomas Hardy, a reader of psychological literature, might be expected to encounter it through his reading and conversation with scientists,[16] but he never uses the word in his published works. (He used other technical terms from psychology, such as the unconscious, magnetism, impulse, hallucination, hypnosis, insanity, reflex, sense-perception, psychic, and psychological.) *Einfühlung,* like empathy, is absent from the written record of Hardy's wide-ranging reading. Though he could have heard Vernon Lee speak about empathy or seen her essays on *Einfühlung* in *The Contemporary Review,* he did not make extracts from them in his *Literary Notebooks.* Because Hardy *did* read and excerpt other essays by Vernon Lee, historical essays and critical works on the novel (*Literary Notebooks* v. 1, 157, 165), it is possible that he also read her psychological studies of empathy and aesthetics. Yet these subjects were not entirely segregated in Lee's early work. In one of Lee's essays from which Hardy copied out a passage, an 1885 essay from *The Contemporary Review,* she broaches an early version of her aesthetics of the beautiful as involving psychological and sympathetic interests ("Dialogue" 387–88). Lee herself would not begin substituting empathy for sympathy for another ten years. Was Hardy was aware of Lee's accounts of contemporary research on empathy? The absence of the word empathy from his published work suggests he may not have known the theorizing connected to the new term, but a cluster of related words, including sympathy, lovingkindness, fellow-feeling, and most importantly, altruism, indicate his parallel interests.[17]

Hardy's discussion of altruism (under this name), suggests that he knew perfectly well the phenomenon of empathy, how it worked, and

16. For instance, Thomas Hardy had a close friend towards the end of his life in Henry Head, the distinguished medical neurologist and editor of the journal *Brain*. See L. S. Jacyna, *Medicine and Modernism: A Biography of Sir Henry Head* (2008). Earlier in his career, Hardy's club, the Athenaeum, provided opportunity for contact with the many scientists and medical men among its members. Many of those conversations naturally went unrecorded, but Hardy did make note of an 1893 conversation with James Crichton-Browne, a medical psychiatrist and co-founder of the journal *Brain* (Millgate, *Life and Work* 275).

17. In his published work, Hardy employs the word *sympathy* 81 times and *sympathetic* 28 times. *Compassion* appears 11 times, clustering in later works with 3 uses of *compassionate*. *Fellow-feeling* appears in the bird-clacker scene of *Jude the Obscure:* in context, the fellows are animals rather than other boys like Jude.

what risks an artist ran in relying upon it. Altruism has been linked with empathy (feeling *with*) by psychologists throughout the twentieth century as a potential consequence of empathetic response.[18] In Hardy's time, sympathy (feeling *for*) was associated with altruism. Indeed, sympathetic emotion and its subsequent benevolent action were often conflated in the single word *altruism*, following Auguste Comte (1798–1857), who coined the term.[19] Hardy was a reader of Comte and Comteans. Amongst the materials prepared near the end of his life for his second wife, Florence Emily Hardy, to incorporate into *The Early Life* and *Later Years* (books that would be published after Hardy's death as biographies by F. E. Hardy) was a manuscript note on "H's Altruism." The note, written in pencil on the back of an envelope postmarked 1927, conflates a definition of empathy with the term altruism:

> It must not be forgotten that H's own life & experiences had been smoother & happier than many—perhaps than the majority. It was his habit, or *strange* power of putting himself in the place of those who endured sufferings from which he himself had been in the main free, or subject to but at brief times. This altruism was so constant with him as to cause a complaint among his readers that he did not say "all's well with the world" because all was well with him. It should really have caused commendation.
>
> (*Personal Notebooks* 291–92, original emphasis)

Following Percy Shelley on the role-taking imagination, Hardy describes his uncanny powers of perspective taking, in which he puts himself in the place of sufferers. Shelley's great goodness, described in his *Defense of Poetry*, requires that a man "imagine intensely and comprehensively" (Shelley 16). For this empathetic process Shelley uses the language of identification, which Hardy augments with the term altruism. Hardy's early

---

18. In twentieth-century psychology, altruism is understood as voluntary helping behavior that benefits another at a sacrifice to the helper, while the emotional response (feeling with another person) that sets up the conditions for helping is called empathy. The empathy–altruism hypothesis, as articulated and investigated by psychologist C. Daniel Batson, demonstrates that empathy can spur prosocial behavior. See C. Daniel Batson, *The Altruism Question: Toward a Social-Psychological Answer* (1991). In the twentieth century feeling with another has one name, while the helping that occurs as a result of the feeling has another name. In the nineteenth-century Comtean sources the two stages were understood to part of one phenomenon, altruism.

19. The first appearance of the term *altruisme* occurred in 1851. Soon afterwards the new label for living for the sake of others was disseminated in English. See Auguste Comte, *The Catechism of Positive Religion, 3rd ed.*, trans. Richard Congreve (1858) 66.

reading of Comte, his indebtedness to Herbert Spencer, and his study of the Darwinian, experimental psychology of Théodule Ribot led him to emphasize the altruism inherent in his "*strange* power of putting himself in the place of those who endured sufferings," that is, in his role-taking imagination, now seen as a core quality of human empathy (*Personal Notebooks* 292).

Altruistic Emotions

Late-nineteenth-century and early-twentieth-century theorists of human emotion such as Herbert Spencer and Théodule Ribot sought to reconcile the philosophical claims of moral sentimentalism, which placed sympathy or fellow-feeling at the start of a set of responses that bound people into families, tribes and nations, with a Darwinian emphasis on the individual organism's success. Working with the older and more traditional term *sympathy,* derived from the influential accounts of David Hume and Adam Smith,[20] Victorian psychologists such as Herbert Spencer[21] strove to explain the evolutionary origin, continuing benefit, and likely future course of tender feelings for others. While the attractive idea of human evolution lending itself to social progress fit well with Victorians steeped in the positivism of Comte, the claims of egoism were bolstered by Darwin, especially as understood by Herbert Spencer, who emphasized survival of the fittest (Spencer, *Psychology* v. 1, 88). Herbert Spencer's influential extension of Darwinian theory in his books *The Principles of Psychology* (1855) and *First Principles* (1862) argued that the human mind developed from organic responses to the environment and that human society was the product of evolution of egoistic individuals into social aggregates based on common interests. Thus, while he acknowledged the natural sympathy of humans for each other, particularly as expressed through the parental instinct, Spencer also thought that unselfish concern for others outside the family, let alone altruism, had developed late in human beings (*Psychology* v. 2, 626).

---

20. On sympathy, see David Hume, *A Treatise of Human Nature* (1739), and Adam Smith, *The Theory of Moral Sentiments* (1759). Hardy had the two-volume 1874 edition of Hume's *Treatise* in his library at the time of his death. See Michael Millgate, "Thomas Hardy's Library at Max Gate."

21. Relevant works by Herbert Spencer include *The Principles of Psychology* (1855); *First Principles* (1862); "Morals and Moral Sentiments," *Fortnightly Review* (1871); and *Essays: Scientific, Political and Speculative* (1891).

This differed somewhat from Comte's view, articulated in 1851 when he coined the term altruism (from the Italian adjective *altrui,* meaning others' or other people's) as a component of his new humanist religion, Positivism. Comte used altruism to mean reflective emotions whose impulses worked to benefit others, with ethical consequences for the altruistic person, whose egoism is subordinated. That is, Comte's altruism conflates the emotion and the subsequent behavior, actions that intend to bring happiness to others. While Herbert Spencer saw altruistic feelings as a late development, emerging out of sympathy through the intermediary "ego-altruistic" blend (*Psychology* v. 2, 592–606), Comte saw self and other-directed feelings as equally innate and always at odds with one other. His Positivist religion sought to create conditions in which egoism could be subordinated to benevolence towards others in the exercise of altruism. This highly influential idea was brought into English by G. H. Lewes in 1853, picked up by John Stuart Mill, and championed by the English positivist Frederic Harrison (whom Hardy knew), and adopted, at least temporarily, by novelists and intellectuals primed by earlier moral sentimentalism.[22]

Hardy was among the Victorians who read G. H. Lewes's Comte with care, and in his recollections of 1874, he acknowledged this commonality with George Eliot, with whom he had been linked in critics' speculations about an unsigned early publication: "He had latterly been reading Comte's Positive Philosophy, and writings of that school, some of whose expressions had thus passed into his vocabulary, expressions which were also common to George Eliot" (*Life and Work* 100). It must be acknowledged that Hardy's notes on Comte do not focus on altruism, though he does jot down a key premise, "Feeling—the great motor force of human life" (*Literary Notebooks* v. 2, 68) from Comte's *Social Dynamics* and notes its importance as a driver of the "fundamental notion of continuous [human] development" (72) towards altruism. Yet Hardy could be skeptical, too. He certainly would not have fallen in with Comte's credulousness about phrenology as proving the physiological basis of altruism. Though Hardy was himself an unbeliever, he faulted Comte for omitting Jesus from his calendar of "worthies," therefore rendering his Positivist religion inimical to many who would have otherwise accepted it (*Life and Work* 150–51). He clipped out a magazine article by John

---

22. See G. H. Lewes, *Comte's "Philosophy of the Sciences"* (1853). For an excellent account of the influence of Comte on Victorian intellectuals, see Thomas Dixon, *The Invention of Altruism: Making Moral Meanings in Victorian Britain* (2008). On Thomas Hardy's knowledge of positivist altruism, see Dixon 234–35.

Morley, criticizing Comte and questioning his religion of Positivism as "hardly more than sympathy under a more imposing name" (*Literary Notebooks* v. 1, 80). This does not suggest that Hardy disapproved of sympathy; to the contrary, it was one of his keywords, appearing in his published work eighty-one times, bolstered by the adjectival sympathetic in twenty-eight instances. Sympathy was a fundamental ingredient of his self-declared "evolutionary meliorism," by which "pain to all upon [the globe], tongued or dumb, shall be kept down to a minimum by loving-kindness" (*LL* v. 2, 319).

As his notebooks reveal, Hardy could have derived his Comtean conflation of sympathetic feeling and altruistic action directly from his reading of the French evolutionary psychologist Théodule Ribot. Hardy made extracts from the English translation of Ribot's *Psychology of the Emotions* (1897),[23] particularly noting Ribot's categorization of types of emotion in the course of accounting for the process of affective degradation. Hardy copied out Ribot's scheme, "(1) the disinterested emotions, (2) the altruistic emotions, (3) the ego altruistic emotions, (4) the purely egoistic emotions" (*Literary Notebooks* v. 2, 63). The social and moral emotions Ribot names "altruistic emotions" consist of general benevolence for the whole human race and family feeling, the absence of which result in "absolute indifference to every one" (*Emotions* 430). Ribot regards sympathy as the basis for the tender emotions (230), including altruistic sentiments and ego-altruistic feelings (in Herbert Spencer's terms). Yet Ribot's explanation of the term sympathy indicates that he applies this older term (used by Alexander Bain, Adam Smith and David Hume) to a set of phases that were already being relabeled by German psychologists as *Einfühlung*/empathy: "The first, or physiological [phase], consists in an agreement of motor tendencies, a *synergia;* the second, or psychological, consists in an agreement of the emotional states, a *synaesthesia;* the third, or intellectual, results from a community of representations or ideas, connected with feelings and movements" (231). Ribot's sympathy (232) contains the automatic motor mimicry, emotional fusion consisting in "feeling an emotion existing in another," marked by bodily movements and facial expressions, and affective perspective taking that leads to action on behalf of another (232). These are all elements of the older "sympathy" that were being assimilated to empathy in the late nineteenth and early twentieth centuries.

---

23. Ribot, *La psychologie des sentiments* (1896), translated as *The Psychology of the Emotions,* ed. Havelock Ellis (1897).

Hardy needed neither the new term, empathy, nor the scientific spec-ulations about how sympathy generated altruism, to arrive at parallel conclusions derived from his study of literature and the behavior of the creatures around him. His novels document his observations of animal and human behavior. His literary allusions (especially to Shakespeare and classical dramatists) reveal his mining of earlier literature for insights into universals of character, such as stoical suffering arousing pity and fear, that he depicted in ordinary folk.[24] His poetry shows his dedication to introspection as a mode of discovery. In other words, these qualities do not require a course of reading in psychology to emerge in Hardy's work. Yet he habitually sought confirmation of his interests and hunches in disparate sources, through steady reading. He often made notes of thinkers whose theories supported his own views. Thus in Ribot's work, Hardy found confirmation of his views that individuals have different underlying emotional dispositions (*Emotions* 166), that affective life develops from childhood (234–35), that animals as well as human beings show feelings (236–37), and that tender emotions are the source "of all altruistic, social, and moral manifestations" (236). Indeed, as historian Thomas Dixon notes, in *Two on a Tower* (1882) Hardy associates the word altruism with love, as transcending egotistical self-love and stimu-lating self-sacrificial impulses (Dixon 235).

But Hardy also shows how the feeling does not guarantee the con-sequent action (that is, he anticipates the separation of empathetic feel-ing and altruistic action into two stages, not invariably linked). For in both instances where the word occurs in *Two on a Tower,* altruism describes a fleeting feeling of Lady Constantine's rather than an action taken, for her love for Swithin is powerful, but her self-love is stronger: "Then the instinct of self-preservation flamed up in her like a fire. Her altruism in subjecting her self-love to benevolence, and letting Swithin go away from her, was demolished by the new necessity, as if it had been a gossamer web" (*TT* 244). Hardy suggests here not only the intensity of altruistic emotion, which stimulates at least temporary commitments to self-abnegation, but warns the reader of its fragility: Self-preservation demol-ishes the strands of the gossamer web.

Théodule Ribot's use of the term altruistic as designating a kind of feeling would have resonated not only with these 1882 representations in *Two on a Tower,* but also with Hardy's earlier reading of Herbert Spen-cer. Ribot borrows the terminology of "altruistic," "ego-altruistic" and

---

24. See Jeanette King, *Tragedy in the Victorian Novel* (1978) 97–126.

"egoistic" emotions, as well as his usage of sympathy, directly from Spencer (*Psychology* v. 2, 578–626). By "ego-altruistic emotion," Spencer meant "sentiments which, while implying self-gratification, also imply gratification in others" (595), while purely altruistic sentiments (such as generosity, pity, justice, and mercy) are uncommon precisely because of their unselfishness (607–16). Spencer agrees with Adam Smith that "the root of all altruistic sentiments is sympathy" (Spencer, "Morals" 430), which "gives rise to superior controlling emotions" (430). However, Spencer questions the inevitability of the process by which sympathy develops from the parental instinct and produces higher sentiments such as justice (430; *Psychology* v. 2, 626). Spencer sees human gregariousness as contributing to the expression of higher sentiments, but he also observes that equally powerful needs, such as the predatory instinct that supports self-preservation, checks the development of justice ("Morals" 430). Thus the scientific Spencer separates the feeling and response that Comte fuses into one term, altruism, by questioning the stages in the process and allowing for the intervention of restraint, caution, and egoism. Spencer calls for an explanation of precisely *how* the expectation has developed, that feelings for others lead to higher moral attributes and sentiments (not an inevitability despite Spencer's optimism about human progress). Spencer's own suggestion is that positive reinforcement (pleasurable feelings), religious sanction and public approbation can combine to make concern for general human welfare habitual in an evolved society (431).

Although Hardy's notes on Spencer's science refer to an earlier work, *Principles of Biology* (1864), not to the essays in which Spencer describes ego-altruistic emotion,[25] Hardy certainly read *First Principles,* extracted from his periodical essays, and owned a copy of Spencer's *Essays: Scientific, Political and Speculative* (1865), as well as his two-volume *Autobiography* (1904) (*Literary Notebooks* v. 1, 335–36). Hardy also testified to Spencer's influence on his thinking in letters (Hardy to Lena Milman, 17 July 1893, in *Selected Letters* 85) and Hardy's view, recorded in spring 1890, that "Altruism, or the Golden Rule, or whatever 'Love your Neighbour as Yourself' may be called, will ultimately be brought about . . . by the pain we see in others reacting on ourselves, as if we and they were part of one body" (*Life and Work* 235) matches the psychology and sociology

---

25. In 1924 Hardy wrote to Ernest Brennecke, "My pages show harmony of view with Darwin, Huxley, Spencer, Comte, Hume, Mill, and others, all of whom I used to read more than Schopenhauer." Thomas Hardy to Ernest Brennecke, 21 June 1924 (*Selected Letters* 386).

of Spencer (*Psychology* v. 2, 618). Hardy was clearly profoundly influenced by the hope of improvement in the species expressed in Spencer, though he was convinced of the limited usefulness of the promptings of feelings, which so often in Hardy's narratives lead characters into ironic traps: Michael Henchard, impetuously offering a job to Donald Farfrae because of his warm feeling towards the younger man, makes an enemy of the applicant Jopp, who will be the agent of the Mayor of Casterbridge's undoing; two brothers allow their disgraceful father to drown to advance their sister's marriage prospects, but live on in suicidal dread in the 1894 story "A Tragedy of Two Ambitions" (from *Life's Little Ironies*).

Throughout his prose and verse, Hardy narrates circumstances in which the impulses of feeling beings get them into trouble, but his stories do not take the form of cautionary tales. Instead, they attempt to bind readers through fellow-feeling into one body, humanity unified by concern for one another's welfare. "Mankind," he concluded in 1890 "may be, and possibly will be, viewed as members of one corporeal frame" (*Life and Work* 235), less likely to be pushed around by the Prime Cause. Thus suffering could lead to the evolution of a better situation for emotional humans. Hardy's ambition, expressed in his notes, prefaces, and poems, was destined to be misunderstood, since many readers responded to his narratives as determinist and to his representations of the wrongness and cruelty of the world as pessimistic, rather than as diagnostic shocks designed to provoke the altruism of the future. To see Henchard's suicide, Tess's execution, Eustacia Vye's drowning, or Farmer Boldwood's shooting of Sergeant Troy as opportunities for the development of human sympathy that would improve the lot of the human species requires extraordinary imaginative extension of the part of readers. Yet this is just what Hardy asks, to some of his contemporaries' incredulity. W. P. Trent protested about Hardy's treatment of his characters in *Two on a Tower*, "it is a painful story. The Genius of Pessimism is slowly rising from the magic jar in which our author has endeavored to imprison him. It is almost too much to ask us to sit quietly by" (Cox 241). Hardy told William Archer in a 1901 interview that his "pessimism, if pessimism it be, does not involve the assumption that the world is going to the dogs. . . . On the contrary, my practical philosophy is distinctly meliorist. What are my books but one plea against 'man's inhumanity to man,'—to woman—and to the lower animals?" (Gibson, *Literary Life* 147–48). Nonetheless, reviewers persisted in calling him a pessimist.[26]

---

26. See the comments by a variety of reviewers in Cox, *Critical Heritage*, xxi, xxii, 69, 146, 239, 241–43, 287–89, 408–9.

This response was hardly inexplicable. Imagine, for instance, what it might have been like to be among the first readers of the poem that Thomas Hardy contributed in May 1912 to the Souvenir Programme for the Dramatic and Operatic matinee in Aid of the *Titanic* disaster fund, held in Covent Garden just a month after the event (*SC* v. 2, 11n). Over fifteen hundred people had died, but Hardy's memorial poem "The Convergence of the Twain" (*SC* v. 2, 11–13) spares neither a word of grief for the dead, nor an expression of consolation for the bereaved. Hardy's fiction demonstrates that he noticed drownings (twenty-two deaths by drowning occur in his novels and stories [Fincham 124]), but not one of the documented losses in the Atlantic rates a mention here. The poem does not address the human cost of the *Titanic*'s sinking, but dispassionately addresses the loss of the ship itself, an inevitability designed by the Immanent Will, a prime mover "that stirs and urges everything" (l. 18), including the iceberg that grows as the ship grows. "No mortal eye could see / The intimate welding of their later history" (ll. 26–27) writes Hardy, as the ship and the iceberg head for each other "by paths coincident" (l. 29) until fate, the Spinner of the Years, commands that they crash together. Though the "consummation" of the accident "jars two hemispheres," suggesting the worldwide response to this first modern disaster story, the poem mentions human feelings only negatively. The sunken ship lies far away from "human vanity, / And the Pride of Life that planned her" (ll. 2–3). "Jewels in joy designed / To ravish the sensuous mind" (ll. 10–11) cannot be seen in the dark. The only voice quoted in the poem belongs to the Spinner of the Years, who commands the moment of the crash; the only thoughts attributed to living beings occur in the minds of "Dim moon-eyed fishes" (l. 12). Emptied out of human sympathy, devoid of compassion, and at odds with the conventions of elegiac commemoration, "The Convergence of the Twain" would seem to illustrate both the determinism and the pessimism that Hardy's critics saw in his work.

However, the poem is saturated with *Einfühlung*. The speaker directs the reader to imagine the circumstances of a lonely cold object on the seafloor. She is abandoned, furnace fires out, with "cold currents" making her steel chambers into "rhythmic tidal lyres" (l. 6) whose music no one hears. Hardy evokes a shudder of disgust on behalf of the dead ship when he describes the sea worm moving over her mirrors (l. 9) and employs plosives to spit out her "bleared and black and blind" jewels (l. 12). Embedded in imagery of burial, invasion of boundaries, and penetration by ice, the *Einfühlung* of the poem invites the reader to ignore the *Titanic*'s cargo of corpses and to suffer instead with the wasted fabric of the ship itself.

Then Hardy's narration shifts in the stanza break between sections VI and VII, and he makes of the ship a romance heroine, personifying her construction as natural growth "In stature, grace, and hue" (l. 23). She does not know it, but she is being prepared for a wedding night that will kill her and send her to the ocean floor. Small consolation that the "intimate welding" (l. 26) of the ship and Shape of Ice "jars two hemispheres" (l. 33). Hardy evades empathy with the drowned or sympathy for the bereaved, employing instead *Einfühlung* with the inanimate, feeling into the sensations of the insensate ship.

"The Convergence of the Twain" narrates the kind of world-shaking shock that, in Hardy's most optimistic moments, he imagined as stimulating the evolution of altruism in the human species and feeling sentience in the Immanent Will. Hardy could incorporate death-dealing disaster into his way of thinking because he was a persuaded Darwinian and reader of Thomas Henry Huxley. He wrote, "The discovery of the law of evolution, which revealed that all organic creatures are of one family, shifted the centre of altruism from humanity to the whole conscious world collectively" (*Life and Work* 373–74). In a note that reflects both his reading of Comte and his Darwinian convictions, Hardy remarks "These venerable philosophers [he had been reading Hegel] seem to start wrong; they cannot get away from a prepossession that the world must somehow have been made to be a comfortable place for man" (185), rather than an uncaring universe. Hardy's strategic empathizing did not assume an androcentric world.

In narrative fiction, authorial strategic empathizing takes three forms. The first is *bounded* empathy on behalf of members of one's own group (here it would be highly unusual not to find other people, but one might also discover an honored object, such as the flag, or location, such as the homeland). Bounded empathy is not expected to move readers from outside the group. The second form, *ambassadorial* empathy, attempts to move more distant others on behalf of those represented empathetically, often but not exclusively other human beings. In the nineteenth century compassionate representations of suffering animals advanced the cause of animal welfare through ambassadorial empathy for pit ponies, cab horses, and other working animals. While he exercised his bounded strategic empathy on behalf of ordinary people, highly recognizable to his compatriots as his rustics, Hardy's ambassadorial strategic empathy stretched to members of despised outgroups and animals, especially horses, dogs, and sheep. Never one to don rose-colored glasses when it came to fellow humans, Hardy did not hesitate to show their cruelty, exclusivity, and domineering authoritarianism as well as their openness, kindness and compassion, studying what has been called "the light side and the dark side of group and intergroup behavior" (Liu and László 101).

But for Hardy it was not just the negative dynamics of prejudice, oppression, and stereotyping emanating from humans towards others that stymied the development of altruism. He also perceived the universe itself as inimical to human beings, as revealed by the workings of chance and coincidence in many of his narratives in prose and verse. This points up the remarkable nature of Hardy's most far-flung, broadcast strategic empathy. This third form, *broadcast* empathy, calls upon every reader and most often evokes compassion for universal objects of concern, such as infants and victims of disasters. As in "The Convergence of the Twain," Hardy's empathy involved imaginative projection into the inanimate objects and abstract forces that make up what he depicted as the unconscious universe in which all humans must exist. Paradoxically, his broadcast strategic empathy shows Hardy at his most hopeful, albeit taking a Darwinian long view. At the end of *The Dynasts* he speculates that the Will might yet evolve to consciousness as human beings already have: "Men gained cognition with the flux of time, / And wherefore not the force informing them" (*Dynasts* v. 5, 252). Through evolution pitiable humans might yet find themselves in a universe run by sentient forces, if not by a loving God. If the Immanent Will can know the effects of its actions, even it could develop altruism eventually. Because for Hardy altruism involved the first feeling phase of empathy (his "*strange* power" [*Personal Notebooks* 291]), a closer look at his empathetic representational strategies follows.

Hardy's Strategic Empathizing

Strategic empathizing may call upon similarity with the reader or familiarity of character types or circumstances; it may attempt to transcend differences and move beyond predictably biased reactions to characters representing outgroups or stigmatized behavior; or it may involve a broad call upon universal human experiences as the basis of its efforts to connect through shared feelings and emotional fusion. The three terms I use to distinguish varieties of authorial strategic empathy emphasize the directional quality of authors' imaginative extension and the potential reach of their representations. *Bounded strategic empathy* addresses an in-group, relies on experiences of mutuality, and stimulates readers' feeling with *familiar* others. For Hardy's readers this meant primarily his charming girls and young lovers, like Bathsheba Everdene and Gabriel Oak, "the faithful, modest, sensible hero" of *Far from the Madding Crowd* (W. P. Trent in Cox 237). This kind of empathy is often called upon by the bards of the dominant culture. While bounded strategic empathy may run the risk of preventing outsiders from joining the empathetic circle, it has advantages of eliciting trust through recognition and a sense of rightness. Though other-directed (like all empathy that does not turn into egoistic personal distress[27]), bounded strategic empathy may be marked by signs of both "similarity" and "here-and-now" bias. Developmental psychologist Martin Hoffman describes the limiting effects of these biases: "Although people tend to respond empathetically to almost anyone in distress, they are vulnerable to bias in favor of victims who are family members, members of their primary group, close friends, and people who are similar to themselves; and to bias in favor of victims who are present in the immediate situation" (Hoffman 13–14).

Ambassadorial strategic empathy addresses distant others with the aim of overcoming both similarity and here-and-now bias, calling forth targeted others' empathy for needy strangers, or for the disenfranchised, despised, or the misunderstood among us, often to with specific end in mind. The term is derived from its description of missions of embassy on behalf of others. Appeals for justice, recognition, and assistance that transcend the self-interest of the group often take this form, and this may be marked by contextual clues, as I have earlier theorized: "ambassadorial empathy is most marked by the relationship between the time of reading and the historical moment of publication, when the text gets sent out in the world to perform its ambassadorial duty by recruiting particular readers to a present cause through emotional fusion. That is, ambassadorial strategic empathy is time sensitive, context and issue dependant" (Keen, "Strategic Empathizing," 486). While bounded strategic empathy may also be dated and may respond to a specific situation, it does not attempt to win the attention of an outside audience. Unlike ambassadorial strategic empathy, which bears a burden of explaining as it renders the situation to strangers as it appeals for their attention, bounded empathy may rely on accustomed, routine, or even proverbial understandings shared by the in-group to which it is addressed.

---

27. Personal distress is an aversive empathetic reaction to another's suffering. It is self-directed rather than other-directed and it causes withdrawal from the stimulus rather than helping behavior. See Nancy Eisenberg and Natalie D. Eggum, "Empathic Responding: Sympathy and Personal Distress" (2009) 71–83.

Historical and contextual analysis, as well as scrutiny of the critical response, can recover the evidence of all three forms of strategic empathy at work. Yet the particularity of both bounded and ambassadorial empathy may dilute the emotional response of a temporally remote audience. That is, a critic may recognize that an emotional appeal has been made to a specific audience—for instance to Christian slave-owners in the antebellum American South—without sharing their feelings at all. The original purpose may be revealed in the text but the feelings remain unactivated. A narrative that survives its original context to evoke readers' empathy in a posterity audience, years or generations after its first appearance, transcends bounded and ambassadorial forms of strategic empathy. For this phenomenon, so noticeable when a reader responds to an ancient text, a third term is helpful.

Broadcast strategic empathy, so named because its appeal is scattered widely like seeds thrown across a field emphasizes our common human experiences, feelings, hopes, and vulnerabilities. Broadcast empathy employs universals to reach everyone, including distant others and later readers. It transmits the particularities that connect a far away subject to a feeling reader of virtually any description. It also attempts to overcome both the similarity and here-and-now biases that can limit the range of less robust empathy effects, but it does so by emphasizing commonalities that persist across time, distance, and cultural barriers. It may be as detailed as its ambassadorial relation, or as confident of recognition as its bounded cousin, but broadcast empathy denies any limit to its appeal.

Gaining a better sense of the narrative techniques employed by authors to effect strategic empathizing is an ongoing project, and empirical verification of readers' empathetic responses to these techniques will require further research. Readers may and do sometimes respond indifferently to appeals to their feelings. This is not a matter of readerly incompetence; it reflects differences in readers' dispositions and experiences. I do not expect to find a neat match between authors' strategic empathy and a record of actual reader-response from the three kinds of audiences (the in group; the remote readership; and the universal audience, including readers from later generations). However, I do anticipate that a combination of rhetorical narrative poetics, contextual analysis of narrative works that attempt to evoke empathy, and case studies of individual writers' aim and techniques will allow the differentiation of bounded, ambassadorial, and broadcast strategic empathy.

The current lack of empirical evidence that any one narrative technique or aspect of craft consistently evokes a predictable response from readers reminds those who would decode narrative empathy at the textual level that readers' identities, dispositions, taste, education levels, experiences, and cultural contexts may act to derail narrative empathy as often as they secure the intended response (Keen, *Empathy* 92–99). Readers bring different levels of commitment, expertise, and effort to their part in reading, as Meir Sternberg and Peter J. Rabinowitz have theorized, with the result that they may opt into an authorial audience or remain at odds with the text's invitation.[28] Even for readers electing to join the authorial audience, the genre of the narrative and readers' individual aims in reading can alter both the speed of evaluation and emotional experience. László and Cupchik's empirical studies show that action-oriented stories "characterized by excitement, curiosity or surprise" receive faster readings, while experience-oriented narratives that "concern empathy or identification" receive slower readings (summarized in László 75). In discourse processing investigations, slower reading pace of emotionally evocative passages is often interpreted as a sign of empathy,[29] but no one has demonstrated that the faster reading associated with strong traits of narrativity (curiosity, suspense, and surprise) is decoupled from empathy. Future empirical investigation will likely reveal that readers' empathy is involved in their responses to narrativity, not just to emotionally charged representations that invite identification with characters. Nor does empathy just pertain to representations of other peoples' feelings in narrative. It may be a factor in the illusion of immersion in fictional worlds, through spatial orientation and directional cues. It may be involved in both curiosity and suspense. It probably will even cause faster reading in response to curiosity and suspense, alternated with slower or even arrested reading in reaction to surprise and the second order sympathetic emotions *for* characters, such as concern, apprehension, pleasure, or satisfaction.

Despite these complications, a comprehensive theory of strategic narrative empathy may still emerge and be subjected to systematic empirical evaluation. To that end, it is worthwhile to examine works of writers who hope to reach multiple audiences, from the immediate in-group or coterie, to the author's contemporary audience, to the potential posterity audiences, for traces of their strategic empathizing. (We may also find evidence

28. See Meir Sternberg, *The Poetics of Biblical Narrative: Ideological Literature and the Drama of Reading* (1985), and Peter J. Rabinowitz, *Before Reading: Narrative Conventions and the Politics of Interpretation* (1987).

29. See, for example, the handling of a slower reading speed in David S. Miall and Don Kuiken, "Foregrounding, Defamiliarization, and Affect: Response to Literary Stories" (1994).

of the three varieties of strategic empathizing within the covers of a single work.) Writers who work in a variety of narrative genres make perceptible choices for such scrutiny. A ballad's generic contract differs from an epic's or a novel's, and an individual author's differentiated forms of expression may reach different readers.

Hardy fits all these characterizations. He wrote in many different narrative subgenres (ballad, dramatic monologue, epic poem, short story, and novel), adopting distinct voices for various audiences. As for multiple audiences for an individual work,[30] Hardy was acutely aware of them. Hardy consciously adapted his work to make it appropriate for first publication in journals such as *Cornhill* or the *Graphic,* with family magazine readerships, but he placed the self-censored excerpts in magazines such as the *Fortnightly Review,* to reach more sophisticated adult readers. He restored bowdlerized passages for later book publication of novels that had first appeared in magazines guarded by anxious editors such as Leslie Stephen.

Not only the textual history, but also the reception history of Hardy's work bears the traces of critical preferences for one of his varieties of strategic empathizing over the others.[31] His critics hesitated neither to sort out their preferred targets of sympathetic representation, nor to criticize Hardy's representational strategies. For instance, many of his reviewers preferred his humorous portraits of Shakespearian rustics to his call to comprehend the fate of disempowered tragic agents in a cold universe. Yet they also often complained about the high-flown philosophical discourse given to these rustics, which made them seem unreal and unlike the peasants of critical preconceptions. For Hardy the task of crafting the expressive language of his agricultural laborers had to avoid the Scylla of dialect transcription (incomprehensible to many readers) and the Charybdis of making them talk like books (Cox xix). He did not want them to appear grotesques, for that worked against his goal

---

30. On multiple audiences, see Brian Richardson, "The Other Reader's Response: On Multiple, Divided, and Oppositional Audiences" (1997) and "Singular Text, Multiple Implied Readers" (2007) 259–74. Empirical evidence of the differing impact of fictional representations on the variable audiences of a work can be found in the work of János László, J. H. Liu, and Ildikó Somogyvári. See J. H. Liu and János László, "A Narrative Theory of History and Identity: Social Identity, Social Representations, Society and the Individual" (2007) 98–101; and János László and Ildikó Somogyvári, "Narrative Empathy and Inter-Group Relations" (2008).

31. This shows in the original reviews of Hardy's novels, collected and excerpted by Cox. For an account of the gap between the responses of Hardy's actual readers and his hopes for his implied audience, see T. R. Wright, *Hardy and His Readers* (2003).

of depicting the men and their natures sympathetically, as he wrote in a letter to the *Athenaeum* in 1878 (30 November, 688).

Few in his own time understood as well as William Lyon Phelps, writing in 1910, that for Hardy two themes, sympathy for ordinary humans and contempt for a heartless God or fate, are intertwined:

> [h]is pessimism is mainly caused by his deep manly tenderness for all forms of human and animal life and by an almost abnormal sympathy. His intense love of bird and beast is well known; many a stray cat and hurt dog have found in him a protector and a refuge. He firmly believes that the sport of shooting is wicked, and he has repeatedly joined in practical measures to waken the public conscience on this subject. As a spectator of human history, he sees life as a vast tragedy, with men and women emerging from nothingness, suffering acute physical and sorrow, and then passing into nothingness again. To his sympathetic mind the creed of optimism is a ribald insult to the pain of humanity. (Cox 413)

By far the majority of Hardy's critics complained about his pessimism rather than recognizing his critique of optimism. Hardy asserted in his preface to the Wessex Edition of his works that he had never intended to advance a consistent philosophy, recording instead impressions of the moment, over the course of a forty-year career. "That these impressions have been condemned as 'pessimistic,'" Hardy complained, "—as if that were a very wicked adjective—shows a curious muddle-mindedness." He sought only the truth, he claimed, but he acknowledged that he was attuned to a certain register: "Differing natures find their tongue in the presence of differing spectacles. Some natures become vocal at tragedy, some are made vocal by comedy, and it seems to me that to whichever of these aspects a writer's instinct for expression the more readily responds, to that he should allow it to respond" ("General Preface to the Wessex Edition" xiii).

That the critical resistance to Hardy's treatment of his tragic characters in his own time has been reversed in subsequent generations reminds us that a novelist's strategic empathizing may only meet a responsive audience in later periods. A novelist's strategic empathizing on behalf of members of despised outgroups may even help to shift the boundaries of a culture's empathetic circle if the fictional representation meets favorable circumstances for translation into political and social change. In his 1912 postscript to the Wessex edition of his 1896 novel, Hardy cited his contemporaries' observation that Ruskin College, founded at

Oxford for workingmen in 1899, "should have been called the College of Jude the Obscure"(*Jude* xlv). Belief in an individual author's ability to effect change through fictional representations, however, can be shattered when the work meets an uncomprehending or hostile audience, unready to stretch beyond a comfort zone hedged about by conventional morality. Thus Hardy had earlier reported "the only effect of [*Jude the Obscure*] on human conduct that I could discover [was] its effect on myself—the experience completely curing me of further interest in novel-writing" (xlv). To rephrase this complaint in a positive form suggests that for Thomas Hardy, novel writing and altering human conduct were ideally linked. As Harvey Curtis Webster long ago observed, "Hardy not only shows us the worst contingencies that a man may be called upon to meet; he also shows us that much of the misery man suffers in remediable by greater social enlightenment" (Webster 189). His strategic empathizing, in bounded, ambassadorial, and broadcast forms, reveals a life-long project of attempting to revise human conduct, in a modest version of the Positivist religion of humanity, tempered by skepticism.

A case study of an individual author's techniques cannot answer all the questions about how strategic narrative empathy works (when it *does* work), but it can provide suggestive patterns and a template for subsequent research on the intersections of authorial temperaments, representational strategies, and evocative content. Hardy makes a good subject for such research because of his artistic temperament, well described by James Gibson, who noted "Hardy's feeling that we lived in a flawed world." Commenting on the word "common lot" in Hardy's poem "To An Unborn Pauper Child" (*PPP* v. 1, 163), Gibson writes of the Hardy's sensitivity to the shared suffering of all living beings:

> This sympathy for individuals and his compassion for all of Nature's creatures (and his sympathy for animals is everywhere present) result from the universality of his vision. We live on a blighted world but we are on it together, and for Hardy, our only hope is that lovingkindness—a word he uses again and again—would spread among the peoples of the world and we would realise that we are all members of one family, one community. (*Literary Life* 6)

To move from this broad view to the particulars of Hardy's artistry of empathetic engagement is the next step. Attention to elements of craft, Hardy's representations, and contexts involved in his strategic empathizing reveals a blend of thematizing of broad topics for general sympathy (the rural poor, the unborn, the mentally or physically ill), targeted representations of individual subjects inviting compassion (a slaughtered pig, starving birds, a fallen woman), and foregrounding operating by way of striking words and phrases (as in "The Convergence of the Twain," discussed above).[32] Hardy's narrative techniques for representation of individual consciousness and intermental minds, his manipulation of pace and location, and his experiments with externalized, behavioral narration augment his sympathetic themes. The variation in the individual targets of Hardy's own empathy and *Einfühlung* highlight his tactics for stimulating altruism, beginning with empathy for a range of sufferers, from people alive and dead, to dumb animals, to insensate fossils and material objects. Hardy's life-long mental habits involved "putting himself in the place of those who endured sufferings from which he himself had been in the main free, or subject to but at brief times" (*Personal Notebooks*, 291–92). Part of what was "strange" about Hardy's empathy was that it did not depend on shared experience or even common humanity. Hardy's self-proclaimed other-directedness prompts a close look at those sufferers in his representations.

Hardy's bounded strategic empathy draws his literate, middle and upper class contemporaries' attention to the individuality and humanity of people they categorized as peasants. To Hardy's contemporaries, his "rustics" or "peasants" were among his most successful representations, both because they were often humorous characters, but also because they were sympathetically drawn. Hardy saw his depictions as portraits and composites made of individuals rather than as representative types. Even when employing them as a Greek chorus commenting on the tragic action of higher-class characters in his narratives, Hardy individuated each member of the group. In his own view this distinguished Hardy from those who would stereotype an agricultural laborer as "Hodge." He worked against such generalization in his fiction and in more polemical writings for magazines. As Hardy writes in his essay, "The Dorsetshire Labourer" (1883), "It seldom happens that a nickname [Hodge] which affects to portray a class is honestly indicative of the individuals composing that class" ("Dorsetshire" 252). Once you get closer to agricultural laborers, Hardy suggests, you do not see a group of undifferentiated Hodges. He goes on

---

32. "The Convergence of the Twain" makes an excellent exhibit of Hardy's diction, which delays reading pace and stalls comprehension as he builds sympathy for the "alien" forms of ship and ice (*SC*, 11–13). For the relation of foregrounding and empathy, see Miall and Kuiken "Foregrounding" 389–407 and David S. Miall, *Literary Reading: Empirical and Theoretical Studies* (2006) 77, 144.

to describe an imaginary stay with rural workfolk that would erase such habits of generalization. His novels and stories provide readers with proxy visits with their countrymen and women, offering a route to the familiarity that would disabuse readers of set views about laborers' uncouth speech, uncleanliness, misery, and laziness. In fact, Hardy's depiction of the speech, individualized dress, beliefs, behavior, work habits, and leisure practices of countrymen and women was one of the most appreciated aspect of his early fiction,[33] in *Under the Greenwood Tree* (1872), *A Pair of Blue Eyes* (1873), *Far from the Madding Crowd* (1874), and *The Return of the Native* (1878). He did not just make exhibits of quaint laborers with their folk customs, however; he emphasized the economic realities that shaped their lives, and even when employing them in a group to provide a Greek chorus as a backdrop to the main action, he insisted on their individual humanity.

This shows in Hardy's depiction of the ailments from which they suffered. Some of his countryfolk, such as Thomas Leaf, exhibit the symptoms of mental retardation (presumably the source of G. K. Chesterton's disparaging remark about Hardy as "the village atheist brooding on the village idiot" (Chesterton v. 16, 262). Others, such as Michael Henchard and Farmer Boldwood, are depressed or monomaniacal (exhibiting symptoms of obsessive-compulsive disorder). Individual characters of Hardy suffer from sleep paralysis, the hearing disorder tinnitus, and Hardy even captures the uncontrollable blurts of speech of a character, Andrew Randle, who is afflicted with Tourette's syndrome. The effect of these fine-grained distinctions of personality among characters who might otherwise blur into an indistinguishable background is to invite recognition of them as individuals, though they are seen from the outside and identified, as flat characters, by their distinctive ailments.

Thus William Worm, a minor servant-class character from *A Pair of Blue Eyes*, complains of the "frying o' fish" and "fizz, fizz, fizz" (*PBE* 211) that he experiences inside his head due to tinnitus, each time he appears in the novel. In a reunion scene in that novel, members of the protagonist Stephen Smith's family gather at his childhood home to welcome him back to the neighborhood. Awkwardly for the anxious and class conscious Stephen, the gathering includes lower class neighbors and servants, including William Worm, doing his comic-pathetic turn as a man afflicted with hearing impairment. Hardy does not focus the reader's attention on

---

33. For a selection of reviews praising the detailed representation of Hardy's workfolk, see Cox.

Worm's ailment, for the bounded empathy exercised by Hardy here does not depend on author or reader being a tinnitus sufferer. Hardy instead counts on recognition of a familiar circumstance in a small nineteenth-century rural community, where people of middling and lower orders rub along together. Writing to more educated, class-conscious contemporaries, Hardy serves up Worm as a version of that local figure, well-known by his typical conversational gambits, who evokes compassion, irritation, and embarrassment from the socially mixed group. Hardy foregrounds Stephen's adolescent embarrassment, emphasizing the social sensitivities of a child who feels he has outgrown his parents' social circle. Hardy calls here on situational empathy, a variety of empathy that requires little imaginative extension, since it depends upon memory and is spurred by recognition of a familiar scenario.[34] All readers need to feel the currents of emotion running through the scene is to know how the return of the educated child to a humble household often involves embarrassment as well as pleasure. Yet if Hardy uses Worm to provoke Stephen's mortified response (allying the reader with the educated young man rather than with the servant), he also preserves Worm's individuality, giving him lines and a role in the scene.

The bounded empathy exercised around the appearance of William Worm combines Hardy's deployment of a character type with the greater complexity afforded by others' responses to him. Worm's suffering elicits affable expressions of interest on the part of the other characters: "Have ye ever tried anything to cure yer noise?" (*PBE* 212), they ask, and Worm explains his Christian resolution to live with the condition (if only he can report on it to his friends at every opportunity). Having warmly conjured up Worm's pitiable and mildly exasperating presence, Hardy deftly sketches Stephen's immature resolution "to avoid the vicinity of that familiar friend" in future (214). Stephen's class-crossing pretensions to the hand of Elfride make him ready to disavow his parents' old friends, and his mother colludes with his discomfort, blaming the "rough nature" of Stephen's father for the awkward social mixture of people from the lower and more respectable classes in their household (217). The invitations to a highly social form of empathy crisscross the passage, ranging from straightforward pity for William Worm, to shared embarrassment with Stephen, to recognition of the currents of feeling provoked

---

34. Patrick Colm Hogan differentiates *categorical* empathy, which relies on matches in identity, and *situational* empathy, which depends on a readers' memory of an experience quite similar to that represented as occurring to a character. See Patrick Colm Hogan, "The Epilogue of Suffering: Heroism, Empathy, Ethics" (2001).

by the returned son who sees the parental home through critical eyes. This bounded empathy makes no stressful demand on readers habituated to the servants' comedy of Shakespearean subplots, but it nudges those readers away from comfortable generalizations about country people towards recognition of their particular qualities.

Ambassadorial empathy asks an audience to stretch beyond immediate experiences and easily recognized situations to feel with others less commonly placed within the empathetic circle. In this regard, Hardy's contemporaries noticed his special attention to the feelings of animals. In the middle of the scene discussed above (from *A Pair of Blue Eyes*), a pig gets slaughtered. This is not an unusual event in a farmhouse of the period. Hardy's straightforward description of the "fatted animal hanging in the back kitchen . . . cleft down the middle of its backbone" refers to a familiar sight. The meditation of the pig-killer on the personalities of his porcine victims adds something different: an odd invitation to regard even pigs as individuals. According to the butcher, specific pigs he has known were afflicted by rheumatism, melancholy, deafness and dumbness (*PBE* 213). Here Hardy gives his own attentiveness to the personalities and experiences of farmyard beasts to a butcher, whom readers might otherwise expect to regard the animals with callousness. Indeed, a disregard for the feelings of intelligent animals could be seen as a prerequisite for the job of killing them.

Famously, Hardy's character Jude Fawley fumbles a job of pig-butchering because of an excess of sympathy for the animal, whom Hardy represents as crying with rage and despair at his situation (*Jude* 58–59). Hardy's text uses impersonal and personal pronouns to mark the boundary between animal and meat: while the pig lives and suffers, it is still a gendered living being. Hardy's empathetic imagination shuttles among three points of a triangle, catching Arabella's exasperation at Jude's tender-heartedness, Jude's horror and relief when the animal dies quickly, and the pig's perspective: "The dying animal's cry assumed its third and final tone, the shriek of agony; his glazing eyes riveting themselves on Arabella with the eloquently keen reproach of a creature recognizing at last the treachery of those who had seemed his only friends" (59). Hardy makes his readers visualize the slaughtered pig as a being with a face, whose "lips and nostrils . . . turned livid, then white" (59). He foregrounds the facial expressions and physiognomy that humans and animals share.[35]

---

35. For another perspective on Hardy's faces, see William A. Cohen, "Faciality and Sensation in Hardy's *The Return of the Native*" (2006).

Though these are not the beautiful lips of doomed Tess, they starkly represent the slaughtered animal in his last moments of life. Hardy's fixation on mouths that issue cross-species communications (Tess whistling to the captive birds; the pig crying to its betrayers) models recognition of commonalities of physiology and feeling that invite the leap from immediate involuntary motor mimicry to all-encompassing sympathy, or compassionate concern.

Hardy's representations of suffering animals and his support for antivivisection activism (a conviction he shared with his first wife, Emma) are well known.[36] From his earliest fiction he described the emotions and motives of dogs, sheep, and horses. Even birds and worms received his affectionate representational attention (in *Jude the Obscure,* in "The Darkling Thrush," and in *The Dynasts,* for example). As Michael L. Campbell observes, Hardy's fictional characters can be classified into three distinct types by noting their attitudes towards animals: The overly sensitive compassionate characters who shrink from the harsh world; those who are one with the natural world and its facts of life and death; and those who are so self-oriented that they scarcely notice nature unless it serves a use to them (Campbell 68). He certainly did not expect everyone to conform to the model of the sensitive Jude, nor even to the competent and attentive Gabriel Oak. However, Hardy hoped that a shift in attitudes, extending the Golden Rule's protection of others to the animal kingdom, could occur: "Few people seem to perceive fully as yet that the most far-reaching consequences of the establishment of the common origin of all species is ethical" (*Life and Work* 376–77).[37] In 1909 Hardy explicitly linked his attitude towards animals to his earlier reading of Darwin, writing "The discovery of the law of evolution, which revealed that all organic creatures are of one family, shifted the centre of altruism from humanity to the whole conscious world collectively. Therefore the practice of vivisection . . . has been left by that discovery without any logical argument in its favor" (373–74). Hardy's reading of Darwin is well attested, but we cannot be certain that it included Darwin's *The Expression of the Emotions in Man and Animals* (1872), from which he

---

36. See Michael L. Campbell, "Thomas Hardy's Attitude towards Animals" (1973); John Marks, "Hardy and Kindness" (1995) 52–59; and Ronald D. Morrison, "Humanity towards Man, Woman, and the Lower Animals: Thomas Hardy's *Jude the Obscure* and the Victorian Humane Movement" (1998).

37. Hardy's reading of T. H. Huxley would have reinforced this point. See for example Huxley's "On the Relations of Man to the Lower Animals" in *Evidence as to Man's Place in Nature* (1863), which denies a psychical distinction between the feelings of men and beasts.

took no notes.[38] Hardy could have found there not only many images of the facial expressions of animal and human emotion, but also confirmation of his materialist view of the human species, since Darwin argues for continuities of human emotions with those of animals. These observations about the relatedness of humans and animals certainly resonate with what Hardy wrote about vivisection: "If the practice, to the extent of merely inflicting slight discomfort now and then, be defended [as I sometimes hold it may] on grounds of it being good policy for animals as well as men, it is nevertheless in strictness a wrong, and stands precisely in the same category as would stand its practice on men themselves" (374). It is no surprise then to discover that in Hardy's ambassadorial empathy we often find feelings for animals and humans entangled, as in *Jude the Obscure.*

While ambassadorial strategic empathy often correlates with a contemporary cause, in this case the prevention of cruelty to animals, Hardy's active empathizing on behalf of fellow-creatures went far beyond anti-vivisection activism. There was no lobby working on behalf of the birds that eat farmers' seed out of the fields or for worms that come to the surface after a rainstorm. Hardy represents young Jude Fawley as overcome by fellow feeling for the hungry birds: "He sounded the clacker till his arm ached, and at length his heart grew sympathetic with the birds' thwarted desire. They seemed, like himself, to be living in a world which did not want them. Why should he frighten them away? They took upon them more and more the aspect of gentle friends and pensioners" (*Jude* 9). Stirred to sympathy with the birds, Jude lets them settle for a meal on Farmer Troutham's field and luxuriates in his charity, linked as it is to self-pity: "A magic thread of fellow-feeling united his own life to theirs. Puny and sorry as their lives were, they much resembled his own" (9). In language that emphasizes the uncanny connection forged by sympathy as described by Adam Smith and David Hume, the magic thread of fellow-feeling overlooks drastic differences between the human boy and the flock of rooks, creating a connection that also reveals Jude's low self esteem. Hardy heightens this effect in the following scene. Beaten by the farmer who employs him for dereliction of duty, the punished child skulks away, his fundamental disposition unaltered: "Though Farmer Troutham had just hurt him, he was a boy who could not himself bear to hurt anything" (11). Beholding "scores of coupled earthworms lying half their length on the surface of the damp ground, as they always did in such weather at

---

38. Hardy could have read a précis of Darwin's work on animal and human emotions in Bettany's *Life of Charles Darwin* or in Ribot's *Emotions,* from which he made extracts.

that time of the year," Jude picks his way through "on tiptoes, without killing a single one" (11). Hardy's empathetic effort in this sequence of scenes uses Jude's pity for animals as a conduit for readers' empathy for Jude himself; a reader who heartlessly crushes bugs on the sidewalk can still receive Hardy's embassy on behalf of a sensitive soul.

Hardy's ambassadorial strategic empathy runs in an elliptical orbit from self out to far-off other, where the threads of fellow-feeling touch the remote lives of worms, birds, pigs, dogs, sheep, fallen women, drunkards, and suicidal children. The extension of the imagination made on behalf of these sufferers flows back in its return trip to the author's self. Hardy is always asking his readers for understanding of his own way of feeling and thinking, through proxies such as his fictional characters. For example, shaken by the realization that grown-up life will bring responsibilities that seem to be fulfilled only through cruelty, Jude wishes "If he could only prevent himself growing up! He did not want to be a man" (*Jude* 12). Critics have identified Jude's death wish with Hardy's reading of Schopenhauer, whose pessimistic philosophy also emphasizes animal rights.[39] Hardy himself documents a source closer to home than his reading, as the textual links between his description of Jude's feelings and his own experiences demonstrate. Comparison of the fictional and autobiographical passages show that Hardy drew Jude's experience from his own boyhood. Of Jude's state of mind, he writes:

> Nature's logic was too horrid for him to care for. That mercy towards one set of creatures was cruelty towards another sickened his sense of harmony. As you got older, and felt yourself to be at the centre of your time, and not at a point in its circumference, as you had felt when you were little, you were seized with a sort of shuddering, he perceived. All around you there seemed to be something glaring, garish, rattling, and the noises and glares hit upon the little cell called your life, and shook it, and warped it. (12)

This description catches the perils of living inside a body endowed with a highly empathetic disposition, subject to the "shuddering" response of empathetic distress (Eisenberg and Eggum 71). The personal distress at perceiving the feelings of others most often causes withdrawal from the stimulus: Jude intuits that as "his existence [is] an undemanded one," he should simply not grow up (*Jude* 12). Hardy went through the same

---

39. See, for example, Robert C. Schweik, "The Influence of Religion, Science, and Philosophy on Hardy's Writings" (1999).

thought process as a child. Lying, like Jude, with the sun shining through the "interstices of the straw" hat with which he has covered his face, the boy Hardy reflected "on his experiences of the world so far as he had got" and came "to the conclusion that he did not want to grow up" (*Life and Work* 20) and would prefer to die while still a child. Callously telling his mother his "conclusions on existence, thinking she would enter into his views," Hardy learned to his great surprise that "she was very much hurt" at her son's death wish, "which was natural enough considering she had been near death's door in bringing him forth" (20).

Although in later life Hardy was to welcome serious illness and regret recovery ("A Wasted Illness"), he was not after all a suicide, and he lived into his eighties. His sensitive disposition remained unchanged. Near his death he recalled his early feeling for animals, as when he picked up a dead bird his father had struck with a stone: "It was light as a feather, all skin and bone, practically starved. He said he had never forgotten how the body of the fieldfare felt in his hand: the memory had always haunted him" (*Life and Work* 479). Another early memory involves an exercise in taking the perspective of an animal: "He recalled how, crossing the ewe-leaze when a child, he went on hands and knees and pretended to eat grass in order to see what the sheep would do. Presently he looked up and found them gathered around in a close ring, gazing at him with astonished faces" (479). Ambassadorial empathy on Hardy's part loops back to the perceptive self, fusing "how do they feel?" with "how does it feel for me to feel with them?'

Rather than succumbing to the empathetic personal distress this dispositional openness to others' perspectives brought on, Hardy channeled it into a productive life of fictional world-making. That his works often brought members of despised outgroups into the representational circle suggests one of the ethical uses of his ambassadorial empathy. Hardy wrote compellingly about suicidal depression, divorce, illegitimate birth, and many other experiences he did not directly share. He did his part in a century of reform to bring attention to neglected individuals whose perspectives were unlikely to command the attention of investigative journalists or compilers of Parliamentary blue books. Lennart Björk rightly emphasizes the relationship between Hardy's psychological vision and his social criticism, which made efforts at ameliorating reforms that would lighten the burden of living for afflicted humanity.[40] Yet an account of

---

40. See Lennart Björk, *Psychological Vision and Social Criticism in the Novels of Thomas Hardy* (1987).

Hardy's empathy that stops with either his feelings for sufferers or his focus on his own sensitive feelings would miss a significant element of his imaginative effort, deployed on behalf of inanimate objects and impersonal forces. For this we must turn to Hardy's strangest, even alienating exercise of strategic empathy.

When strategic empathizing invites character identification in particular, it may be prompted by recognition, shared experience, narratorial instructions to engage in perspective-taking, or far simpler invitations to travel with a character, in Wayne Booth's phrase. A common strategy of authorial empathizing involves revelation of characters' inner thought and feelings, but as I have argued earlier, Thomas Hardy employs what Dorrit Cohn calls quoted monologue and narrated monologue (free indirect discourse, *erlebte Rede*) far less often than his contemporaries, relying instead on dialogue, description of behavior and bodily states, and psycho-narration (or narrator's summaries of characters' thoughts and inward states) (Cohn 11–14). Study of Hardy's characters shows the author directing attention to externals of speech and behavior rather than providing thought-transcripts, and detailing circumstances that place his fictional people in highly recognizable *milieux*.

In the novel *A Pair of Blue Eyes,* in the famous "Cliff without a Name" scene, Knight, Stephen's rival, clings to a cliff face while Elfride runs for help (*PBE* 199–206). During her several minutes' absence, Knight's thoughts are detailed by Hardy in a blend of techniques: His usual psycho-narration; uncommon outbreaks of narrated monologue ("Was he to die? . . . He had hoped for deliverance, but what could a girl do?" [201]); and extremely rare quoted monologue ("'She will never come again; she has been gone ten minutes,' he said to himself. . . . 'As many more minutes will be my end,' he thought" [202]). In a situation of extremity, pelted by rain and fatigued, Hardy's character certainly evokes empathy and also sympathy from readers. Those who have physical experience of rock climbing or who have had near-death experiences may be especially primed to feel *with* Knight. Hardy's narrative technique charts the increasing desperation of Knight by providing more and more direct thought transcript until the narrator decorously closes access to the character's mind when he gives up hope of rescue: "Into the shadowy depths of these speculations we will not follow him" (203). The remarkable aspect of this passage resides not in Hardy's modest experiments with mixing modes of representation of consciousness, though that is a striking feature of the episode, but with its invocation of *Einfühlung* for inanimate objects in the natural environment.

Hardy's broadcast strategic empathy ambitiously employs *Einfüh-lung* with dead (no longer animate) creatures and with inanimate objects that never lived, in order to evoke a salutary awareness of human insignificance in the universe. Hanging by his arms on the cliff face, Knight "could only look sternly at nature's treacherous attempt to put an end to him, and strive to thwart her" (*PBE* 199). Right in front of his eyes he sees "an imbedded fossil, standing forth in low relief from the rock. It was a creature with eyes. The eyes, dead and turned to stone, were even now regarding him" (200). Face to face with the embodied, though fossilized perspective of the trilobite, Knight perceives its regard and feels himself into its long lost animation: "It was the single instance within reach of his vision of anything that had ever been alive and had had a body to save, as he himself had now" (200). Sufficiently "fair geologist" to identify the trilobite, its phylum, and its period, Knight's *Einfühlung* extends beyond the individual fossil to the "extremity of the years, face to face with the beginning and all the intermediate centuries simultaneously" (200). Rather than the conventional life-review of near-death experiences, time itself collapses "like a fan before him" (200). Knight's mind projects a temporally elliptical sequence of images that moves backwards from prehistoric humans to "the lifetime scenes of the fossil" animating its stone surroundings, round to the "present and modern condition of things" (201). Scientifically minded Victorians were primed to contemplate "the immense lapses of time each formation represented . . . know[ing] nothing of the dignity of man" (200), but to ponder geologic time at the moment of one's death enacts an extraordinary dissociation from humanity through association with rock remnants of prehistoric life: "He was to be with the small in his death" (200).

Knight's empathetic enlivening of the inanimate trilobite into "lifetime scenes of the fossil" (*PBE* 200), his attribution of agency to the torturing rain and the cliff whose features speak grimness and desolation could seem like a recurrence of animism or superstition, but Hardy makes clear that they are imaginary, an effect brought on by the physical circumstances: "There is no place like a cleft landscape for bringing home such imaginings as these" (200). A rejoinder to the faithful testimony of the eighteenth-century hymn "Rock of Ages," by Augustus Montague Toplady, in which the mortal clinging to the rock finds refuge and hopes for salvation, Hardy's scene on the cliff emphasizes the insignificance of human life in a material world that seems bent on extinguishing it. This is neither the first nor last time in Hardy's writing where he juxtaposes vastnesses of time and space with the perspectives of the feeling human creatures inhabiting them. It is not a consoling vision. He refers to himself as a "time-torn man" in his poetry ("A Broken Appointment" [*PPP* v. 1, 172]). Space was no kinder than time in Hardy's imagination. When Hardy enlivens wastes, endowing landscapes such as Egdon Heath with facial features and personalities, animates abstract forces such as the Phantom Intelligences, and feels into the perspectives of fossils or worn church pavement stones, he exercises *Einfühlung* that is not reciprocated. As we have earlier seen, Hardy was committed to the altruism that follows in the Comtean model from the exercise of the role-taking imagination. Yet he disbelieved in a benevolent God or even a sentient Creator, so he could not pretend that his feelings were returned by the universe. Indeed, he imagined worse.

Hardy bends his perceptions to explore the point of view of The Spirit of the Years in *The Dynasts,* who places human action in the long view of historical narrative. This voice conveys that humans, even world-historical figures, neither understand nor control the meaning of their actions, which are driven by the unconscious Immanent Will. Personifying compassion in the person of The Spirit of the Pities, Hardy worries in *The Dynasts* that the evidence suggests not simply an indifferent universe but a sadistic Creator:

> *The tears that lie about this plightful scene*
> *Of heavy travail in a suffering soul,*
> *Mocked with the forms and feints of royalty*
> *While scarified by briery Circumstance,*
> *Might drive Compassion past her patiency*
> *To hold that some mean, monstrous ironist*
> *Had built this mistimed fabric of the Spheres*
> *To watch the throbbings of its captive lives,*
> *(The which may Truth forfend), and not thy said*
> *Unmaliced, unimpassioned, nescient Will!* (Dynasts v. 4, 386, ll. 50–59)

A "mean, monstrous ironist" for a Creator, who watches "captive lives" suffer in a misaligned universe would be worse even than an unknowing and unfeeling Immanent Will. The fact that anyone in this universe has evolved to feel for self and others is either a cruel joke or worse, a vicious design. Though the Spirit of the Years chides the Pities, "Mild one, be not too touched with human fate" (386, l. 60), Hardy glosses in the passage quoted above a negative ethical consequence of the exercise of *Einfühlung*. If projective imagining on the part of humans endows the lifeless and motiveless universe with feelings, then it transforms the Immanent Will from an indifferent force into a torturer.

Hardy extrapolated from his own experience as an empathizer to the whole human species. He plans in one of his notebook entries for a representation of life in which "The human race [is] to be shown as one great network or tissue, which quivers in every part when one point is shaken" (*Life and Work* 183). For Hardy this unity of the human species in one fabric simultaneously guarantees its interconnection and renders it vulnerable to pains suffered by its members. For full altruism to come out of human role-taking imagination requires further evolution and not only of human beings. Hardy's own *Einfühlung* shows in his projection that the Immanent Will, "the dreaming dark, dumb Thing / That turns the handle of this idle Show" (*Dynasts* v. 5, 254, ll. 79–80), should one day break out of blindness, wake to feeling sentience, and tend "To Its mending / In a genial germing purpose, and for loving-kindness' sake" (255, ll. 98–99). To bring on this evolution of a feeling and conscious Force out of an "Inadvertent Mind" (252, l. 17), according to Hardy, requires the gradual amelioration of human suffering that he called Altruism and described in terms of empathy.

Conclusion

As early as 1873, then, the year of Vischer's discussion of *Einfühlung,* Hardy was already employing all three modes of strategic empathy in his narrative fiction. Rather than surmising a *Zeitgeist* that would explain Hardy's prescience about empathy and *Einfühlung,* I have emphasized evidence of Hardy's reading drawn from his journals and reflections in his ghosted biography to confirm the importance of Darwin, Huxley, and Spencer on the commonalities of humans and animals, the French Darwinian psychologist Ribot on egoistic and altruistic emotion, and the early influence of Comte's positivism on Hardy's evolutionary meliorism.

That altruism, a term so often coupled with empathy in twentieth-century investigations of human social psychology, should *precede* the terminology and theorizing of both empathy and *Einfühlung* it is vital to recall. The early formulations of other-directed emotion that Hardy read, starting with Comte and including Spencer and Ribot, described altruism as a feeling for others that would lead to actions on their behalf. In late-twentieth-century psychology, the feeling and the action would be separated, as C. Daniel Batson's "empathy–altruism hypothesis" indicates.

This separation allows for investigations of the conditions under which empathy does (or does not) lead to altruism, as well as consideration of more self-interested motivations for altruistic action, such as expectation of reciprocity. It also opens up a way of studying failures of empathy, because of egoistic personal distress and withdrawal, or because of diffusion of responsibility, by which an individual in a crowd absolves himself of responsibility to act and becomes a bystander rather than a helper. I have argued elsewhere that the empathy–altruism hypothesis, which has been demonstrated by psychologists to work among real people, does not automatically function in the same way when it comes to narrative empathy (Keen, *Empathy* 90–92, 99). That is, I am in agreement with Meir Sternberg's caution against package-dealing, in resisting the analogy that would equate the use of empathetic narrative techniques in fiction with real-life empathy–altruism. We should not expect, and we do not in fact find, reliable evidence of altruistic results in the social and political realm of tens of thousands of empathy-inducing narratives. We should ask instead what interferes with the transmission of fellow feeling induced by narrative fiction and/or the altruism that was Comte's Positivist dream.

In Hardy's narratives of self-thwarting characters, driven by impulsions that they scarcely register, we find clear delineations of the obstacles to altruism that balk even the most feeling beings, such as Tess and Jude. Hardy depicts the near irresistible force of class prejudice, limiting gender roles, legal and economic obstacles, group pressure to conform, as well as his characters' vulnerability to criminal manipulations, sexual desire, and emotional natures to explain why things just can't improve as quickly as we might wish. That humans live such short lives, in the evolutionary time-scale, made an impression on Hardy that is reflected in his faith in meliorism; it is *evolutionary* meliorism, and may be helped along, but cannot be rushed. We find in Thomas Hardy's notes of 1881 evidence of his struggle to reconcile his Darwinism with his observation of human's emotional natures. He names here Law what in later narratives he calls Cause and Immanent Will, an unthinking motive force:

> May 9. After infinite trying to reconcile a scientific view of life with the emotional and spiritual, so that they may not be interdestructive I come to the following:
>
> General Principles. Law has produced in man a child who cannot but constantly reproach its parent for doing much and yet not all, and constantly say to such parent that it would have been better never to have

begun doing than to have *over*done so indecisively; that is, than to have created so far beyond all apparent first intention (on the emotional side), without mending matters by a second intent and execution, to eliminate the evils of the blunder of overdoing. The emotions have no place in a world of defect, and it is a cruel injustice that they should have developed in it.

If Law itself had consciousness, how the aspect of its creatures would terrify it, fill it with remorse! (*Life and Work* 153)

Though he deplores the injustice of evolved feelings, Hardy never abjures the emotional nature that time and again leads his characters into traps they cannot escape. Bathsheba Everdene impulsively teases Farmer Boldwood with a valentine, starting a chain of events that leads from Boldwood's obsession to his murder of his rival for Bathsheba's affections. Eustacia Vye flees into Egdon Heath in an escape attempt that leads to her drowning. Michael Henchard sells his wife in drunken exasperation and can never evade the consequences of his action. Jude entangles himself disastrously with Arabella and Sue Bridehead with tragic results for himself and his offspring. Though readers have found his narratives pessimistic or deterministic, they have rarely complained that Hardy's characters' plights are unmoving. Hardy's narratives take advantage of readers' emotional dispositions to involve them in the experience of his fictional beings. Though we may point to areas of potential reform where Hardy's fiction might have influenced readers' attitudes (workingmen's access to education, availability of divorce, treatment of unwed mothers), his aim was grander still. By mobilizing readers' empathy on behalf of others, Hardy's lovingkindness and altruism might look like grim responsibilities. He should be congratulated, he asserts, for sticking to the task of perspective-taking, as in the long run, the universe itself could be awakened to its senses, learn to pity, and evolve into a feeling Prime Mover.

WORKS CITED

Ablow, Rachel. "Victorian Feelings and the Victorian Novel." *Literature Compass* 4.1 (2007): 298–316. Web.

Arabatzis, Theodore. *Representing Electrons: A Biographical Approach to Theoretical Entities.* Chicago: University of Chicago Press, 2006. Print.

Arcana of Science and Art: Or, An Annual Register of Useful Inventions and Improvements. 4 v. London: John Limbird, 1830–33. *Google Book Search.* 15 February 2010.

Armstrong, Tim. *Haunted Hardy: Poetry, History, Memory.* Basingstoke: Palgrave Macmillan, 2000. Print.

Asquith, Mark. *Thomas Hardy, Metaphysics and Music.* Basingstoke: Palgrave Macmillan, 2005. Print.

Auden, W. H. "A Literary Transference." *Hardy: A Collection of Critical Essays.* Ed. Albert Guérard. Englewood Cliffs: Prentice-Hall, 1963. 135–42. Print.

Auerbach, Erich. *Mimesis: The Representation of Reality in Western Literature.* Trans. Willard Trask. Princeton: Princeton University Press, 1953. Print.

Austen, Jane. *Pride and Prejudice.* 1813. Rpt. Norton Critical Edition, 3rd ed. Ed. Donald Gray. New York: Norton, 2001. Print.

Austin, Linda M. "Reading Depression in Hardy's 'Poems of 1912–13.'" *Victorian Poetry* 36.1 (Spring 1998): 1–15. Print.

Bäckman, Sven. *The Manners of Ghosts: A Study of the Supernatural in Thomas Hardy's Short Poems.* Göteborg: Acta Universitatis Gothoburgensis, 2001. Print.

Bailey, J. O. *The Poetry of Thomas Hardy: A Handbook and Commentary* (Chapel Hill: University of North Carolina Press, 1970). Print.

———. *Thomas Hardy and the Cosmic Mind: A New Reading of* The Dynasts. Chapel Hill: University of North Carolina Press, 1956. Print.

Banfield, Ann. *Unspeakable Sentences: Narration and Representation in the Language of Fiction.* London: Routledge, 1982. Print.

Bate, Jonathan. "Culture and Environment: From Austen to Hardy." *New Literary History* 33.3 (Summer 1999): 541–60. Print.

Batson, C. Daniel, ed. *The Altruism Question: Toward a Social-Psychological Answer.* Hillsdale: Erlbaum, 1991. Print.

Beckmann, John. *A History of Inventions, Discoveries and Origins.* 4th ed. 2 v. London: Bohn Library, 1846. *Google Book Search.* 15 February 2010.

Beer, Gillian. *Darwin's Plots: Evolutionary Narrative in Darwin, George Eliot, and Nineteenth-Century Fiction.* 2nd ed. Cambridge: Cambridge University Press, 2000. Print.

———. *Open Fields: Science in Cultural Encounter.* Oxford and New York: Oxford University Press, 1996. Print.

———. "Origins and Oblivion in Victorian Narrative." *Sex, Politics, and Science in the Nineteenth-Century Novel.* Ed. Ruth Bernard Yeazell. Baltimore: Johns Hopkins University Press, 1986. 63–87. Print.

Berrios, G. E. "Body and Mind: W. K. Clifford." *History of Psychiatry* 11 (2000): 311–38. Print.

Bettany, G. T. *The Life of Charles Darwin.* London: Walter Scott, 1887. *Google Book Search.* 15 February 2010.

Björk, Lennart A. "Hardy's Reading." *Thomas Hardy: The Writer and his Background.* Ed. Norman Page. New York: St. Martin's Press, 1980. 102–27. Print.

———. "Psychological Vision and Social Criticism in *Desperate Remedies* and *Jude the Obscure.*" *Budmouth Essays on Thomas Hardy.* Ed. F. B. Pinion. Dorchester: Thomas Hardy Society, 1976. 86–105. Print.

———. *Psychological Vision and Social Criticism in the Novels of Thomas Hardy.* Stockholm: Almqvist and Wiksell International, 1987. Print.

Björk, Lennart A., ed. *The Literary Notebooks of Thomas Hardy.* 2 v. New York: New York University Press, 1985. Print.

Booth, Wayne C. *The Rhetoric of Fiction,* 2nd ed. Chicago: University of Chicago Press, 1983. Print.

Boumelha, Penny. *Thomas Hardy and Women: Sexual Ideology and Narrative Form.* Brighton: Harvester Press; Totowa: Barnes and Noble, 1982. Print.

Bray, Joe. "The Source of 'Dramatized Consciousness': Richardson, Austen, and Stylistic Influence." *Style* 35.1 (Spring 2001): 18–33. Print.

Brooke-Rose, Christine. "Ill Wit and Sick Tragedy: *Jude the Obscure.*" *Alternative Hardy.* Ed. Lance St. John Butler. New York: St. Martin's Press, 1989. 26–48. Print.

Browne, Sir James Crichton. "Dreamy Mental States." *Lancet* 3749–50 (1895): 1–5, 73–75. Print.

Bullen, J. B. *The Expressive Eye: Fiction and Perception in the Work of Thomas Hardy.* Oxford: Clarendon Press, 1986. Print.

Burdett, Carolyn. "'The Subjective Inside Us Can Turn into the Objective Outside': Vernon Lee's Psychological Aesthetics." *19: Interdisciplinary Studies in the Long Nineteenth Century* 12 (2011). Web. Accessed 17 January 2012.

Campbell, Matthew. *Rhythm and Will in Victorian Poetry.* Cambridge: Cambridge University Press, 1999. Print.

Campbell, Michael L. "Thomas Hardy's Attitude towards Animals." *Victorians Institute Journal* 2 (1973): 61–71. Print.

Casagrande, Peter J. "The Shifted 'Centre of Altruism' in *The Woodlanders:* Thomas Hardy's Third 'Return of a Native.'" *ELH* 38.1 (March 1971): 104–25. Print.

———. *Tess of the D'Urbervilles: Unorthodox Beauty.* New York: Twayne, 1982. Print.

Chesterton, G. K. *The Autobiography of G. K. Chesterton.* 1936. V. 16, *The Collected Works of G. K. Chesterton.* San Francisco: Ignatius Press, 1988. Print.

Chudler, E. H. "Milestones in Neuroscience Research." Web. 18 September 2009.

Clarke, Edwin, and L. S. Jacyna. *Nineteenth-Century Origins of Neuroscientific Concepts.* Berkeley and London: University of California Press, 1987. Print.

Clausius, Rudolph. "On the Moving Force of Heat, and the Laws Regarding the Nature of Heat Itself Which Are Deducible Therefrom." *London, Edinburgh and Dublin Philosophical Magazine and Journal of Science* 2 (1851): 1–21, 102–19. Print.

Clifford, W. K. "Body and Mind." 1874. *Lectures and Essays.* Ed. Leslie Stephen and Frederick Pollack. London: Macmillan, 1879. V. 2, 31–70. Print.

———. "Cosmic Emotion." *Nineteenth Century* (October 1877): 411–29. Print.

———. *Lectures and Essays.* Ed. Leslie Stephen and Frederick Pollack. 2 v. London: Macmillan, 1904. Print.

———. "On the Nature of Things-in-Themselves." *Mind* 3.9 (January 1878): 57–67. Print.

Cohen, William A. "Faciality and Sensation in Hardy's *The Return of the Native.*" *PMLA* 121.2 (March 2006): 437–52. Print.

Cohn, Dorrit. *Transparent Minds: Narrative Modes for Presenting Consciousness in Fiction.* Princeton: Princeton University Press, 1983. Print.

Colby, Vineta. *Vernon Lee: A Literary Biography.* Charlottesville: University of Virginia Press, 2003. Print.

Coleman, S. M. "'Two on a Tower': An Analytical Study." *British Journal of Medical Psychology* 11 (1931): 55–77. Print.

Compton-Burnett, Ivy. *Manservant and Maidservant.* 1947. New York: New York Review of Books, 2001. Print.

Comte, Auguste. *The Catechism of Positive Religion,* 3rd ed. Trans. Richard Congreve. London: Chapman, 1858. Print.

———. *A General View of Positivism.* Trans. J. H. Bridges. London: Trübner, 1865. *Google Book Search.* 15 October 2009.

———. *System of Positive Polity.* 1854. 4 v. London: Longman, Green, 1875–77. Print.

Cox, R. G. *Thomas Hardy: The Critical Heritage.* London and New York: Routledge, 1979. Print.

Creighton, Charles. *Illustrations of Unconscious Memory in Disease, Including a Theory of Alternatives.* London: Lewis, 1886. Print.

Dale, Peter Allan. *In Pursuit of a Scientific Culture: Science, Art, and Society in the Victorian Age.* Madison: University of Wisconsin Press, 1989. Print.

Dalziel, Pamela, and Michael Millgate, eds. *Thomas Hardy's "Poetical Matter" Notebook.* Oxford and New York: Oxford University Press, 2009. Print.

Dames, Nicholas. *Amnesiac Selves: Nostalgia, Forgetting, and British Fiction, 1810–1870.* Oxford and New York: Oxford University Press, 2001. Print.

———. "The Clinical Novel: Phrenology and *Villette.*" *Novel* 29.3 (1996): 367–90. Print.

———. *The Physiology of the Novel: Reading, Neural Science, and the Form of Victorian Fiction.* New York: Oxford University Press, 2007. Print.

———. Rev. of Anne Stiles, ed., *Neurology and Literature, 1860–1920. Victorian Studies* 51.3 (Spring 2009): 552–54. Print.

Darwin, Charles. *The Expression of the Emotions in Man and Animals.* London: John Murray, 1872. *Google Book Search.* 1 June 2010.

———. *The Expression of the Emotions in Man and Animals.* 1872. Ed. Paul Ekman. Oxford and New York: Oxford University Press, 1998. Print.

Davis, Michael. *George Eliot and Nineteenth-Century Psychology: Exploring the Unmapped Country.* Aldershot and Burlington: Ashgate, 2006. Print.

Dean, Susan. *Hardy's Poetic Vision in "The Dynasts": The Diorama of a Dream.* Princeton: Princeton University Press, 1977. Print.

Dessner, Lawrence Jay. "Space, Time, and Coincidence in Hardy." *Studies in the Novel* 24.2 (1992): 154–72. Print.

Dixon, Thomas. *The Invention of Altruism: Making Moral Meanings in Victorian Britain.* Oxford and New York: Oxford University Press, 2008. Print.

Dolin, Tim. "A History of the Text." *The Hand of Ethelberta: A Comedy in Chapters.* 1896, 1912. Ed. Tim Dolin, Penguin Classics. Harmondsworth: Penguin, 1997. Print.

Dry, Helen. "Syntax and Point of View in Jane Austen's *Emma.*" *Studies in Romanticism* 16.1 (1977): 87–99. Print.

Eagleton, Terry. "Flesh and Spirit in Thomas Hardy." *Thomas Hardy and Contemporary Literary Studies.* New York: Palgrave Macmillan, 2004. 14–22. Print.

Efron, Arthur. *Experiencing* Tess of the D'Urbervilles: *A Deweyan Account.* Amsterdam and New York: Rodopi, 2005. Print.

Eisenberg, Nancy, and Natalie D. Eggum. "Empathic Responding: Sympathy and Personal Distress." *The Social Neuroscience of Empathy.* Ed. Jean Decety and William Ickes. Cambridge, MA, and London: MIT Press, 2009: 71–83. Print.

Ekman, Paul. "Introduction." *The Expression of the Emotions in Man and Animals,* by Charles Darwin. Oxford and New York: Oxford University Press, 1998. xxi–xxxvi. Print.

Elliott, Ralph W. V. *Thomas Hardy's English.* Oxford: Blackwell and André Deutsch, 1984. Print.

Ellis, Havelock. "The Logic of Dreams." *The Contemporary Review* 98 (1910): 353–59. Print.

———. *The World of Dreams.* London, Constable: 1911. Print.

[Ellis, Havelock.] "Thomas Hardy's Novels." *Westminster Review* (April 1883): 163–77. Print.

Enstice, Andrew. *Thomas Hardy: Landscapes of the Mind.* New York: St. Martin's Press, 1979. Print.

Erlich, Susan. *Point of View: A Linguistic Analysis of Literary Style.* London: Routledge, 1990. Print.

Fayen, George. "Hardy's Woodlanders: Inwardness and Memory." *Studies in English Literature, 1500–1900* 1.4 (Autumn 1961): 81–100. Print.

Federico, Annette. *Masculine Identity in Hardy and Gissing.* Cranbury: Associated University Presses, 1991. Print.

Ferguson, Frances. "Jane Austen, *Emma,* and the Impact of Form." *Modern Language Quarterly: A Journal of Literary History* 61.1 (March 2000): 157–80. Print.

Fincham, Tony. *Hardy the Physician: Medical Aspects of the Wessex Tradition.* Houndmills, Basingstoke, and New York: Palgrave Macmillan, 2008. Print.

Flavin, Louise. "*Mansfield Park*: Free Indirect Discourse and the Psychological Novel." *Studies in the Novel* 19.2 (Summer 1987): 137–59. Print.

Fludernik, Monika. *The Fictions of Language and the Languages of Fiction: The Linguistic Representation of Speech and Consciousness.* London: Routledge, 1993. Print.

Fogle, Richard Harter. *The Imagery of Keats and Shelley: A Comparative Study.* Chapel Hill: University of North Carolina Press, 1949. Print.

Fourier, Charles. *The Passions of the Human Soul.* Trans. John Reynell Morell. London: Hippolyte Bailliere, 1851. *Google Book Search.* 16 October 2009.

Freud, Sigmund. *The Interpretation of Dreams.* 1900. 3rd ed. Trans. A. A. Brill. London: George Allen & Unwin; New York: Macmillan, 1913. *Google Book Search.* 2 February 2010.

———. *The Psychopathology of Everyday Life.* Trans. A. A. Brill. London: T. Fisher Unwin, 1914. Print.

Friedman, Melvin. *Stream of Consciousness: A Study in Literary Method.* New Haven: Yale University Press, 1955. Print.

Friedman, Susan Stanford., ed. *Analyzing Freud: Letters of H. D., Bryher, and Their Circle.* New York: New Directions, 2002. Print.

Galton, Francis. *Hereditary Genius: An Inquiry into Its Laws and Consequences.* London: Macmillan, 1869. Print.

Garrison, Chester A. *The Vast Venture: Hardy's Epic Drama* The Dynasts. Salzburg: Universität Salzburg, 1973. Print.

Garwood, Helen. *Thomas Hardy: An Illustration of the Philosophy of Schopenhauer.* Philadelphia: Winston, 1911. Print.

Gatrell, Simon. "Wessex." *The Cambridge Companion to Thomas Hardy.* Ed. Dale Kramer. Cambridge: Cambridge University Press, 1999. 19–37. Print.

Gauld, Alan. "Myers, Frederic William Henry, 1843–1901." *The Oxford Dictionary of National Biography.* Online edition, May 2006. Web. 23 September 2009.

Gibson, James. "'The Characteristic of All Great Poetry—The General Perfectly Reduced in the Particular' Thomas Hardy." *New Perspectives on Thomas Hardy.* Ed. Charles P. C. Pettit. London: St. Martins, 1994. 1–15. Print.

———. *Thomas Hardy: A Literary Life.* Basingstoke and New York: Macmillan and St. Martin's Press, 1996. Print.

Gibson, James, ed. *Thomas Hardy: Interviews and Recollections.* Houndmills: Macmillan, 1999. Print.

Giordano, Frank R., Jr. *"I'd Have My Life Unbe": Thomas Hardy's Self-destructive Characters.* University: University of Alabama Press, 1984. Print.

———. "Hardy's Farewell to Fiction: The Structure of 'Wessex Heights.'" *Thomas Hardy Yearbook* 5 (1975): 58–66. Print.

Gittings, Robert. *Young Thomas Hardy.* London: Heinemann, 1975. Print.

Goldstein, Thalia R. "The Pleasure of Unadulterated Sadness: Experiencing Sorrow in Fiction, Nonfiction, and 'In Person.'" *Psychology of Aesthetics, Creativity, and the Arts.* 3.4 (2009): 232–37. Print.

Gosse, Philip Henry. *Evenings at the Microscope.* New York: Collier, 1859. Print.

Gossin, Pamela. *Thomas Hardy's Novel Universe: Astronomy, Cosmology, and Gender in the Post-Darwinian World.* Aldershot and Burlington: Ashgate, 2007. Print.

Greenslade, William, ed. *Thomas Hardy's "Facts" Notebook: A Critical Edition.* Aldershot: Ashgate, 2004. Print.

Griffin, Ernest G. "Hardy and the Growing Consciousness of the Immanent Will: A Study in the Relationship of Philosophy to Literary Form." *Cairo Studies in English* (1961): 121–33. Print.

Guérard, Albert. *Thomas Hardy: The Novels and Stories.* Cambridge, MA: Harvard University Press, 1949. Print.

Gunn, Daniel P. "Free Indirect Discourse and Narrative Authority in *Emma*." *Narrative* 12.1 (January 2004): 35–54. Print.

Hardy, Barbara. "Literary Allusion: Hardy and Other Poets." *Thomas Hardy Reappraised: Essays in Honor of Michael Millgate.* Ed. Keith Wilson. Toronto: University of Toronto Press, 2006. 55–77. Print.

Hardy, Evelyn. *Thomas Hardy: A Critical Biography.* London, Hogarth Press, 1954. Print.

Hardy, F. E. *The Early Life of Thomas Hardy, 1840–1891.* London and New York: Macmillan, 1928. Print.

———. *The Later Years of Thomas Hardy, 1892–1928*. London and New York: Macmillan, 1930. Print.

Hardy, Thomas. "Candour in English Fiction." *New Review* (January 1890). Rpt. *Thomas Hardy's Personal Writings*. Ed. Harold Orel. London: Macmillan, 1966. 125–33. Print.

———. *A Changed Man and Other Tales*. London: Macmillan, 1913. Print.

———. *The Collected Letters of Thomas Hardy*. Ed. Richard Little Purdy and Michael Millgate. 7 v. Oxford: Clarendon Press, 1978–88. Print.

———. *The Complete Poems*. Ed. James Gibson. Houndmills, Basingstoke: Palgrave Macmillan, 2001. Print.

———. *Desperate Remedies*. 1871. Ed. Patricia Ingham. Oxford World's Classics. Oxford and New York: Oxford University Press, 2009. Print.

———. "The Dorsetshire Labourer." *Longman's Magazine* 2 (1883): 252–69. Print.

———. *The Dynasts: Parts First and Second*. 1904, 1906. *The Complete Poetical Works of Thomas Hardy*, v. 4. Ed. Samuel Hynes. Oxford: Clarendon Press, 1995. Print.

———. *The Dynasts: Part Third*. 1908. *The Complete Poetical Works of Thomas Hardy*, v. 5. Ed. Samuel Hynes. Oxford: Clarendon Press, 1995. Print.

———. *The Dynasts: An Epic-Drama of the War with Napoleon, in Three Parts, Nineteen Acts, and One Hundred and Thirty Scenes*. London: Macmillan, 1913. Print.

———. *Far from the Madding Crowd*.1874. Ed. Suzanne B. Falck-Yi. Oxford World's Classics. Oxford and New York: Oxford University Press, 2008. Print.

———. "General Preface to the Wessex Edition." *Tess of the d'Urbervilles*. v. 1. The Wessex Edition, London: Macmillan, 1912. vii–xiii. Print.

———. *A Group of Noble Dames*. London: James Osgood, McIlvaine, & Co., 1891. Print.

———. *The Hand of Ethelberta: A Comedy in Chapters*.1876. New Wessex Edition. Introduction by Robert Gittings. London: Macmillan, 1975. Print.

———. *The Hand of Ethelberta: A Comedy in Chapters*. 1896, 1912. Ed. Tim Dolin, Penguin Classics. Harmondsworth: Penguin, 1997. Print.

———. "H's Altruism." 1927. *The Personal Notebooks of Thomas Hardy, with an Appendix Including the Unpublished Passages in the Original Typescripts of* The Life of Thomas Hardy. Ed. Richard H. Taylor. New York: Columbia University Press, 1979. 291–92. Print.

———. *Human Shows*. 1925. *The Complete Poetical Works of Thomas Hardy*, v. 3. Ed. Samuel Hynes. Oxford: Clarendon Press, 1985. Print.

———. *Jude the Obscure*. 1895. Ed. Patricia Ingham. Oxford World's Classics. Oxford and New York: Oxford University Press, 2008. Print.

———. *A Laodicean: Or, The Castle of the De Stancys*.1881. Ed. John Schad. London and New York: Penguin Books, 1997. Print.

———. *Late Lyrics and Earlier*. 1922. *The Complete Poetical Works of Thomas Hardy*, v. 2. Ed. Samuel Hynes. Oxford: Clarendon Press, 1984. Print.

———. Letter, *Athenaeum* (30 November 1878): 688. Print.

———. *The Life and Work of Thomas Hardy*. Ed. Michael Millgate. Athens: University of Georgia Press, 1985. Print.

———. *Life's Little Ironies*. 1894. Ed. Alan Manford. Oxford World's Classics. Oxford and New York: Oxford University Press, 2008. Print.

———. "Life's Opportunity." *Wayfarer's Love: Contributions from Living Poets*. Ed. Millicent, Duchess of Sutherland. Westminster: Constable, 1904. 16. Print.

———. *The Literary Notebooks of Thomas Hardy*. Ed. Lennart A. Björk. 2 v. New York: New York University Press, 1985. Print.

————. *The Mayor of Casterbridge.* 1886. Ed. Dale Kramer. Oxford World's Classics. Oxford and New York: Oxford University Press, 2008. Print.

————. "The Midnight Baptism." *Fortnightly Review* 55 o.s./49 n.s. (May 1891): 695–701. Print.

————. *Moments of Vision.* 1917. *The Complete Poetical Works of Thomas Hardy,* v. 2. Ed. Samuel Hynes. Oxford: Clarendon Press, 1984. Print.

————. *A Pair of Blue Eyes.* 1873. Ed. Alan Manford. Oxford World's Classics. Oxford and New York: Oxford University Press, 2009. Print.

————. "The Profitable Reading of Fiction." *Forum* (New York) (March 1888): 57–70. Rpt. *Thomas Hardy's Personal Writings.* Ed. Harold Orel. London: Macmillan, 1966. 110–25. Print.

————. *Poems of the Past and the Present.* 1901[2]. *The Complete Poetical Works of Thomas Hardy,* v. 1. Ed. Samuel Hynes. Oxford: Clarendon Press, 1982. Print.

————. *The Return of the Native.* 1878. Ed. Simon Gatrell. Oxford World's Classics. Oxford and New York: Oxford University Press, 2008. Print.

————. *Satires of Circumstance.* 1914. *The Complete Poetical Works of Thomas Hardy,* v. 2. Ed. Samuel Hynes. Oxford: Clarendon Press, 1984. Print.

————. "Schools of Painting" notebook. 1863. *The Personal Notebooks of Thomas Hardy, with an Appendix Including the Unpublished Passages in the Original Typescripts of* The Life of Thomas Hardy. Ed. Richard H. Taylor. New York: Columbia University Press, 1979: 103–14. Print.

————. "The Science of Fiction." *New Review* (April 1891). Rpt. *Thomas Hardy's Personal Writings.* Ed. Harold Orel. London: Macmillan, 1966. 134–38. Print.

————. *Tess of the d'Urbervilles.* 1891. Ed. Juliet Grindle and Simon Gatrell. Oxford World's Classics. Oxford and New York: Oxford University Press, 2008. Print.

————. *Thomas Hardy: Selected Letters.* Ed. Michael Millgate. Oxford: Clarendon Press, 1990. Print.

————. *Time's Laughingstocks.* 1909. *The Complete Poetical Works of Thomas Hardy,* v. 1. Ed. Samuel Hynes. Oxford: Clarendon Press, 1982. Print.

————. *The Trumpet Major.* 1880. Ed. Richard Nemesvari. Oxford World's Classics. Oxford and New York: Oxford University Press, 1998. Print.

————. *Two on a Tower.* 1882. Ed. Sulieman M. Ahmad. Oxford World's Classics. Oxford and New York: Oxford University Press, 1998. Print.

————. *Under the Greenwood Tree.* 1872. Ed. Simon Gatrell. Oxford World's Classics. Oxford and New York: Oxford University Press, 2009. Print.

————. *The Well-Beloved.* 1897. Ed. Tom Hetherington. Oxford World's Classics. Oxford and New York: Oxford University Press, 1998. Print.

————. *The Woodlanders.* 1887. Ed. Dale Kramer. Oxford World's Classics. Oxford and New York: Oxford University Press, 2009. Print.

————. *The Woodlanders.* 1887. Ed. James Gibson. 1981. Rpt. Penguin Classics. Harmondsworth and New York: Penguin, 1986. Print.

————. "The Woodlanders. Chapter 1." *Harper's Bazaar* 19.20 (May 1886): 318–19. Print.

————. *Wessex Poems.* 1898. *The Complete Poetical Works of Thomas Hardy,* v. 1. Ed. Samuel Hynes. Oxford: Clarendon Press, 1982. Print.

————. *Wessex Tales.* 1888. Ed. Kathryn R. King. Oxford World's Classics. Oxford and New York: Oxford University Press, 2009. Print.

————. *Winter Words.* 1928. *The Complete Poetical Works of Thomas Hardy,* v. 3. Ed. Samuel Hynes. Oxford: Clarendon Press, 1985. Print.

Harris, Jose. "Mill, John Stuart (1806–1873), Philosopher, Economist, and Advocate of Women's Rights." *Oxford Dictionary of National Biography*. Online edition, October 2008. Web. 28 September 2009.

Hartmann, Eduard von. *The Philosophy of the Unconscious*. 1869. Trans. William C. Coupland. 1884. 3 v. London: Kegan Paul, Trench, 1893. Print.

Heaney, Seamus. "Place, Pastness, Poems: A Triptych." *The New Salmagundi Reader* (1996): 14–31. Print.

Henchman, Anna. "Hardy's Stargazers and the Astronomy of Other Minds." *Victorian Studies* 51.1 (Autumn 2008): 37–64. Print.

Herman, David, ed. *The Emergence of Mind: Representations of Consciousness in Narrative Discourse in English*. Lincoln: University of Nebraska Press, 2011. Print.

Hernadi, Paul. "Dual Perspective: Free Indirect Discourse and Related Techniques." *Comparative Literature* 24 (1972): 32–43. Print.

Higonnet, Margaret. Ed. *The Sense of Sex: Feminist Perspectives on Hardy*. Urbana: University of Illinois Press, 1993. Print.

Hoffman, Martin. *Empathy and Moral Development*. Cambridge and New York: Cambridge University Press, 2000. Print.

Hogan, Patrick Colm. "The Epilogue of Suffering: Heroism, Empathy, Ethics." *SubStance* 30.1–2 (2001): 199–243. Print.

Hornback, Bert G. "Thomas Hardy: The Poet in Search of His Voice." *Victorian Poetry* 12.1 (Spring 1974): 55–63. Print.

Hughes, John. "Visual Inspiration in Hardy's Fiction." *Palgrave Advances in Thomas Hardy Studies*. Ed. Phillip Mallett. Basingstoke: Palgrave Macmillan, 2004. 229–54. Print.

Hume, David. 1739. *A Treatise of Human Nature*. Ed. L. A. Selby-Bigge, Oxford: Clarendon Press, 1978. Print.

———. *A Treatise on Human Nature: Being an Attempt to Introduce the Experimental Method of Reasoning into Moral Subjects and Dialogues Concerning Natural Religion*. Ed. T. H. Green and T. H. Grose. 2 v. London: Longmans, Green, 1874. Print.

Huxley, T. H. *Lessons in Elementary Physiology*. London: Clay, Son, and Taylor, 1866. Print.

———. "On the Hypothesis That Animals are Automata, and Its History." *Fortnightly Review* 95 (1874): 555–80. Print.

———. "On the Relations of Man to the Lower Animals." *Evidence as to Man's Place in Nature*. London: Williams and Norgate, 1863. Print.

Hyde, William J. "Theoretic and Practical Unconventionality in *Jude the Obscure*." *Nineteenth-Century Fiction* 20.2 (September 1965): 155–64. Print.

Hynes, Samuel. "On *The Dynasts* as an Example." *Hardy: A Collection of Critical Essays*. Ed. Albert Guérard. Englewood Cliffs: Prentice-Hall, 1963. 160–74. Print.

———. *The Pattern of Hardy's Poetry*. Chapel Hill: University of North Carolina Press, 1961. Print.

Irwin, Michael. *Reading Hardy's Landscapes*. New York: St. Martins Press, 2000. Print.

Jacyna, L. S. *Medicine and Modernism: A Biography of Sir Henry Head*. London: Pickering and Chatto, 2008. Print.

Jahn, Manfred. "Contextualizing Represented Speech and Thought." *Journal of Pragmatics* 17 (1992): 347–67. Print.

James, William. *Human Immortality: Two Supposed Objections to the Doctrine*. Westminster: Archibald Constable, 1898. Print.

———. *The Meaning of Truth: A Sequel to Pragmatism*. London: Longmans, Green, 1909. Print.

————. *A Pluralistic Universe: Hibbert Lectures at Manchester College on the Present Situation in Philosophy.* London: Longmans, Green, 1909. Print.

Joh, Byunghwa. *Thomas Hardy's Poetry: A Jungian Perspective.* New York: Peter Lang, 2002. Print.

Joyce, James. *Dubliners.* 1914. Ed. Robert Scholes and A. Walton Litz. London and New York: Penguin, 1996. Print.

Keen, Suzanne. *Empathy and the Novel.* Oxford and New York: Oxford University Press, 2007. Print.

————. "Introduction: Narrative and the Emotions." *Poetics Today* 32.1 (Spring 2011): 1–53. Print.

————. "Psychological Approaches to Thomas Hardy." *Ashgate Research Companion to Thomas Hardy.* Ed. Rosemarie Morgan. Aldershot and Burlington: Ashgate, 2010. Print.

————. "Strategic Empathizing: Techniques of Bounded, Ambassadorial, and Broadcast Narrative Empathy." *Deutsche Vierteljahrs Schrift für Literaturwissenschaft und Geistesgeschichte* 82.3 (2008): 477–93. Print.

————. "A Theory of Narrative Empathy." *Narrative* 14.3 (2006): 207–36. Print.

————. *Victorian Renovations of the Novel: Narrative Annexes and the Boundaries of Representation.* Cambridge: Cambridge University Press, 1998. Print.

Kiely, Robert. "Vision and Viewpoint in *The Mayor of Casterbridge.*" *Nineteenth-Century Fiction* 23.2 (September 1968): 189–200. Print.

King, Jeanette. *Tragedy in the Victorian Novel.* Cambridge and New York: Cambridge University Press, 1978. Print.

Kern, Stephen. *The Culture of Time and Space, 1880–1918.* Cambridge, MA: Harvard University Press, 1983. Print.

Kramer, Dale, ed. *The Cambridge Companion to Thomas Hardy.* Cambridge: Cambridge University Press, 1999. Print.

Kucich, John. "Scientific Ascendancy." *A Companion to the Victorian Novel.* Ed. Patrick Brantlinger and William B. Thesing, Oxford: Blackwell, 2002. 119–36. Print.

Lakoff, George, and Mark Turner. *More Than Cool Reason: A Field Guide to Poetic Metaphor.* Chicago and London: University of Chicago Press, 1989. Print.

Laming, Richard. *On the Primary Forces of Electricity.* London and Edinburgh Philosophical Magazine and Journal of Science. London and Edinburgh: Taylor, 1838. Print.

Lane, Christopher. *The Burdens of Intimacy: Psychoanalysis and Victorian Masculinity.* Chicago: University of Chicago Press, 1999. Print.

Larkin, Philip. *Collected Poems.* Ed. Anthony Thwaite. New York: Farrar, Straus and Giroux, 1989. Print.

László, Janos. *The Science of Stories: An Introduction to Narrative Psychology.* London and New York: Routledge, 2008. Print.

László, János, and Ildikó Somogyvári. "Narrative Empathy and Inter-Group Relations." *Directions in Empirical Literary Study.* Ed. Sonia Zyngier, Marisa Bortolussi, et. al. Amsterdam and Philadelphia: John Benjamins, 2008. 113–25. Print.

Lee, Vernon. *The Beautiful: An Introduction to Psychological Aesthetics.* Cambridge: Cambridge University Press, 1913. Print.

————. "A Dialogue on Novels." *Contemporary Review* 48 (1885): 378–401. Print.

————. *The Handling of Words and Other Studies in Literary Psychology.* London: John Lane, 1923. Print.

Lee, Vernon, and C. Anstruther-Thomson. "Beauty and Ugliness." *Contemporary Review* 72 (October 1897): 544–69; (November 1897): 669–88. Print.

Levine, George Lewis. *Darwin and the Novelists: Patterns of Science in Victorian Fiction.* Cambridge, MA: Harvard University Press, 1988. Print.

———. *Dying to Know: Scientific Epistemology and Narrative in Victorian England.* Chicago: University of Chicago Press, 2002. Print.

———. "*The Woodlanders* and the Darwinian Grotesque." *Thomas Hardy Reappraised: Essays in Honor of Michael Millgate.* Ed. Keith Wilson. Toronto: University of Toronto Press, 2006. 174–98. Print.

Levinson, Marjorie. "Object-Loss and Object-Bondage: Economies of Representation in Hardy's Poetry." *ELH* 73 (2006): 549–80. Print.

Lewes, G. H., *Comte's Philosophy of the Sciences: Being an Exposition of the Principles of the Cours De Philosophie Positive of Auguste Comte.* London: Henry G. Bohn, 1853. Print.

———. *The Physical Basis of Mind: The Second Series of Problems of Life and Mind.* 1877. Rpt. London: Kegan Paul, Trench, Trubner, 1893. Print.

Lipps, Theodor. *Äesthetik: Psycholgie des Schönen und der Kunst.* 2 v. Hamburg and Leipzig: Voss, 1903, 1906. Print.

———. "Das Wissen von Fremden Ichen." *Psychologische Untersuchungen* 1 (1906): 694–722. Print.

———. *Zur Einfühlung.* Leipzig: Engleman, 1913. Print.

Liu, J. H., and János László. "A Narrative Theory of History and Identity: Social Identity, Social Representations, Society and the Individual." *Social Representation and Identity: Content, Process, and Power.* Ed. G. Maloney and I. Walker. London and New York: Palgrave Macmillan, 2007. 85–108. Print.

Lock, Charles. "Hardy Promises: *The Dynasts* and the Epic of Imperialism." *Reading Thomas Hardy.* Ed. Charles C. Pettit. London: Macmillan, 1998. 83–116. Print.

Lodge, David. "Introduction." *The Woodlanders,* by Thomas Hardy. Ed. David Lodge. London: Macmillan, 1975. 13–22. Print.

———. "Thomas Hardy and the Cinematographic Form." *Novel* 7.3 (1974): 246–54. Print.

Lothe, Jakob. "Hardy's Authorial Narrative Method in *Tess of the D'Urbervilles.*" *The Nineteenth-Century British Novel.* Ed. Jeremy Hawthorn. London: Edward Arnold, 1986. 157–70. Print.

Malane, Rachel. *Sex in Mind: The Gendered Brain in Nineteenth-Century Literature and Mental Sciences.* New York: Peter Lang, 2005. Print.

Mallett, Phillip. "Hardy and Philosophy." *A Companion to Thomas Hardy.* Ed. Keith Wilson. Oxford: Blackwell, 2009. 21–35. Print.

———. "Noticing Things: Hardy and the Nature of Nature." *The Achievement of Thomas Hardy.* Ed. Phillip Mallett. Houndmills and New York: Macmillan and St. Martin's Press, 2000. 155–69. Print.

Mallett, Phillip, ed. *The Achievement of Thomas Hardy.* Houndmills and New York: Macmillan and St. Martin's Press, 2000. Print.

———. *Thomas Hardy: Texts and Contexts.* Houndmills and New York: Palgrave Macmillan, 2002. Print.

Marks, John. "Hardy and Kindness." *Thomas Hardy Journal* 11.1 (1995): 52–59. Print.

Marsh, Joss. "Dickensian 'Dissolving Views': The Magic Lantern, Visual Story-Telling, and the Victorian Technological Imagination." *Comparative Critical Studies* 6.3 (2009): 333–46. Print.

Matsuoka, Mitsuharu. *The Victorian Literary Studies Archive Hyper-Concordance.* Web. 29 August 2007.

Matus, Jill L. *Shock, Memory and the Unconscious in Victorian Fiction.* Cambridge: Cambridge University Press, 2009. Print.

———. "Victorian Framings of the Mind: Recent Work on Mid-Nineteenth Century Theories of the Unconscious, Memory, and Emotion." *Literature Compass* 4.4 (2007): 1257–76. Web.

Maudsley, Henry. *Body and Mind: An Inquiry into Their Connection and Mutual Influence, Specially in Reference to Mental Disorders.* London: Macmillan, 1870. Rpt. New York: Appleton, 1871. Print.

———. *Natural Causes and Supernatural Seemings.* London: Kegan Paul, Trench, 1886. Print.

———. *The Physiology and Pathology of Mind.* New York: Appleton, 1867. Print.

Maynard, Katherine Kearney. *Thomas Hardy's Tragic Poetry: The Lyrics and* The Dynasts. Iowa City: University of Iowa Press, 1991. Print.

McHale, Brian. "Free Indirect Discourse: A Survey of Recent Accounts." *PTL* 3 (1978): 249–87. Print.

Menke, Richard. "Victorian Interiors: The Embodiment of Subjectivity in English Fiction, 1836–1901." Ph.D. dissertation, Stanford University, 1999.

Meynell, G. G. "Freud Translated: An Historical and Bibliographical Note." *Journal of the Royal Society of Medicine* 74 (April 1981): 306–9. Print.

Meynert, Theodor. *Psychiatry: A Clinical Treatise on Diseases of the Forebrain Based upon a Study of Its Structure, Function, and Nutrition.* London: G. P. Putnam, 1885. *Google Book Search.* 30 September 2009.

Miall, David S. *Literary Reading: Empirical and Theoretical Studies.* New York: Peter Lang, 2006. Print.

Miall, David S., and Don Kuiken. "Foregrounding, Defamiliarization, and Affect: Response to Literary Stories." *Poetics* 22 (1994): 389–407. Print.

Mill, John Stuart. *Essays on Ethics, Religion and Society.* V. 10 of *The Collected Works of John Stuart Mill.* Ed. John M. Robson. Toronto: University of Toronto Press, 1969. Print.

———. *Essays on Politics and Society.* V. 18 of *The Collected Works of John Stuart Mill.* Ed. John M. Robson. Toronto: University of Toronto Press, 1977. Print.

Miller, J. Hillis. "'Wessex Heights': The Persistence of the Past in Hardy's Poetry." *Critical Quarterly* 10.4 (1968): 339–59. Print.

———. *Thomas Hardy: Distance and Desire.* Cambridge, MA: Belknap Press of Harvard University Press, 1970. Print.

Miller, Susan M. "Thomas Hardy and the Impersonal Lyric." *Journal of Modern Literature* 30.3 (Spring 2007): 95–115. Print.

Millgate, Michael. "Hardy, Thomas (1840–1928), Novelist and Poet." *Oxford Dictionary of National Biography.* September 2004; online edition, May 2006. Web. 5 February 2010.

———. *Thomas Hardy: A Biography Revisited.* Oxford and New York: Oxford University Press, 2004. Print.

———. "Thomas Hardy's Library at Max Gate: Catalogue of an Attempted Reconstruction." University of Toronto Library. Web. 26 May 2008.

Millgate, Michael, ed. *The Life and Work of Thomas Hardy.* Athens: University of Georgia Press, 1985. Print.

Milton, John. *Milton's Poetical Works.* Halifax: Milner and Sowerby, 1865. Print.

———. *Paradise Lost, as Originally Published by John Milton, Being a Facsimile Reproduction of the First Edition.* Introduction by David Masson. London: Elliot Stock, 1877. Print.

————. The Poetical Works of John Milton. A New Edition, Carefully Revised. Ed. Theodore Alois Buckley. London and New York: Routledge, Warne, and Routledge, 1864. Google Book Search. 8 June 2010.

Morgan, Rosemarie. Women and Sexuality in the Novels of Thomas Hardy. London and New York: Routledge, 1988. Print.

Morrison, Ronald D. "Humanity towards Man, Woman, and the Lower Animals: Thomas Hardy's Jude the Obscure and the Victorian Humane Movement." Nineteenth Century Studies 12 (1998): 64–82. Print.

————. "Love and Evolution in Thomas Hardy's The Woodlanders." Kentucky Philological Review 6 (1991): 32–37. Print.

[Moule, Horace.] "Under the Greenwood Tree." Saturday Review 34 (1872): 417–18. Google Book Search. 15 February 2013.

Myers, F. W. H. "Modern Poets and the Meaning of Life." Nineteenth Century 33 (January 1893): 93–111. Print.

Nemesvari, Richard. "'Genres Are Not to Be Mixed. . . . I Will Not Mix Them': Discourse, Ideology, and Generic Hybridity in Hardy's Fiction." A Companion to Thomas Hardy. Ed. Keith Wilson. Oxford: Wiley-Blackwell, 2009. 102–16. Print.

Neumann, Anne Waldron. "Characterization and Comment in Pride and Prejudice: Free Indirect Discourse and 'Double-Voiced' Verbs of Speaking, Thinking, and Feeling." Style 20.3 (Fall 1986): 364–94. Print.

Oberndorf, Clarence Paul. A History of Psychoanalysis in America. New York: Grune & Stratton: 1953. Print.

Orel, Harold, ed. Thomas Hardy's Personal Writings. London: Macmillan, 1966. Print.

Page, Norman, ed. Oxford Reader's Companion to Hardy. Oxford and New York: Oxford University Press, 2000. Print.

Palmer, Alan. Fictional Minds. Lincoln: University of Nebraska Press, 2004. Print.

————. Social Minds in the Novel. Columbus: Ohio State University Press, 2010. Print.

Paris, Bernard J. Imagined Human Beings: A Psychological Approach to Character and Conflict in Literature. New York: New York University Press, 1997. Print.

Pascal, Roy. The Dual Voice: Free Indirect Speech and Its Functioning in the Nineteenth-Century European Novel. Manchester: Manchester University Press, 1977. Print.

Paulin, Tom. Thomas Hardy: The Poetry of Perception. London: Macmillan; Totowa: Rowman and Littlefield, 1975. Print.

Paterson, John. "Lawrence's Vital Source: Nature and Character in Thomas Hardy." Nature and the Victorian Imagination. Ed. U. C. Knoepflmacher and G. B. Tennyson. Berkeley: University of California Press, 1977. 455–69. Print.

Pereira, Marcos Emanoel. "History of Psychology Timeline." Web. 18 September 2009.

Pinion, F. B. A Hardy Companion. London: Macmillan, 1968. Print.

Pite, Ralph. Thomas Hardy: The Guarded Life. New Haven: Yale University Press, 2007. Print.

Proctor, Richard A. Science Byways. London: Smith, Elder & Co., 1875. Google Book Search. 8 February 2010.

Purdy, Richard Little, and Michael Millgate, eds. The Collected Letters of Thomas Hardy. 7 v. Oxford: Clarendon Press, 1978–88. Print.

Rabinowitz, Peter J. Before Reading: Narrative Conventions and the Politics of Interpretation. Ithaca: Cornell University Press, 1987. Print.

Radford, Andrew D. Thomas Hardy and the Survivals of Time. Aldershot and Burlington: Ashgate, 2003. Print.

Ramazani, Jahan. Poetry of Mourning: The Modern Elegy from Hardy to Heaney. Chicago: University of Chicago Press, 1994. Print.

Ray, Martin, comp. *A Variorum Concordance to the "Complete Poems."* New Haven, CT: The Thomas Hardy Association, 1999. CD-ROM.

Ribot, Théodule. *Heredity: A Psychological Study of Its Phenomena, Laws, Causes, and Consequences.* London: H. S. King & Co., 1875. Print.

———. *The Psychology of the Emotions.* 1896. Trans. *La psychologie des sentiments.* Ed. Havelock Ellis. London: Walter Scott, 1897. Print.

Richardson, Alan. *British Romanticism and the Science of the Mind.* Cambridge: Cambridge University Press, 2001. Print.

———. *The Neural Sublime: Cognitive Theories and Romantic Texts.* Baltimore: Johns Hopkins University Press, 2010. Print.

Richardson, Alan, and Ellen Spolsky, eds. *The Work of Fiction: Cognition, Culture, and Complexity.* Aldershot and Burlington: Ashgate, 2004. Print.

Richardson, Angelique. "Hardy and Biology." *Thomas Hardy: Texts and Contexts.* Ed. Phillip Mallett. Houndmills and New York: Palgrave Macmillan, 2002. 156–79. Print.

———. "Hardy and Science: A Chapter of Accidents." *Palgrave Advances in Thomas Hardy Studies.* Ed. Phillip Mallett. Houndmills, Basingstoke: Palgrave Macmillan, 2004. 156–80. Print.

Richardson, Brian. "The Other Reader's Response: On Multiple, Divided, and Oppositional Audiences." *Criticism* 39.1 (1997): 31–53. Print.

———. "Singular Text, Multiple Implied Readers." *Style* 41 (2007): 259–74. Print.

Richardson, James. *Thomas Hardy: The Poetry of Necessity.* Chicago: University of Chicago Press, 1975. Print.

Rimmer, Mary. "A Feast of Language: Hardy's Allusions." *The Achievement of Thomas Hardy.* Ed. Philip Mallett. Houndmills and New York: Macmillan and St. Martin's Press, 2000. 58–71. Print.

———. "'My Scripture Manner': Reading Hardy's Biblical and Liturgical Allusion." *Thomas Hardy Reappraised: Essays in Honor of Michael Millgate.* Ed. Keith Wilson. Toronto: University of Toronto Press, 2006. 20–37. Print.

Rivers, W. H. R. *Conflict and Dream.* London: Kegan Paul, Trench, Trubner; New York: Harcourt, Brace, 1923. Print.

Romanes, George John. *Mental Evolution in Man: Origin of Human Faculty.* London: Kegan Paul, Trench, 1888. Print.

———. *Mind and Motion and Monism.* London: Longmans, Green, 1895. Print.

———. *Thoughts on Religion.* London: Longmans, Green, 1895. Print.

———. "The World as an Eject." 1886. *Mind and Motion and Monism.* London: Longmans, Green, 1895. Print.

Roose, Robson. *Nerve Prostration and Other Functional Disorders of Daily Life,* 2nd ed. London: H. K. Lewis, 1891. Print.

Rutland, William R. *Thomas Hardy: A Study of His Writings and Their Background.* New York: Russell and Russell, 1962. Print.

Ryan, Vanessa L. *Thinking without Thinking in the Victorian Novel.* Baltimore: Johns Hopkins University Press, 2012. Print.

Rylance, Rick. *Victorian Psychology and British Culture, 1850–1880.* Oxford and New York: Oxford University Press, 2000. Print.

The Savile Club, 1868–1923. Great Britain: Privately printed for the committee of the club by Neill, 1923. Print.

Saxelby, F. Outwin. *Thomas Hardy Dictionary.* London: Routledge, 1911. Print.

Scarry, Elaine. "The Difficulty of Imagining Other Persons." *The Handbook of Interethnic Coexistence.* Ed. Eugene Weiner. New York: Continuum, 1998. 40–62. Print.

———. "Work and the Body in Hardy and Other Nineteenth-Century Novelists." *Representations* 3 (Summer 1983): 90–123. Print.

Schur, Owen. *The Regulation of Consciousness in the English Novel: Desire and Power.* Lewiston: Edwin Mellen Press, 2002. Print.

Schweik, Robert C. "The Ethical Structure of Hardy's '*The Woodlanders.*'" *Thomas Hardy Journal* 12.3 (October 1996): 31–44. Print.

———. "The Influence of Religion, Science, and Philosophy on Hardy's Writings." *The Cambridge Companion to Thomas Hardy.* Ed. Dale Kramer. Cambridge and New York: Cambridge University Press, 1999. 54–72. Print.

———. "Mill's Images of Justice in Utilitarianism: The Influence of Bain and Darwin." Unpublished paper, c. 2005. TS.

Shelley, Percy Bysshe. *A Defense of Poetry.* 1840. *Essays, Letters from Abroad, Translations and Fragments.* Ed. Mrs. Shelley. V. 1. London: Bradbury and Evans, 1852. Google Book Search. 1 June 2010.

Shepherd, Gordon. *Foundations of the Neuron Doctrine.* Oxford and New York: Oxford University Press, 1991. Print.

Shires, Linda. "'And I Was Unaware': The Unknowing Omniscience of Hardy's Narrators." *Thomas Hardy: Texts and Contexts.* Ed. Phillip Mallett. Houndmills and New York: Palgrave Macmillan, 2002. 31–48. Print.

———. "The Radical Aesthetic of *Tess of the d'Urbervilles.*" *The Cambridge Companion to Thomas Hardy.* Ed. Dale Kramer. Cambridge and New York: Cambridge University Press, 1999. 145–63. Print.

Shuttleworth, Sally. *The Mind of the Child: Child Development in Literature, Science, and Medicine, 1840–1900.* Oxford and New York: Oxford University Press: 2010. Print.

———. "Psychological Definition and Social Power: Phrenology in the Novels of Charlotte Brontë." *Nature Transfigured: Science and Literature, 1700–1900.* Ed. John Christie and Sally Shuttleworth. Manchester and New York: Manchester University Press, 1989. 121–51. Print.

Silverman, Kaja. "History, Figuration and Female Subjectivity in *Tess of the D'Urbervilles.*" *Novel: A Forum on Fiction* 18 (1984): 5–28. Print.

Slater, Michael D. "Entertainment Education and the Persuasive Impact of Narratives." *Narrative Impact: Social and Cognitive Foundations.* Ed. Melanie C. Green, Jeffrey J. Strange, and Timothy C. Brock. Mahwah and London: Lawrence Erlbaum, 2002. 157–82. Print.

———. "Processing Social Information in Messages: Social Group Familiarity, Fiction versus Nonfiction, and Subsequent Beliefs." *Communications Research* 17.3 (1990): 327–43. Print.

Small, Helen. "Chances Are: Henry Buckle, Thomas Hardy, and the Individual at Risk." *Literature, Science, Psychoanalysis, 1830–1970.* Ed. Helen Small and Trudi Tate. Oxford and New York: Oxford University Press, 2003. 64–85. Print.

Smith, Adam. *The Theory of Moral Sentiments.* 1759. Ed. D. D. Raphael and A. L. Macfie. *Glasgow Edition of the Works and Correspondence of Adam Smith.* V. 1. Oxford and New York: Oxford University Press, 1976. Print.

Snow, C. P. *The Two Cultures and the Scientific Revolution.* Cambridge: Cambridge University Press, 1961. Print.

Sorum, Eve. "Hardy's Geography of Narrative Empathy." *Studies in the Novel* 43.2 (Summer 2011): 179–99. Print.

Southerington, F. R. *Hardy's Vision of Man.* New York: Barnes and Noble, 1971. Print.

Spence, James. *Lectures on Surgery.* Edinburgh: Adam and Charles Black, 1882. Print.

Spencer, Herbert. *An Autobiography.* 2 v. London: Williams and Norgate, 1904. *Google Book Search* 2 June 2010.

———. *Essays: Scientific, Political and Speculative.* 1891. Rpt. New York: Appleton, 1892. Print.

———. *First Principles.* London: Williams and Norgate, 1862. Print.

———. *First Principles,* 4th edition. London: Williams and Norgate, 1880. Print.

———. "Morals and Moral Sentiments." *Fortnightly Review* 9 n.s. (1 April 1871): 419–32. Print.

———. *Principles of Biology.* 1862. Rpt. New York: Appleton, 1904. *Google Book Search.* 2 June 2010.

———. *The Principles of Psychology.* London: Longman, Brown, Green, and Longmans, 1855. Print.

———. *The Principles of Psychology.* V. 1. 3rd ed. New York: Appleton, 1910. *Google Book Search.* 2 June 2010.

———. *The Principles of Psychology.* V. 2. 2nd ed. New York: Appleton, 1897. *Google Book Search.* 2 June 2010.

———. *Social Statics: Or, The Conditions Essential to Happiness Specified, and the First of Them Developed.* London: John Chapman, 1851. *Google Book Search.* 12 August 2010.

Springer, Marlene. *Hardy's Use of Allusion.* Lawrence: University of Kansas Press, 1983. Print.

Stephen, Leslie. *An Agnostic's Apology and Other Essays.* London: Smith, Elder, 1893. Print.

———. *Essays on Freethinking and Plainspeaking.* 1873. Rpt. New York: G. P. Putnam's Sons, 1877. Print.

———. *History of English Thought in the Eighteenth-Century.* London: Smith, Elder, 1876. Print.

———. *The Science of Ethics.* London, Smith, Elder, 1882. Print.

Sternberg, Meir. *The Poetics of Biblical Narrative: Ideological Literature and the Drama of Reading.* Bloomington: Indiana University Press, 1985. Print.

———. "Proteus in Quotation-Land: Mimesis and the Forms of Reported Discourse." *Poetics Today* 3.2 (1982): 107–56. Print.

Stiles, Anne. "Victorian Psychology and the Novel." *Literature Compass* 5 (2008): 1–13. Web.

Stiles, Anne, ed. *Neurology and Literature, 1860–1920.* Basingstoke: Palgrave Macmillan, 2007. Print.

Sumner, Rosemary. *Thomas Hardy: Psychological Novelist.* New York: St. Martin's Press, 1981. Print.

Sumpter, Caroline. "On Suffering and Sympathy: *Jude the Obscure,* Evolution, and Ethics." *Victorian Studies* 53.4 (Summer 2011): 665–87. Print.

Tan, Ed. *Emotion and the Structure of Narrative Film: Film as an Emotion Machine.* Trans. Barbara Fasting. Mahwah: Lawrence Erlbaum, 1996. Print.

Taylor, Dennis. "Hardy and Hamlet." *Thomas Hardy Reappraised: Essays in Honor of Michael Millgate.* Ed. Keith Wilson. Toronto: University of Toronto Press, 2006. 38–54. Print.

———. *Hardy's Literary Language and Victorian Philology.* Oxford: Clarendon Press, 1993. Print.

———. *Hardy's Metres and Victorian Prosody: With a Metrical Appendix of Hardy's Stanza Forms.* Oxford; Clarendon Press, 1988. Print.

———. *Hardy's Poetry, 1860–1928.* New York: Columbia University Press, 1981. Print.

———. "The Riddle of Hardy's Poetry." *Victorian Poetry* 11.4 (Winter 1973): 263–76. Print.

Taylor, Richard H., ed. *The Personal Notebooks of Thomas Hardy, with an Appendix Including the Unpublished Passages in the Original Typescripts of* The Life of Thomas Hardy. New York: Columbia University Press, 1979. Print.

Thurley, Geoffrey. *The Psychology of Hardy's Novels: The Nervous and the Statuesque.* St. Lucia: University of Queensland Press, 1975. Print.

Titchener, Edward Bradford. *Lectures on the Experimental Psychology of the Thought-Processes.* New York: Macmillan, 1909. *Google Book Search.* 1 June 2010.

Tomalin, Claire. *Thomas Hardy: The Time-Torn Man.* New York: Viking, 2006. Print.

Tucker, Herbert F. *Epic: Britain's Heroic Muse, 1790–1910.* Oxford and New York: Oxford University Press, 2008. Print.

Turner, T. H. "Maudsley, Henry (1835–1918)." *Oxford Dictionary of National Biography.* Online edition 2004. Web. 24 September 2009.

Van Wyhe, John. "The History of Phrenology: A Chronology." *The Victorian Web.* Ed. George Landow. Web. 26 May 2008.

Vermeule, Blakey. *Why Do We Care about Fictional Characters?* Baltimore: Johns Hopkins University Press, 2010. Print.

VICTORIA Archives. "Re: Periodicals in London Athenaeum Club Library?" Web. 24 February 2006.

Vischer, Robert. *Über das optische Formgefühl: Ein Beitrag zur Ästhetik (On the Optical Sense of Form: A Contribution to Aesthetics).* 1873. *Empathy, Form, and Space: Problems in German Aesthetics, 1873–93.* Trans. Harry Francis Mallgrave and Eleftherios Ikonomou. Los Angeles: Getty Trust Publications, 1993. 89–123. Print.

Vrettos, Athena. "Displaced Memory in Victorian Fiction and Psychology." *Victorian Studies* 49.2 (2007): 99–107. Print.

Watt, Ian. *The Rise of the Novel: Studies in Defoe, Richardson, and Fielding.* Berkeley: University of California Press, 1957. Print.

Webster, Harvey Curtis. *On a Darkling Plain: The Art and Thought of Thomas Hardy.* Chicago: University of Chicago Press, 1947. Print.

Wellek, René. *Discriminations: Further Concepts of Criticism.* New Haven and London: Yale University Press, 1970. Print.

Wickens, Glen. *Thomas Hardy, Monism and the Carnival Tradition: The One and the Many in* The Dynasts. Toronto: University of Toronto Press, 2002. Print.

Wilson, Keith. "'Flower of Man's Intelligence': World and Overworld in *The Dynasts.*" *Victorian Poetry* 17.1/2 (Spring–Summer 1979): 124–33. Print.

———. "'We Thank You . . . Most of all, Perhaps, for *The Dynasts*': Hardy's Epic Drama Re-evaluated." *Thomas Hardy Journal* 22 (2006): 235–54. Print.

Wilson, Keith, ed. *Thomas Hardy Reappraised: Essays in Honor of Michael Millgate.* Toronto: University of Toronto Press, 2006. Print.

Winter, Alison. *Mesmerized: Powers of Mind in Victorian Britain.* Chicago: University of Chicago Press, 1998. Print.

Wispé, Lauren. "History of the Concept of Empathy." *Empathy and Its Development.* Ed. Nancy Eisenberg and Janet Strayer. Cambridge: Cambridge University Press, 1987. 17–37. Print.

Wittenberg, Judith Bryant. "Early Hardy Novels and the Fictional Eye." *Novel: A Forum on Fiction* 16.2 (Winter 1983): 151–64. Print.

Wright, T. R. "From Bumps to Morals: The Phrenological Background to George Eliot's Moral Framework." *Review of English Studies* 33.129 (1982): 35–46. Print.

———. *Hardy and His Readers.* Houndmills, Basingstoke: Palgrave Macmillan, 2003. Print.

———. *The Religion of Humanity: The Impact of Comtean Positivism on Victorian Britain.* Cambridge and New York: Cambridge University Press, 1986. Print.

Wright, Walter. *The Shaping of* The Dynasts: *A Study in Thomas Hardy.* Lincoln: University of Nebraska Press, 1967. Print.

Wundt, Wilhelm. *Vorlesungen über die Menschen- und Thierseele.* Leipzig: Leopold Voss, 1863. Print.

Young, Edward. *The Complaint: Or, Night-Thoughts on Life, Death, and Immortality.* 1742. Rpt. London: H. Setchel, 1776. Print.

Young, Kay. *Imagining Minds: The Neuro-Aesthetics of Austen, Eliot, and Hardy.* Columbus: Ohio State University Press, 2010. Print.

———. "*Middlemarch* and the Problem of Other Minds Heard." *Literature Interpretation Theory* 14 (2003): 223–41. Print.

Zietlow, Paul. *Moments of Vision: The Poetry of Thomas Hardy.* Cambridge, MA: Harvard University Press, 1974. Print.

Zunshine, Lisa. "What Is Cognitive Cultural Studies?" *Introduction to Cognitive Cultural Studies.* Ed. Lisa Zunshine. Baltimore: Johns Hopkins University Press, 2010. 1–33. Print.

INDEX

THEORY AND INTERPRETATION OF NARRATIVE

James Phelan, Peter J. Rabinowitz, and Robyn Warhol, Series Editors

Because the series editors believe that the most significant work in narrative studies today contributes both to our knowledge of specific narratives and to our understanding of narrative in general, studies in the series typically offer interpretations of individual narratives and address significant theoretical issues underlying those interpretations. The series does not privilege one critical perspective but is open to work from any strong theoretical position.

Understanding Nationalism: On Narrative, Cognitive Science, and Identity
PATRICK COLM HOGAN

The Rhetoric of Fictionality: Narrative Theory and the Idea of Fiction
RICHARD WALSH

Experiencing Fiction: Judgments, Progressions, and the Rhetorical Theory of Narrative
JAMES PHELAN

Unnatural Voices: Extreme Narration in Modern and Contemporary Fiction
BRIAN RICHARDSON

Narrative Causalities
EMMA KAFALENOS

Why We Read Fiction: Theory of Mind and the Novel
LISA ZUNSHINE

I Know That You Know That I Know: Narrating Subjects from Moll Flanders *to* Marnie
GEORGE BUTTE

Bloodscripts: Writing the Violent Subject
ELANA GOMEL

Surprised by Shame: Dostoevsky's Liars and Narrative Exposure
DEBORAH A. MARTINSEN

Having a Good Cry: Effeminate Feelings and Pop-Culture Forms
ROBYN R. WARHOL

Politics, Persuasion, and Pragmatism: A Rhetoric of Feminist Utopian Fiction
ELLEN PEEL

Telling Tales: Gender and Narrative Form in Victorian Literature and Culture
ELIZABETH LANGLAND

Narrative Dynamics: Essays on Time, Plot, Closure, and Frames
EDITED BY BRIAN RICHARDSON

Breaking the Frame: Metalepsis and the Construction of the Subject
DEBRA MALINA

Invisible Author: Last Essays
CHRISTINE BROOKE-ROSE

Ordinary Pleasures: Couples, Conversation, and Comedy
KAY YOUNG

Narratologies: New Perspectives on Narrative Analysis
EDITED BY DAVID HERMAN

Before Reading: Narrative Conventions and the Politics of Interpretation
PETER J. RABINOWITZ

Matters of Fact: Reading Nonfiction over the Edge
DANIEL W. LEHMAN

The Progress of Romance: Literary Historiography and the Gothic Novel
DAVID H. RICHTER

A Glance Beyond Doubt: Narration, Representation, Subjectivity
SHLOMITH RIMMON-KENAN

Narrative as Rhetoric: Technique, Audiences, Ethics, Ideology
JAMES PHELAN

Misreading Jane Eyre: *A Postformalist Paradigm*
JEROME BEATY

Psychological Politics of the American Dream: The Commodification of Subjectivity in Twentieth-Century American Literature
LOIS TYSON

Understanding Narrative
EDITED BY JAMES PHELAN AND PETER J. RABINOWITZ

Framing Anna Karenina: *Tolstoy, the Woman Question, and the Victorian Novel*
AMY MANDELKER

Gendered Interventions: Narrative Discourse in the Victorian Novel
ROBYN R. WARHOL

Reading People, Reading Plots: Character, Progression, and the Interpretation of Narrative
JAMES PHELAN